Feb. 11, 1993

For Emily,

May you have many
wonderful moments with these
desserts.

Best Wishes,

Jim Dodge

Also by Jim Dodge with Elaine Ratner

THE AMERICAN BAKER

Baking with Jim Dodge

JIM DODGE

WITH

ELAINE RATNER

ILLUSTRATIONS BY

LAUREN JARRETT

PHOTOGRAPHS BY

CHRIS SHORTEN

SIMON & SCHUSTER

NEW YORK • LONDON • TORONTO • SYDNEY • TOKYO • SINGAPORE

SIMON & SCHUSTER
Simon & Schuster Building
Rockefeller Center
1230 Avenue of the Americas
New York, New York 10020

10   9   8   7   6   5   4   3   2   1

Library of Congress Cataloging in Publication Data

Dodge, Jim, date-
  Baking with Jim Dodge / Jim Dodge with Elaine Ratner :
illustrations by Lauren Jarrett.
      p.   cm.
   Includes index.
   1. Desserts.   2. Baking.   3. Ice cream, ices, etc.   I. Ratner,
Elaine.   II. Title.
TX773.D632   1991
641.8'6—dc20   90-26747
ISBN 0-671-68100-1   CIP

For my parents,
    James W. Dodge
    and Arlene Dodge Avigdor.
JD

For Jay Harlow,
    my partner in business and in life.
ER

Contents

1

Desserts
in the American Tradition

MORE THAN ANYTHING ELSE, Americans love their freedom. We have always been a hearty, freewheeling nation, glorying in the abundance of our natural resources and inventing new ways to use them. Freedom loving in our cooking as in everything else, American cooks have never felt themselves bound by European traditions that dictate the "correct" way to flavor a certain sauce or decorate a particular cake. American desserts developed from the ground up—determined by the fruits, nuts, and dairy products offered by the land itself.

Because the American land is so vast, both the country and its desserts developed regional styles. Blueberry pie was an early New England staple, as were maple-flavored sauces and ice creams, while peach pie was synonymous with the South. Gradually, as transportation and refrigeration improved, the produce of one region became easily available to all the others, and favorite regional desserts became national. Now, no matter where you live, every imaginable kind of fruit is in the market, and many fruits are there even when they are not in season.

Modern technology is both wonderful and terrible. In supplying ourselves with all kinds of ingredients all year round, we have begun to forget the basic truth on which our rich baking heritage is based: that the time to enjoy any fruit is when it is at the peak of its season, ripe and luscious and so abundant it begs to be picked and eaten. We have been so charmed by the exotic that we sometimes pass over local produce, which always has been best for baking. Before finding my own way as an American baker, I was painstakingly trained by a European pastry chef. I think perhaps the most important thing the European cooking tradition can teach Americans today is the value of local ingredients. If you travel through Europe, the first thing you notice about the food is that regions have their own distinctive cooking styles, and that each region's style is based on the foods that are raised locally. At the same time, wherever you go, the food is amazingly good.

Although I would never advocate going back to using only locally grown produce (after all, I love mangoes and bananas too), I do encourage my students, and the readers of my books, to rediscover the fruits that abound in your own area, often literally in your own back-yard. Local produce is likely to be fresher and riper than what you'll find in most big supermarkets because it doesn't have to be picked underripe to survive shipping. If you have to buy fruits rather than pick them, local varieties should also be cheaper (again because they don't need to be packed or shipped). American pies, cobblers, and crisps call for large quantities of fruit; they originated as celebrations of the season and its bounty. The season is today; the bounty is what's being picked right now in your state. Some seasons are more exciting than others, but what's fresh and in season is always best.

Besides the wonderful and plentiful produce, what makes American desserts distinctive is their simplicity. This country was settled by simple folk, and their down-to-earth ways established our baking tra-ditions. What could be more American than a pound cake? And what could be simpler? In the beginning the recipe simply called for a pound of each ingredient: flour, sugar, eggs, and butter. Today we prefer to bake in smaller quantities, but the stunningly simple concept remains the same. We may add a little spice or lemon for flavor, but two hundred years later no one has found a way to improve on the original recipe for pound cake.

The same holds true of so many traditional American desserts. A good fruit pie has always been a good, flaky crust filled with lots of lightly sweetened fruit. A crisp is likewise lots of fresh fruit, a little sugar, and a very simple topping made of flour, butter, and sugar. Ice cream is fresh, unadulterated cream, eggs, fruit, and sugar. When the ingredients are excellent and fresh, they don't need much done to them.

That is not to say we Americans have ignored European desserts. In fact, we have adopted some of the best as our own. When I began assembling recipes for this book, I thought of it as a book of purely American desserts. Then foreign-born recipes began finding their way onto my list. I couldn't do a cookie chapter without including my beloved madeleines and florentines. The chapter on individual pastries, such as brownies and bars, made me think of cannoli; and next to the shortcakes I caught myself jotting down a recipe for napoleons made with strawberries. Finally I admitted that American desserts today, like the American people, include many that were born in Europe, and that is part of the strength of our baking tradition. I inserted a chapter on tarts—a traditionally French dessert—right after the pie chapter. But you will find that many of the tarts here are American in concept. The Cranberry Crumb Tart on page 61 stems from my own New England roots, as does my longtime love for blueberries and cream, translated into the Blueberry and Cream Tart on page 62.

Regardless of the source of various desserts, all of the recipes in this book reflect what I consider the hallmarks of American baking: freshness; simplicity; and clean, bold flavors. Although there are ele-gant cakes and tarts as well as simple, unadorned ones, nothing here is fussy or decorative. And nothing is difficult to make.

In keeping with my love of fresh, homemade baked goods, I have included a chapter of my favorite breakfast pastries and breads. Muf-fins, like pies, are traditionally American; so are biscuits. I have also included some of their European cousins—crumpets and scones—which are appearing more and more in American bakeries and on American breakfast tables.

I see more and more Americans returning to home-baked bread, which is wonderful. Perhaps it is because technology has now given us electric mixers with dough hooks, food processors that can knead doughs effortlessly, and even little bread-baking machines that take in raw ingredients at night and pop out finished loaves in the morning. If these machines are the reason for the revival of home-baked bread, I welcome them most heartily. Perhaps we have come full circle; technology enticed us away from our culinary roots, and now it is bringing us back.

I don't think Americans' enthusiasm for freshly baked breads and desserts has ever waned. We just got busier and had less time to spend in the kitchen. Now some of the more time-consuming aspects of baking have been simplified by appliances, and good smells are wafting again from kitchens all over America. I hope the recipes in this book will inspire you and reacquaint you, if you have forgotten, with the incredible heritage of American baking.

Ingredients

There are a few basic rules for buying dessert ingredients that take precedence over all else: Buy fresh. Buy in season. Buy pure and natural. Always remember that the better the ingredients you put into a dessert, the better the dessert will be. There is no way to put back flavor that isn't there, and attempts to mask inferior ingredients are bound to fail.

The following guidelines will help you to select the best ingredients.

APPLES

When you are thinking about making an apple dessert, remember that apples are seasonal fruits. To get the best taste and texture, you should choose an apple that's in season. If possible, check each apple before buying. It should have smooth, unbruised skin. When you pick it up it should feel heavy and firm.

For desserts that will cook for a long time use Pippins, Baldwins, Cortlands, or any other local, firm apple. The pie apples I use most often are Baldwins, Cortlands, Gravensteins, Royal Galas, and Pippins.

Soft apples or apples with high moisture, such as Granny Smiths, are best for quick-baking desserts. They should have smooth, unbruised skins and a sweet apple smell near the stem. Some of my favorite soft apples are Jonathans, Winesaps, McIntoshes, and Empires.

During off seasons when I want to use apples even though none are at their best, I select the greenest Golden Delicious I can find. They are quite a bit more tart than they would be if fully ripe and yellow.

BAKING POWDER

Never use baking powder that has aluminum in it; it has a strong chemical flavor that will come through in your desserts. I buy Rumford, which is aluminum free, or any from a health or natural food store. Always buy baking powder in small cans unless you use it a lot; it goes flat rather quickly. Check old baking powder by dropping ½ teaspoon into a glass of warm water. If it foams to the top, it is still active. Never put a wet spoon into the can; moisture will cause the baking powder to go flat.

BAKING SODA

To be effective, baking soda should be fresh. It will lose some power after about nine months and should be replaced.

BUTTER

Butter is one of the most taken for granted of all baking ingredients. All butter is not the same, and the firmness of the butter you use is very important. The firmer the butter the more air it will hold, and the lighter the buttercreams and cakes it will make. The firmer the butter the more pliable it is, enabling doughs to hold together longer and be easier to handle and roll.

Buy only unsalted butter for baking. When shopping, choose the butter that feels the firmest. Smell the wrapper to check for freshness. (If butter hasn't been stored properly you can smell an off odor right through the wrapping.) Of course, you should also check the date on the carton. On the West Coast, Challenge, Gilt Edge, and Dairy Gold are the best butters I've found for baking. In the East, Breakstone is very good.

Remember that fat picks up flavors easily, so when baking it is always best to add extracts and other flavorings to the butter. Soft butter (butter that has been left out to soften but is still cool) is pliable and will accept air easily and whip to its maximum. Cold butter is best for making doughs, as it keeps the dough firm, tender, and easy to roll.

If you don't want to wait for butter to soften at room temperature, you can soften it in a microwave. Place it on a plate and heat it on high for 15 seconds; repeat until it becomes soft to the touch. It is acceptable to have a small amount of the butter melt.

BUTTER, CLARIFIED

Clarified butter lasts longer than solid butter and can be heated to a higher temperature without burning. To clarify butter, heat it slowly until the moisture and milk solids separate from the fat. The solids will float to the top; the moisture, or water, will settle to the bottom. Strain the solids from the fat by pouring the melted butter slowly through cheesecloth into a container, stopping before you pour the water from the bottom of the pan. Discard the solids and the water. Keep the clarified butter refrigerated.

CHOCOLATE

It is important to remember that chocolate is not a single ingredient but a recipe; it is a highly processed food. Different brands of chocolate vary considerably in taste and texture. Your best choice will depend on your personal preference.

When you buy chocolate you are paying for the quality of the beans from which it was made and the texture of the finished product. Look for chocolate that is shiny on the outside; it should have a good snap when you break it and uniform color and texture throughout. When you taste it (and by all means taste it if you can before buying) it should melt like butter on your tongue and leave a pleasant lingering flavor.

Watch out for chocolate that has not been carefully processed and stored. Because of its high fat content chocolate picks up odors easily, and if not properly handled may smell of mold or smoke. Chocolate that is cooled too fast during processing may have isolated fats that form "oysters"—grainy or chalky white spots that make the chocolate more difficult to temper and to work with. It's best to find a brand of chocolate you like that is consistent in quality and stick with it. Some of the better domestic chocolates are Van Leer, Guittard, Ghirardelli, and Wilbur's.

Never store chocolate in plastic wrap! It will give the chocolate an offensive taste. Wrap chocolate in freezer paper then in foil. Never freeze chocolate and be sure to keep it away from moisture. Store in a dark cool place away from anything with a strong odor, like onions.

CITRUS ZEST   Zest is the colored outside of the peel on any citrus fruit. It is full of flavorful citrus oil, which imparts subtle fruit flavor to desserts. The white pith directly beneath the zest is bitter; remove as much of it as possible before using the zest. All citrus fruits, such as oranges, lemons, limes, and grapefruits, should be scrubbed with dishwashing detergent and a brush, then rinsed well to remove pesticides and wax before using; they are unpleasant to eat and will give the peel a bitter, chemical flavor. Zest can be effectively removed from citrus fruit with a special zester, a vegetable peeler, a box grater, or a small, sharp knife.

CREAM   See Milk and Cream.

CREAM OF TARTAR   Cream of tartar is made from a deposit left in wine barrels after the grapes have fermented. It is used to balance the harsh flavors of baking soda when an acid isn't present in baking. If you find yourself out of baking powder you can substitute ½ teaspoon of cream of tartar and ¼ teaspoon of baking soda for each teaspoon of baking powder called for in a recipe.

EGGS   All of my recipes are developed using large eggs. I use large eggs because they generally have the hardest shells. Always buy eggs from a refrigerated case; eggs deteriorate quickly at room temperature. Choose grade AA eggs. When cracked, the yolk should be firm and stand tall. The white should spread little and there should be more thick than thin white. Before buying, open the carton and feel the eggs; they should be cold. I always take mine from the back of the case. Check the shells. There shouldn't be any cracks and the shells should be thick, not thin. Thick shells mean the chickens had a good diet. Once you get the eggs home, keep them refrigerated in the carton they came in. It is designed to keep unwanted odors away from the eggs and to keep them from dehydrating.

Fresh eggs are best for baking. They will whip to their maximum, giving you higher and lighter cakes and meringues. Never leave eggs at room temperature; they will not stay fresh as long as eggs that have been kept refrigerated. Warm eggs are also more susceptible to the growth of bacteria. This is confusing to most people because they have been told to keep eggs out for an hour or so before using. It is true that eggs will whip faster when warm, because the protein is relaxed, but they will not rise to their maximum if they are no longer fresh.

For the best results, keep eggs refrigerated, then just before using warm them briefly in a bowl of warm water or in the top of a double boiler, stirring continuously until warm. When separating eggs, wash them first, then use the eggshell, not your hands. Bacteria on your hands may contaminate the eggs.

Equivalents
5 large whole eggs equal 1 cup
7 large egg whites equal 1 cup
14 large egg yolks equal 1 cup

FLOUR

It is important to use the right kind of flour when baking. If you substitute one flour for another, you will significantly change the texture of a dessert, bread, or pastry.

All-purpose flour is a blend of wheats and can be used for both bread and cakes, although it gives cakes a coarser and heavier texture than cake flour. It has the perfect protein content for pie doughs, making them easy to roll without crumbling or getting tough. Because it is a blend, all-purpose flour varies from manufacturer to manufacturer.

Bread flour has the highest protein content of any flour. It is best used for bread doughs. The extra protein supports the dough as it rises giving it better texture and shape. When you buy bread flour, look for a package that says either Bread Flour or Hi-Protein Flour, not all-purpose.

Cake flour has the lowest protein content of any flour and is milled the finest. It costs more because it takes a very expensive mill to mill cake flour. Very light and soft, it makes light, tender cakes and tender cookies.

FRUIT

(See also Apples.) Wash all fruit before using. Select fruit that is ripe and full of flavor. Freshness is only half the battle; fruit can be fresh and still be bland or flavorless. Fresh local seasonal fruit is always the best bet. When there is no fresh local fruit, it is wise to buy fresh-frozen fruit packed loose in bags. This fruit is picked ripe and frozen immediately, usually with very little if any sugar added. Allow frozen fruit to partially defrost in the refrigerator before using.

FRUIT PECTIN

Pectin is a natural starch that comes from fruit. It needs to be cooked to remove its cloudy appearance and starchy taste. It is a great way to thicken fruit sauces without lightening their color. Both granular and liquid forms are available in most supermarkets.

LM Pectin is a low-methoxyl pectin, which means it jells with calcium, instead of sugar. This pectin is used to make preserves without sugar or with a low sugar content. It is available in health food stores. The brand I prefer is Pomona's Universal Pectin. When using LM Pectin always follow instructions included with the product. It can be substituted for regular pectin.

LIQUEURS

When buying liqueurs always buy the best quality you can find. They will have purer flavors and will last longer.

MILK AND CREAM

It amazes me how much cream varies in this country. In some cities, such as Los Angeles, it is impossible to buy cream that hasn't been ultrapasteurized. In San Francisco, where I do most of my baking, many grocery stores and supermarkets carry pure cream, with nothing added. When you shop for cream, look at the list of ingredients on the carton. It should say cream, and nothing else. Cream with stabilizers and chemical preservatives added has a bitter aftertaste that has to be masked with sugar and vanilla. If your favorite market doesn't carry pure, fresh cream, ask the manager to add it to the shelves.

Some dairies say on the carton what kind of cows the cream has come from. The best cream and milk come from brown jersey or guernsey cows; black and white holstein cows produce the most milk, but not the best. The best cream on the West Coast comes from the Clover-Stornetta Dairy in Petaluma, California.

Adding a small amount of gelatin to whipped cream will prevent it from weeping or becoming soft if it has to stand a while before serving. Use a very small amount. Too much gelatin will give a dessert or pastry the offensive texture and flavor we have all found from time to time in a pretty but bland dessert.

Scalded milk is milk that has been heated to just below the simmering point. When a recipe calls for scalded milk, heat the milk slowly in a saucepan until a chalky white ring appears around the edge. Remove the milk from the heat before it starts to simmer.

PEANUT BUTTER

Choose a peanut butter that is low in sugar and added fat or a natural one that is fresh. Natural peanut butters separate when left standing, but that is not a problem. Simply stir the oil back into the peanut butter before using.

SALT

Table salt has chemicals added to it to prevent it from clumping together. Those chemicals give it an offensive, harsh aftertaste. I use kosher salt because it is pure salt and has a cleaner flavor. All of the recipes in this book were developed with kosher salt. If you use table salt, use half as much salt as is called for because it is twice as salty as kosher salt. Sea salt is four times as salty as table salt and is a good substitute for table salt. If using sea salt, use one-eighth the amount of salt called for.

SUGAR

When making caramel it is best to use pure cane sugar. Cane sugar doesn't foam when cooked as beet sugar does. Foaming carries sugar crystals above the water line; crystals thus isolated can cause the entire caramel to crystallize. I use C&H pure cane sugar.

Most manufacturers make brown sugar by adding molasses to plain sugar, which colors the outside of the sugar and will rub off on your hands. C&H is the only manufacturer I know that makes brown sugar by not removing the molasses from the sugar in the first place. This gives the sugar a better flavor and a different color.

When measuring brown sugar, pack it tightly into the cup for an accurate measure.

VANILLA BEANS

I prefer the flavor of Mexican vanilla beans. I find them richer, sweeter, sharper, and more pungent than Tahitian vanilla beans, which have a perfumy flavor.

**VANILLA
EXTRACT**

If you don't have pure vanilla extract, substitute lemon or orange zest or leave the flavoring out altogether. Don't use imitation vanilla; it has an offensive taste that will ruin the flavor of your dessert. Buy pure vanilla extract in a dark glass bottle, preferably a large bottle. It will improve with age. Plastic bottles impart a plastic flavor to the vanilla. I use Nielsen-Massey vanillas.

YEAST

One envelope of active dry yeast is equivalent to 2 teaspoons of bulk active dry yeast or one fresh yeast cake.

When buying fresh yeast always check the date on the package and check for cuts accidently made during transport or shelving. Fresh yeast should be uniform in color and clay-like, without mold or any dry crust.

When using dry yeast, follow the directions on the package. The most common mistake people make with dry yeast is not allowing enough time for the yeast to become activated. This causes the dough to rise slowly and gives it an unpleasant, bitter taste. When properly activated, dry yeast will slowly float to the top of the dissolving liquid, forming a light "raft" that tells you it is ready to use. Fresh yeast can be mixed directly into doughs without being dissolved or activated first.

Equipment

It really doesn't take a lot of special equipment to make wonderful desserts. Most of the pots, pans, and tools already in your kitchen will work very well. If you decide to replace old equipment or buy some things you've never owned before, just follow this advice: buy the best quality you can find (and remember that high quality and high price do not always go together). Poorly made tools will break just when you need them most. Buy what appeals to you, what feels comfortable in your hands, and what promises to last a long time.

As a professional baker, I use professional equipment, and I enjoy the convenience of a food processor and a large tabletop electric mixer equipped with a paddle, a whisk, and a dough hook. If you have that kind of equipment, it will make many tasks easier for you. But you certainly do not have to have them. I tested many of the recipes in this book with a small hand-held electric mixer because I wanted to be sure they would come out equally well when made with that simple, inexpensive appliance. They did.

What follows is by no means a complete list of recommended kitchen equipment or even a list of everything you may need for the recipes in this book. It is, rather, a list of those things that I have strong feelings about or that I suspect the average home kitchen may not contain and should. Purchase only the equipment necessary for the kind of baking you intend to do.

BENCH SCRAPER

A bench scraper—a blunt, rectangular metal blade with a wooden handle—is used to move and cut dough. It is a great tool for cleaning stuck dough from a work surface after dough or pastry work is finished.

CANDY THER-MOMETER

I recommend a candy thermometer over other kinds of thermometers because it is easier to read than most and is very accurate.

CHERRY PITTER

Pitting cherries by hand is pretty tedious. A cherry pitter makes the job quick and easy—although it is still messy. Choose a pitter that feels comfortable in your hand. The type that you squeeze like a paper punch is best. If you hold the pitter inside a large paper bag when pitting, the cherry juices will splatter the bag and not you or your kitchen. If you bake a lot with cherries, consider buying a semiautomatic pitter that has an enclosed compartment for the pits and a bowl and trough for the cherries. Then you simply stem the cherries and place them in the bowl on top. Each time you push a plunger a cherry rolls into position and gets pitted.

CHINESE KNIFE (CLEAVER)

The straight, thin blade of a Chinese knife is perfect for chopping nuts or cutting cookies and pastries. Turned on its side, the broad blade is very good for crushing toasted nuts.

COOKIE SHEETS

Heavy baking sheets are best because they temper the heat from the bottom of the oven. If your sheets are thin, you can double them to prevent cookies and pastries from burning on the bottom. When buying new cookie sheets, choose the type with four sides rather than the completely flat ones, so that they can also be used as jelly-roll pans.

CUTTING PIN

Rolling pins should never be used to trim the excess dough from tart shells. The sharp edge of the pan will cut into the wood, leaving cut marks that will catch the dough as you roll; your pin will be ruined. Buy an inexpensive wooden dowel about 18 inches long and 2 to 3 inches in diameter and use that for trimming. To trim off excess dough, simply roll the cutting pin over the edge of the tart pan; the sharp metal edge of the pan will do the cutting.

DOUBLE BOILER

Double boilers are designed to cook delicate sauces that would burn in saucepans placed over direct heat. A small amount of water is placed in the bottom saucepan and placed over heat. The second saucepan is placed over the top with the sauce or filling inside. The water between the two pans heats to provide the sauce with a gentler heat source.

Sets can be purchased that include two saucepans and one lid. I prefer the one made by Vision Glass that is see-through and has rounded inside edges for easy stirring. You can also use a saucepan with a bowl that fits on top, but these can be awkward, so be careful.

ELECTRIC MIXER

For whipping cream, eggs, or butter, a hand-held mixer works as well as a large upright, but it will take twice as long. A large mixer with a paddle attachment is excellent for making doughs. If you don't have one, use your hands. A hand-held mixer won't do this job right. If using your hands, make sure the butter is cold, or the heat from your hands will make the dough too soft to work with. In the summer, freeze your work bowl with the flour in it for an hour before mixing the dough, then work quickly.

FLUTED OR PLAIN PASTRY WHEELS

Pastry wheels are used for cutting thin pieces of dough. Used with a yardstick, they allow you to cut long, straight strips for pastries and cookies. Select a wheel that rolls easily in a straight line and has a sharp edge. Be sure it fits comfortably in your hand.

PARCHMENT PAPER AND PARCHMENT CIRCLES

Parchment paper comes in a roll like foil. It is heavier than waxed paper and doesn't bake into food as waxed paper does. I use it for lining cake pans and cookie sheets, and sometimes for wrapping ingredients. To line a cake pan with a parchment circle, set the pan on a piece of parchment that is slightly larger. Trace the pan, then cut inside the drawn circle with scissors. Butter the pan, and lay the circle in the bottom; be sure it lies smooth. The cake will come out of the pan easily; when the cake is cool, peel the parchment off.

PASTRY BAG AND TIPS

You should have a sturdy cloth pastry bag and a few metal tips. Buy a large bag that feels comfortable in your hand and is easy to rinse clean. Buy a few professional tips (at least one plain and one star), not the small ones sold in sets for cake decorating. Always rinse the bag immediately after using; later it will be much harder to clean. If possible, hang it up to dry. If you have never used a pastry bag before, it may seem awkward at first. With a little practice it gets a lot easier.

PASTRY BRUSH

Use a 3- to 4-inch-wide pastry brush to brush extra flour from doughs. Use a 1- to 2-inch brush to spread glazes over tarts or fruit. When choosing a brush it does not matter if it is made from natural bristles or synthetic. What is important is that it has soft bristles that will not tear your dough or drag across your tarts. To test the brush, draw the tip of the bristles across the inside of your wrist, where the skin is tender. If it scratches, don't buy the brush; if it feels soft, it is okay to buy.

PASTRY CUTTERS

Pastry cutters are metal rings used to cut circles of dough to exact sizes. You can buy them singly or in sets. Choose cutters that are made out of strong metal and have a curved top for easy handling. Sizes vary depending on the manufacturer. The sizes I use most often are 1½ inches, 1¾ inches, and 2 inches. If you don't have a pastry cutter, you can do very well with the top of a small glass.

PIE PANS

Use only metal pie pans; glass pans do not bake the crust as evenly. If you can find them, buy the kind of pie pans that have small holes all over the bottom. They are the kind used most often by professional bakers because they provide the most evenly browned crusts. The pies in this book are baked in either a 9-inch or an 8-inch pie pan.

PIZZA STONE OR KILN SHELF

The problem most home bakers have with pies is that the bottom crust comes out soggy. Baking the pie on a pizza stone or kiln shelf solves this problem. The stone brings heat in direct contact with the bottom of the pie pan and assures that the bottom crust bakes through. Place the stone in the oven while it preheats. When the oven reaches the desired temperature, set the pie pan directly on the stone. Pizza stones are available at most cookware shops; kiln shelves are available at ceramic supply stores. Either will work well.

ROLLING PIN

I like to use a French-style tapered rolling pin for rolling out pie and tart doughs and a heavy ball bearing–type pin with handles for puff pastry and other large pieces of dough. Whichever style you use, it should be of maple and should be very smooth and polished. If it is porous, doughs will stick to it. A rolling pin should never be washed. Immediately after using it, wipe it clean with a towel. If something has stuck to it, gently scrape it clean with a plastic bowl scraper, then wipe it. Never allow dough to dry on the pin.

RUBBER SCRAPER

Use a wide-blade rubber spatula with a strong handle for scraping down bowls during mixing. Buy one with a slightly stiff blade; it will soften as you use it. Keep a scraper just for desserts. If you use it for general cooking, it may pick up strong odors, such as onion or garlic, and transmit them to a delicate batter.

2

Pies

I LOVE ALL KINDS of pies—double-crusted pies, crumb-topped pies, meringue pies, cream pies. In summer, when berries are sweet and plentiful, I pile basket after basket of them into my pies. If two pints of blueberries are good, three pints are better. I don't believe in skimpy pies.

In the fall I turn to apples. Over the past few years the number of varieties of apples in the markets has grown amazingly. Now it's not just a question of whether to bake an apple pie, it's a question of what kind of apple to use. I've done a lot of experimenting, and have found that I like the way some apples bake better than others. I've included recipes for a few of my favorite pies here. Don't be dismayed if you can't get the kind of apples called for in a recipe. The best bet is always to use the apples that are grown locally. You probably have access to varieties I can't get. So conduct your own experiments and find your own favorites.

Although I've always liked meringue pies, I get tired of the same two or three kinds. So I set out to create some new ones. In this chapter you'll find not only the expected, year-round lemon and lime, but also some seasonal, fruit-filled meringue pies made with pineapples, nectarines, sour plums, rhubarb, and cherries.

Just about any fruit that's ripe and juicy can be baked into a fine pie. I hope my experiments will inspire you to try some of your own. Follow your instincts, and just be careful not to oversweeten or overthicken. Too much sugar will mask the wonderful flavor of fresh fruit. Too much thickening will ruin the texture.

I have purposely not specified a pie dough in most of my pie recipes. Some people prefer a butter-based crust, others like to use shortening or lard. Choose the dough you like best and use it in any of the pies.

Flaky Pie Dough

The secret of a flaky dough is to leave the shortening in flakes rather than working it all in. As the dough bakes, the flakes of shortening melt, creating pockets of air, and thus thin layers in the crust. Because the ingredients are not completely blended, their flavors remain somewhat isolated and create a melody of separate flavors in the final pastry. The texture and taste of the crust will vary according to which shortening you use. Vegetable shortening will give you a crust that is light in both flavor and texture. Butter will give a more flavorful crust that will also bake to a deeper brown. Either version produces a delicate crust perfect for fruit pies and very American.

MAKES 1 DOUBLE-CRUST PIE (FOR A SINGLE-CRUST PIE, DIVIDE RECIPE IN HALF)

2 cups plus 2 tablespoons all-purpose flour
14 tablespoons unsalted butter
*   or pure vegetable shortening*
5 tablespoons cold tap water
½ teaspoon kosher salt
1 tablespoon apple cider vinegar

Freeze 2 cups of flour in a bowl for ½ hour. After 15 minutes, cut the butter or shortening into 1-inch cubes and place it in the freezer with the flour. Combine the water, salt, and vinegar in a 1-cup measuring cup. Set aside.

Toss the butter or shortening with the flour to coat it. Dump them out onto a work surface and roll them with a rolling pin. Keep sweeping the two ingredients into a pile with your hands and rolling them out with the pin until all of the butter or shortening is in large flakes about 2 to 3 inches long. The dough will stick to the rolling pin; whenever necessary, scrape it back onto the table and continue rolling.

Lift the dough with a bench scraper and drop it into a bowl. Add the vinegar water and mix with a rubber spatula, turning the dough over and scraping it up from the bottom of the bowl until all the water is absorbed. There will be some large clumps; not all the dry ingredients will come together. Press the dough into the bottom of the bowl with an open hand.

Sprinkle your work surface with the remaining 2 tablespoons of flour and turn the dough out onto it. Roll the dough out. Lift one side with a bench scraper and fold the dough in half. Roll it into a 9- × 14-inch rectangle, then fold the rectangle into thirds. Roll it out to an 8- × 9-inch rectangle. Use the scraper to fold it in half again. The dough will be loose and crumbly, not smooth. Carefully lift it onto a sheet of plastic wrap and wrap it. Press the dough together by gently rolling the pin back and forth over it. Chill the dough 30 minutes before rolling it out for the pie.

FORMING
THE PIE
SHELL

If you are making a double-crust pie, divide the dough in half. Work on a well-floured table or board. Have a rolling pin, a soft brush, and your pie pan close at hand.

Put the dough for the shell (half the dough for a double-crust pie) down on the board and sprinkle a little flour on top. Shape the dough into a thick patty, about 6 inches in diameter. Beginning in the middle and working to opposite sides, roll the dough into an elongated oval, about 12 inches long. Lift it carefully, with straight fingers under both ends to support it, and swirl it a little on the table to coat the bottom again with flour as you give it a quarter turn. Sprinkle a little more flour on top, then roll to opposite sides as you did before, shaping the dough into a circle. Continue rolling gently, from the center to the edges, until you have a smooth circle of uniform thickness. You can locate too-thick places by running your fingers gently over the dough. Work them out with a back and forth motion of the pin. The finished circle should be about 12 inches in diameter.

Brush the flour off the dough. Fold it into quarters, brushing any excess flour from the bottom, and transfer it gently to the pie pan. Unfold it so that it covers the bottom and sides of the pan. Work your way around the pan, gently lifting the edges of the dough so that it settles into the pan without stretching. Gently press the dough against the side of the pan; trim off any excess with scissors.

If you are making a double-crust pie, leave about 1 inch of overlap all the way around when you trim the shell. When it is time to add the top crust, roll the second half of the dough as you did the first, this time rolling it into a 13-inch circle. Brush the edge of the shell lightly with beaten egg and lay the top crust over the filling.

Egg seals crusts better than water. You can use the whole egg, just the yolk, or just the white. To keep leftover beaten egg for future pies, add a pinch of salt and a teaspoon of sugar to preserve it.

CRIMPING
(OR FLUTING)
THE EDGES

Lift the overlapping top and bottom edges and press them together all around the pie to seal them. If there is more than 1 inch of overlap, trim it to 1 inch. Lift the sealed overlap and fold it under so that the

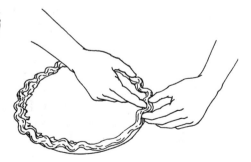

edge rests on the rim of the pie plate. For crimping, use the index finger on the right hand and a finger and thumb on the left. Place the tips of the finger and thumb of your left hand against the inside of the sealed edge; with the right index finger push the dough gently into a point between finger and thumb. Move the thumb and finger and repeat. Work your way all around the pie, making a zigzag pattern in the edge. When you are done, go back and pinch the outer points to make them more distinct. The fluted edge should not overlap the pan; overlapping edges get too much direct heat and can burn.

If the recipe calls for sprinkling the top of the pie with sugar, keep the sugar off the fluted edge; it may burn there. Before baking, cut 4 to 8 slashes in a circle in the center of the pie to let steam escape. Bake as directed.

PREBAKING A PIE SHELL

Preheat the oven to 400°. Set another pie pan of the same size on top of the shell. Invert the two pans and bake upside down. After 10 minutes, press down on the top pan firmly but gently; otherwise, the shell may shrink away from the pan and not fit snugly against the bottom when you turn it right side up. Continue baking until the bottom of the shell no longer looks raw, about 10 more minutes. Turn the shell right side up, remove the top pie plate, and continue baking until golden brown, about 15 minutes.

Lard Dough

I make most of my pie crusts with butter, but I sometimes like to use a lard dough for apple pie. Lard makes a tender crust, and adds just a hint of pork flavor, which goes well with apples. I add a little butter, because I think it improves both texture and flavor.

MAKES 1 DOUBLE-CRUST PIE (FOR A SINGLE-CRUST PIE, DIVIDE RECIPE IN HALF)

½ cup lard
1½ cups plus 1 teaspoon all-purpose flour
1 tablespoon butter
⅓ cup cold water

Cut the lard into ½-inch cubes. Combine it with 1½ cups of flour and the butter; mix by hand, with the paddle attachment on an electric mixer, or in a food processor until clumpy but not to the coarse-meal stage. Mix the water in a little at a time until it is completely absorbed. Dust the dough with 1 teaspoon of flour and work it gently until it comes together. Remove the dough from the bowl and divide it in half.

Form each half into an inch-thick patty. Refrigerate the dough for 15 minutes before rolling it out.

To complete the pie crust, see "Forming the pie shell," page 24.

Graham Cracker Crust

A graham cracker pie crust is sweeter than most crusts, and has its own special kind of crunchiness. Some pies just don't taste right with any other crust.

MAKES 1 9-INCH PIE SHELL

1 packet (5⅓ ounces) graham crackers
¼ cup cake flour
3 tablespoons sugar
8 tablespoons (¼ pound) unsalted butter
   (melted)

Crush the graham crackers with a rolling pin or chop them in a food processor until fine. Add the flour and sugar and mix (4 pulses in a food processor). Add the butter and mix well (30 seconds in a food processor).

Butter a 9-inch pie pan and cover the bottom and sides evenly with the crumbs. Chill for 15 minutes.

Preheat the oven to 350°. Bake the crust in the middle of the oven until it is slightly firm and brown, 15 to 20 minutes. Cool on a wire rack. If you're not going to use the crust right away, cover it with plastic wrap and freeze it until needed. Defrost the crust before filling it.

Baldwin Apple Pie

Red and gold Baldwin apples are crisp, juicy, and just slightly tart. They are best for pie when still a little green; when fully ripe they are a bit too sweet for my taste. This pie contains no butter or thickener; the apples have a naturally rich flavor, and their juices thicken nicely on their own.

SERVES 10

1 recipe pie dough (page 23 or 25)
6 Baldwin apples
¼ cup plus 1 teaspoon sugar
½ teaspoon cinnamon
⅛ teaspoon ground mace
1 egg, beaten

Prepare either pie dough as directed.

Preheat the oven to 425°. Peel and core the apples. Cut each apple into 8 wedges, then cut each wedge in half crosswise. Put the apple chunks in a bowl and sprinkle them with ¼ cup of sugar, the cinnamon, and the mace. Toss with a spoon to coat the fruit.

Divide the pie dough in half. On a lightly floured surface, roll one half into a 12-inch circle. Line a 9-inch pie pan with it (see "Forming the pie shell," page 24). The dough should overlap about 1 inch all around.

Heap the apples in the pie shell, piling them higher in the center. Scrape any sugar left in the bowl over them.

Roll the remaining pie dough into a 13-inch circle. Brush the edge of the pie shell lightly with beaten egg. Lay the circle of dough over the pie. Fold and flute the edges as instructed on page 24. When fluting, push your thumb toward your index finger to create a slanted design around the edge.

Brush the top of the pie (but not the edges) with water and sprinkle on the remaining 1 teaspoon of sugar. Cut 4 small slashes in the top to let steam escape. Bake on the lowest shelf in the oven. Check the pie after the first 10 minutes of baking. If the top is already brown and looks as if it might burn, turn the heat down immediately to 375°. Otherwise, rotate the pie after the first 15 minutes and turn the oven temperature down to 375°. Continue baking until the crust is golden brown and the fruit juices have begun to thicken, about 1 hour. Cool on a wire rack. Serve warm or at room temperature.

Gala Apple Pie

Royal Gala apples are sweet and rich, with a full flavor. I like them better for pies than many other cooking apples because they hold up well during baking and don't get mushy.

SERVES 10

1 recipe pie dough (page 23 or 25)
7 Royal Gala apples
½ cup plus 1 tablespoon sugar
1 teaspoon cinnamon
1 tablespoon tapioca
⅛ teaspoon ground mace
2 tablespoons unsalted butter
1 egg, lightly beaten

Prepare either pie dough as directed.

Preheat the oven to 425°. Peel the apples, cut them in half, and remove the cores. Place an apple half cut side down on a cutting board and cut it in half. Turn both pieces 90 degrees and cut it in half again, giving you four roughly equal pieces. Cut each piece into thirds. Repeat with the rest of the apple halves.

Combine ½ cup of sugar with the cinnamon, tapioca, and mace. Sprinkle over the apples and toss to coat the fruit.

Divide the pie dough in half. On a lightly floured surface, roll one half into a 12-inch circle. Line a 9-inch pie pan with it (see "Forming the pie shell," page 24).

Heap the apples in the pie shell, piling them higher in the center. Scrape any sugar mixture left in the bowl over them. Cut the butter into 6 pats and scatter it over the fruit.

Roll the remaining pie dough into a 13-inch circle. Brush the edge of the pie shell lightly with beaten egg. Lay the circle of dough over the pie. Fold and crimp the edges as instructed on page 24.

Brush the top of the pie (but not the edges) with water and sprinkle on the remaining 1 teaspoon of sugar. Cut 8 small slashes in the top to let steam escape. Bake on the lowest shelf in the oven for 20 minutes, then rotate the pie and turn the oven temperature down to 350°. Continue baking until the crust is golden brown and the fruit is bubbling, about 1 hour. Cool on a wire rack. Serve warm or at room temperature.

Apple-Walnut Pie

This is an unusual apple pie. It is denser and more complex than the average apple pie because it has a layer of spiced walnuts beneath the apples. I developed the recipe with ripe Cortland apples, but you can use any of the softer, sweeter apples. Tart apples, however, will not combine well with the vinegar.

SERVES 8 TO 10

1 recipe Flaky Pie Dough (page 23)
4 medium apples
2 tablespoons plus 1 teaspoon sugar
1 cup brown sugar
2 teaspoons ground cinnamon
2 large eggs
2 tablespoons unsalted butter
2 cups walnut pieces
1 teaspoon apple cider vinegar

Prepare the flaky pie dough as directed.

Peel and core the apples; cut them into 1-inch chunks. Toss the apple chunks with 2 tablespoons of sugar in a bowl. Set them aside.

Sift the brown sugar and cinnamon into another bowl. Add 1 egg and stir until smooth. Melt the butter and stir it in. Stir in the walnuts and vinegar.

Preheat the oven to 450°.

Divide the pie dough in half and roll each half into a 12-inch circle. Fold one of the circles into quarters and transfer it gently to an 8-inch pie pan. Unfold the dough so that it lines the bottom and sides of the pan. Work your way around the edge, gently lifting the dough to settle it into the pan. Press the dough gently against the sides of the pan.

Spoon the walnuts evenly into the pie shell. Add the apple chunks, pressing them carefully into a shallow dome shape. Lightly beat the remaining egg and brush the edges of the dough with part of it; lay the second circle of dough over the fruit. Press the top and bottom circles together around the edge of the pie, then trim off the overlapping dough, leaving about 2 inches of overlap all the way around. Work your way around the pan, lifting the overlapping dough and folding it under so that the cut edge rests on the rim of the pan. Crimp the edge as instructed in the pie dough recipe.

Brush the top of the pie lightly with water and sprinkle it with the remaining teaspoon of sugar. Cut 4 small slashes near the center to let steam escape. Bake on the bottom oven shelf for 10 minutes. Reduce the temperature to 375° and rotate the pie to reverse front and back. Continue baking until the crust is golden brown and the fruit bubbles, 35 to 40 minutes more. Cool on a wire rack for at least 30 minutes before serving; as the pie cools, the fruit reabsorbs much of the liquid it has released during baking. Serve warm or at room temperature.

Apple-Almond Pie

A rich almond cream lies beneath the apples in this unusual pie. As the apples bake, they release juices that are absorbed by the almond cream, infusing it lightly with apple flavor and keeping it moist.

SERVES 10

1 recipe Flaky Pie Dough (page 23)
8 ounces almond paste
8 tablespoons (¼ pound) unsalted butter (soft)
2 tablespoons all-purpose flour
3 large eggs
4 large apples (about 2 pounds)
1 tablespoon lemon juice
2 tablespoons sugar

Prepare the flaky pie dough as directed.

Preheat the oven to 450°. Blend the almond paste and butter together in a food processor until smooth and free of lumps. Add the flour and 2 eggs and continue mixing until well blended.

Peel, quarter, and core the apples. Cut each quarter into ½-inch-thick wedges, then cut each wedge crosswise into thirds. Toss the apple pieces in a bowl with the lemon juice and sugar.

Divide the pie dough in half. Refrigerate one half; on a lightly floured surface, roll the other half into a 12-inch circle. Fold the circle in half and lay it over half of a 9-inch pie pan. Unfold the dough so that it covers the pie plate. Work your way around the pan, gently lifting the edges to let the dough settle into the bottom of the pan, then press the dough gently against the sides and bottom. Lightly beat the remaining egg and brush the rim of the pie shell with part of it.

Spoon the almond cream evenly into the bottom of the shell. Spread the apples over the almond cream. Roll the remaining dough into a 12-inch circle and lay it over the fruit. Press the edges of the dough together to seal them, then cut away any excess dough, leaving a clean edge. Cut 6 holes in the top of the pie to let steam escape.

Place the pie in the preheated oven and immediately lower the temperature to 375°. Continue baking until the crust is golden brown and the apples are tender, about 45 minutes. Cool on a wire rack. Serve warm or at room temperature.

Autumn Fruit Pie

Although I think of this pie as a celebration of autumn, it really draws on the bounty of two seasons, combining the fall harvest of apples and walnuts with two varieties of dried summer figs.

SERVES 8 TO 10

CRUST

2½ cups all-purpose flour
1 teaspoon kosher salt
1 tablespoon sugar
16 tablespoons (½ pound) unsalted
      butter (cold)
¼ cup cold water

FILLING

1 cup dried mission figs
1 cup dried calimyrna figs
2 cups cold water
2 medium apples
1½ cups walnut pieces
¼ teaspoon ground cinnamon
2 teaspoons grated orange zest
2 tablespoons sugar
1 large egg, beaten, for brushing

CRUST

To begin the pie crust, combine the flour, salt, and sugar in a large bowl. Cut the butter into 1-inch cubes and cut them into the flour or mix them in with the paddle attachment of an electric mixer until the mixture resembles coarse meal. Add the water and toss gently to blend. Press the dough together. Wrap it in plastic wrap and refrigerate until needed.

FILLING

With a small knife, remove the hard bit of stem at the tip of each fig. Place all the figs in a medium saucepan with water and bring it to a boil. Reduce it to a simmer and cook until the figs are tender, 15 to 20 minutes. Strain them, discarding the liquid, and set aside to cool.

Preheat the oven to 425°. Chop the cooled figs into ½-inch chunks. Peel, quarter, and core the apples; cut them into ½-inch pieces. Combine the fruits and walnuts in a large bowl. Blend the cinnamon, orange zest, and 1 tablespoon of sugar and sprinkle the mixture over the fruit; toss to blend evenly.

Cut the chilled pie dough in half. On a lightly floured surface, roll each half into a 13-inch circle. Line the bottom of a 9-inch pie pan with one circle. Spoon the fruit mixture into the shell, gently pressing it into place. Brush the rim of the shell with beaten egg, and top the pie with the other circle of dough. Crimp the edges (see page 24). Brush the top of the pie (but not the edges) lightly with water; sprinkle on the remaining tablespoon of sugar. Cut 4 small slashes in the top crust to allow steam to escape.

Bake the pie on the lowest oven shelf for 15 minutes, then reduce the temperature to 375°. Continue baking until the top is golden brown, about 30 minutes. Cool on a wire rack.

Blueberry Pie

As apple pie is the essence of autumn, blueberry pie and peach pie are summer to me. When blueberries, wild or cultivated, are at their peak, get yourself a generous amount, and mound them into a pie shell. This is no time for frugality; blueberry pie should be *full* of blueberries.

SERVES 10

1 recipe pie dough (page 23 or 25)
3 pints blueberries
1 tablespoon lemon juice
3 tablespoons tapioca
¾ cup plus 1 teaspoon sugar
1 egg, lightly beaten

Prepare either pie dough as directed.

Preheat the oven to 400°. Divide the pie dough in half. On a lightly floured surface, roll one half into a 12-inch circle. Line a 9-inch pie pan with it (see "Forming the pie shell," page 24).

Wash and drain the blueberries. Sprinkle them with the lemon juice, tapioca, and ¾ cup of sugar; toss to coat the berries. Heap the berries in the pie shell, piling them higher in the center. Scrape any sugar and tapioca left in the bowl over them.

Roll the remaining pie dough into a 13-inch circle. Brush the edge of the pie shell lightly with beaten egg. Lay the circle of dough over the pie. Fold and crimp the edges as shown on page 24.

Brush the top of the pie (but not the edges) with water and sprinkle on the remaining 1 teaspoon of sugar. Cut 8 small slashes in the top to let steam escape. Bake for 20 minutes, then rotate the pie, slip a cookie sheet under it, and lower the oven temperature to 350°. Continue baking until the crust is golden brown and the fruit is bubbling, about 40 minutes. Cool on a wire rack. Serve warm or at room temperature.

Peach Pie

Juicy, ripe, sweet peaches make a glorious pie. Lively in both color and flavor, it is the perfect summer dessert. Serve it warm or at room temperature, either plain (can peach pie ever be plain?!) or accompanied by a scoop of vanilla ice cream.

SERVES 10

1 recipe pie dough (page 23 or 25)
8 medium peaches, ripe and firm
2½ tablespoons tapioca
¾ cup plus 1 teaspoon sugar
1 egg, lightly beaten

Prepare either pie dough as directed.

Preheat the oven to 400°. Wash the peaches. Cut each peach into 8 wedges, then cut each wedge crosswise into thirds. Put the pieces in a bowl and sprinkle on the tapioca and ¾ cup of sugar. Toss with a spoon to coat the fruit.

Divide the pie dough in half. On a lightly floured surface, roll one half into a 12-inch circle. Line a 9-inch pie pan with it (see "Forming the pie shell," page 24).

Put the peaches in the pie shell and scrape any sugar and tapioca left in the bowl over them.

Roll the remaining pie dough into a 13-inch circle. Brush the edge of the pie shell lightly with beaten egg. Lay the circle of dough over the pie. Fold and crimp the edges as shown on page 24.

Brush the top of the pie (but not the edges) with water and sprinkle on the remaining 1 teaspoon of sugar. Cut 8 slashes in the top to let steam escape. Place the pie pan on a cookie sheet and bake until the crust is golden brown and the fruit is bubbling, about 1½ hours. Cool on a wire rack. Serve warm or at room temperature.

Blackberry Pie

If you are lucky enough to have blackberries growing in your yard, or you know a place to gather them wild, treat yourself to one of summer's great treasures—a luscious, juicy blackberry pie. Even if you have to buy the berries, which can be expensive, this pie is worth it.

SERVES 10

1 recipe Tart Dough (page 23) or Lard Dough
    (page 25)
6 cups blackberries (2 dry pints)
3 tablespoons tapioca
⅔ cup sugar
½ teaspoon lemon zest
½ teaspoon orange zest
1 tablespoon unsalted butter
1 egg, lightly beaten
1 tablespoon whipping cream

Prepare either dough as directed.

Preheat the oven to 500°. Wash and drain the berries and put them in a bowl. Sprinkle on the tapioca, sugar, and lemon and orange zest. Toss to coat the berries.

Divide the dough in half. On a lightly floured surface, roll one half into a 12-inch circle. Line a 9-inch pie pan with it (see "Forming the pie shell," page 24). Fill the pie shell with the berries; scrape in any sugar and tapioca left in the bowl. Cut the butter into 5 pieces and dot the fruit with them.

Roll the remaining pie dough into a 13-inch circle. Brush the edge of the pie shell lightly with beaten egg. Lay the circle of dough over the pie. Fold and crimp the edges as shown on page 24.

Brush the top of the pie (but not the edges) with the cream. Cut 8 small slashes in the top to let steam escape. Bake for 10 minutes, then rotate the pie, slip a cookie sheet under it, and lower the oven temperature to 375°. Continue baking until the crust is golden brown and the fruit is bubbling, about 1 hour and 10 minutes. Slip the tip of a knife in through one of the slashes; the juices should look syrupy, not thin.

Cool on a wire rack. Serve warm or at room temperature, plain or with lightly whipped unsweetened cream or vanilla ice cream.

Rhubarb and Peach Pie

The tartness of rhubarb combines wonderfully with the smooth sweetness of ripe peaches. And the red of the rhubarb gives the peaches a rosy glow. As the pie cools, the juices thicken and the fruit reabsorbs some of the liquid, so resist the temptation to cut a slice while the pie is still piping hot.

SERVES 10

1 recipe Tart Dough (page 50)
1 pound rhubarb (4 or 5 stalks)
4 medium peaches, ripe and firm
¾ cup plus 1 teaspoon sugar
3 tablespoons tapioca
1 egg, lightly beaten

Prepare the tart dough as directed.

Trim the rhubarb, being sure to remove all the leaves and any green stem ends. Wash and dry the stalks and cut them crosswise into ¾-inch pieces.

Wash the peaches and cut them into ½-inch chunks. Combine the rhubarb, peaches, ¾ cup of sugar, and the tapioca in a bowl. Toss to coat the fruit and set aside for 15 minutes.

Preheat the oven to 400° and set an oven rack in the lowest possible position. Divide the tart dough in half. On a lightly floured surface roll half the dough into a 12-inch circle. Line a 9-inch pie pan with it (see "Forming the pie shell," page 24). Heap the fruit in the pie shell, mounding it higher in the center. Scrape in any sugar and tapioca left in the bowl.

Roll the rest of the dough into a 13-inch circle. Brush the edge of the pie shell lightly with beaten egg. Lay the circle of dough over the fruit; fold and crimp the edges as shown on page 24. Brush the top of the pie (but not the edges) with water, and sprinkle on the remaining 1 teaspoon of sugar. Cut 8 small slashes to let steam escape. Bake 20 minutes.

Rotate the pie, slip a cookie sheet under it, and lower the oven temperature to 350°. Continue baking until the crust is golden brown, the fruit juices have thickened slightly, and the fruit is bubbling, about 50 minutes. Cool on a rack for at least 20 minutes before serving.

Fig and Nectarine Pie

A combination of figs and nectarines gives this pie a particularly lush and fragrant filling. The not-too-sweet crumb topping adds crunch.

SERVES 10

½ recipe pie dough (page 23 or 25)
6 or 7 fresh figs
4 medium nectarines
1½ cups sugar
2 tablespoons tapioca
⅛ teaspoon almond extract
1 cup all-purpose flour
10 tablespoons unsalted butter (cold)

Prepare either pie dough as directed.

Preheat the oven to 450°. On a lightly floured surface, roll the pie dough into a 13-inch circle (see "Forming the pie shell," page 24). Fold the circle into quarters and transfer it gently to a 9-inch pie pan. Unfold the dough so that it lines the bottom and sides of the pan. Work your way around the edge, gently lifting the dough to settle it into the pan. Press the dough gently against the sides of the pan. Trim off any excess.

Wash the figs, remove the stems, and cut each fig into 8 wedges; you should have about 2 cups. Wash the nectarines and cut each into 8 wedges, then cut each wedge in half crosswise. Toss the figs and nectarines together in a bowl.

In another bowl combine ½ cup of sugar and the tapioca. Add the almond extract and toss the ingredients together until they look and feel like moist sand. Add the mixture to the fruit and toss to mix. Heap the fruit in the unbaked pie shell, being sure to scrape in all the sugar syrup from the bottom of the bowl.

Blend the remaining cup of sugar and the flour in a bowl. Cut the butter into small pieces. Using the paddle attachment on a tabletop mixer or a hand-held mixer, blend the butter with the flour and sugar until large clumps form. Cover the fruit with the topping. Place the pie in the oven and reduce the heat to 425°. After 15 minutes reduce it to 375°, and continue baking until the topping is golden brown, about 55 minutes. Cool before serving

Butterscotch Pie

The distinctive flavor of butterscotch comes from blending butter and brown sugar. I add vinegar to my butterscotch to cut the sweetness; it must be added last, or its acidity can cause the milk to curdle. Apple cider vinegar is the only vinegar suitable for desserts; never substitute another kind.

SERVES 8

½ recipe pie dough (page 23 or 25)
2 large eggs
1 tablespoon cornstarch
1 tablespoon all-purpose flour
1 cup dark brown sugar, firmly packed
2½ cups milk
4 tablespoons unsalted butter
½ teaspoon apple cider vinegar
1 cup whipping cream

Prepare a 9-inch pie shell as directed and prebake according to the directions on page 25.

Preheat the oven to 350°. Whisk the eggs, cornstarch, flour, and ⅓ cup of brown sugar together in a large bowl. Scald the milk. In a separate, heavy saucepan, heat the remaining ⅔ cup of brown sugar over medium heat until it liquifies. Stir occasionally with a wire whisk as the sugar melts. When the sugar is completely melted, turn off the heat under it. Meanwhile, bring some water to a simmer in the bottom of a double boiler.

Whisk the hot milk into the egg mixture, then pour it slowly into the melted sugar, stirring constantly. When it is smooth, pour the entire mixture into the top of the double boiler. Cook, stirring constantly, until it starts to thicken. Remove the top of the boiler from the heat and stir in the butter. When the butter is incorporated, stir in the vinegar.

Pour the filling into the prebaked pie shell and bake in the middle of the oven until the filling starts to set, about 20 minutes. Cool the pie on a wire rack, then refrigerate until firm.

Whip the cream to soft peaks. Spoon it into a pastry bag with a #7 star tip. Pipe whipped cream rosettes, close together, all around the edge of the pie. Refrigerate until ready to serve.

Boston Lemon Pie

I collect old menus and I like to read old cookbooks. I first came across this pie in a turn-of-the-century book for professional bakers. It is very unusual because the filling is really a soufflé. Like a soufflé, it rises high when baked, then collapses somewhat as it cools.

SERVES 8

½ recipe pie dough (page 23 or 25)
4 large eggs
6 tablespoons lemon juice
1 teaspoon grated lemon zest
½ cup sugar
1 tablespoon powdered sugar

Prepare a 9-inch pie shell as directed and prebake according to the directions on page 25.

Preheat the oven to 350°. Separate the eggs. Beat the yolks in the top of a double boiler with the lemon juice, lemon zest, and ¼ cup of sugar. Cook over simmering water, stirring occasionally, until quite thick. Set aside.

Beat the egg whites with the remaining ¼ cup of sugar to soft peaks. Stir the egg yolk mixture until smooth, then fold in about 1 cup of the whites. Fold the entire mixture into the rest of the whites. Spoon the filling into the prebaked pie shell and dust the top with powdered sugar. Bake for 15 minutes, then rotate the pie to help it bake more evenly. Continue baking until the top rises and browns, about 5 minutes more. (The top may also crack, like a soufflé.)

Cool on a wire rack; serve at room temperature.

Lemon Meringue Pie

Lemon meringue pie is a longtime American favorite. This one is light and not too sweet.

SERVES 10

½ recipe pie dough (page 23 or 25)
4 large eggs
1 cup plus 2 teaspoons sugar
¼ cup cornstarch
½ cup lemon juice
Zest of 1 lemon
1 cup boiling water
4 tablespoons unsalted butter
⅛ teaspoon vanilla extract

Prepare a 9-inch pie shell as directed and prebake according to the directions on page 25.

Preheat the oven to 250°. Separate the eggs, putting the yolks in one bowl and two whites in each of two other bowls. Beat the yolks and set them aside.

Bring some water to a simmer in the bottom of a double boiler. Meanwhile, combine ¾ cup of sugar with the cornstarch in the top of the double boiler off the heat. Stir in the lemon juice with a whisk. Stir in the lemon zest and the cup of boiling water. Set the top of the double boiler over the simmering water. Whisk in the egg yolks; cut the butter into 4 pieces and stir it in. Cook, stirring occasionally with the whisk, until the mixture is thick and bright yellow. Remove it from the heat.

Beat 2 egg whites until foamy. Add 2 teaspoons of sugar and beat until thick (not all the way to soft peaks). Stir the lemon mixture and fold the beaten whites into it, one half at a time. Pour the mixture into the prebaked pie shell and smooth the top. Set aside to cool.

To make the meringue, beat the remaining 2 egg whites until foamy. Beat in the remaining ¼ cup of sugar, a tablespoon at a time. Add the vanilla and continue beating to stiff peaks. Spoon the meringue onto the pie and smooth it with the back of the spoon. Using the side of the spoon, make 5 parallel lines across the pie to create a ribbon-like pattern of ridges. Bake until the meringue is lightly browned, about 40 minutes. Cool on a wire rack. Serve at room temperature or chilled.

Orange Meringue Pie

This is a tasty variation on lemon meringue pie. Freshly squeezed orange juice tastes far better than prepackaged or frozen juice. You'll need 4 or 5 juice oranges for this recipe; I prefer Valencias. Their bright flavor is well worth the small amount of extra work it takes to juice them.

SERVES 10

½ recipe pie dough (page 23 or 25)
1¼ cups sugar
¼ cup cornstarch
3 large eggs
1½ cups freshly squeezed orange juice
1 teaspoon orange zest
1 tablespoon Grand Marnier liqueur
2 large egg whites
⅛ teaspoon vanilla extract

Prepare a 9-inch pie shell as directed and prebake according to the directions on page 25. Set aside.

To make an orange curd, combine 1 cup of sugar with the cornstarch. Beat in the 3 eggs. Stir in the orange juice and zest. Transfer the mixture to the top of a double boiler and cook it over simmering water, stirring occasionally, until it is pudding-thick. Stir in the Grand Marnier. Set aside to cool.

When cool, pour the mixture into the prebaked, cooled pie shell.

To make the meringue, preheat the oven to 350°. Beat the egg whites until foamy. Beat in the remaining ¼ cup of sugar, one tablespoon at a time. Add the vanilla and continue beating to stiff peaks. Spoon the meringue onto the pie. Bake until the meringue is lightly browned, about 15 minutes. Cool on a wire rack. Serve at room temperature or chilled.

Pineapple Meringue Pie

The dense texture and tropical flavor of ripe pineapple contrasts beautifully with a sweet, airy meringue. This is a somewhat unusual and very delicious pie that is showy enough for special occasions.

SERVES 10

½ recipe pie dough (page 23 or 25)
1 medium pineapple, ripe and firm
¼ cup cornstarch

1⅛ cups sugar
3 large eggs
1 tablespoon lemon juice
4 tablespoons unsalted butter

Prepare a 9-inch pie shell as directed and prebake according to the directions on page 25. Set aside.

Peel the pineapple, cut it into quarters, and remove the core. Grate it coarsely (using the large round holes on the grater or grate in a food processor); you need 2 cups of grated pineapple.

Combine the cornstarch and ¾ cup of sugar. Separate the eggs. Beat the egg yolks with an electric mixer. Slowly beat in 1 cup of grated pineapple, then the cornstarch and sugar and the lemon juice. Transfer the mixture to the top of a double boiler and cook over simmering water, stirring occasionally, until hot. Cut the butter into 1-inch cubes and stir it in. Cook until thick, then remove from the heat and stir in the remaining cup of grated pineapple. Set the filling aside to cool.

To make the meringue, preheat the oven to 350°. Beat the egg whites until foamy. Beat in the remaining 6 tablespoons of sugar, one tablespoon at a time. Continue beating until stiff peaks form. If you underbeat the egg whites they will shrink after baking.

Pour the pineapple filling into the prebaked pie shell and smooth the top. Spoon on the meringue, swirling it into blunt peaks if you wish (pointed tips will burn). Bake until the meringue is lightly browned, about 15 minutes. Cool on a wire rack. Serve at room temperature or chilled.

Rhubarb-Cherry Meringue Pie

Rhubarb and cherries make for a happy combination I discovered one day when both were irresistibly fresh and enticing in the market. The pie is topped with Italian meringue, which I find to be lighter and of a finer texture than the usual American version. It is made by beating a hot sugar syrup, instead of plain sugar, into beaten egg whites; a small amount of gelatin stabilizes the meringue so that it keeps quite nicely for several days (although the pie is unlikely to last that long).

SERVES 10

1 recipe Graham Cracker Crust (page 26)
1 pound rhubarb (4 or 5 stalks)
1¼ cups sugar
¼ teaspoon almond extract
1 pound bing cherries
1 envelope plus ½ teaspoon unflavored
gelatin

3 large egg whites
1 tablespoon lemon juice
Powdered sugar for dusting

Prepare the graham cracker crust and prebake as directed. Set aside.

Trim the rhubarb, removing all the leaves and the green ends of the stalks. Wash the stalks and cut them crosswise into ¾-inch pieces. Put the rhubarb in the top of a double boiler with ½ cup of sugar and the almond extract. Toss with a spoon to coat the pieces with sugar. Cook, covered, over simmering water, removing the cover occasionally to turn the rhubarb over with a spoon.

While the rhubarb cooks, wash and pit the cherries and put them in a bowl. When the rhubarb has cooked for 15 minutes, add the cherries and any cherry juice that has leaked into the bowl. Turn the mixture with a spoon until all the cherries are coated with sugar syrup and are well mixed with the rhubarb. Cover the pot and continue cooking, removing the cover to stir well every 5 minutes.

After 40 minutes total cooking time (25 minutes after adding the cherries), sprinkle the envelope of gelatin over 1 tablespoon of cold water in a small bowl. Stir to soften the gelatin. Transfer 2 tablespoons of hot liquid from the cooking fruit to the bowl of gelatin and work it in with the back of a spoon until the gelatin is dissolved. Add the gelatin mixture to the fruit and stir in well. The liquid from the rhubarb and cherries will begin to bind immediately; it will thicken more as it cools. Transfer the fruit mixture to a clean bowl and chill. When the mixture is cool to the touch, pour it into the prebaked, cooled pie shell. Refrigerate.

To make the meringue, preheat the oven to 425°. Sprinkle the remaining ½ teaspoon of gelatin over 1 tablespoon of cold water; set aside.

Bring ¾ cup of sugar and ¼ cup of water to a boil in a small, heavy pot. Continue cooking until the syrup registers 238° on a candy thermometer. Remove from the heat, add the gelatin, and stir until it dissolves. When you lift the spoon, the syrup should run off.

Beat the egg whites with an electric mixer at high speed until they form stiff peaks. With the mixer running, add the sugar syrup in a slow, steady stream. Add the lemon juice, and beat to soft peaks. Spread about ½ cup of the meringue over the pie, bringing it all the way to the edges. Draw a rubber scraper lightly over the perimeter of the shell to seal the meringue. Then spoon on the rest of the meringue, dropping it from the spoon to form peaks, but do not give them sharp tips (they will burn in the oven). If you want a more formal design, instead of making peaks, smooth the meringue with the back of a spoon, then draw the spoon through the meringue in a repeating zigzag pattern.

Dust the meringue lightly with powdered sugar and bake the pie until the top is lightly browned, about 10 minutes. Cool on a wire rack. Serve at room temperature or chilled.

Sour Plum Meringue Pie

Plums are not often baked in pies, but I especially like the way this one tastes. The dense sour-plum filling contrasts beautifully with the sweet, light cloud of Italian meringue. The filling has to be well chilled before the meringue goes on, and chilled again before serving, or else it can be runny.

SERVES 10

½ recipe pie dough (page 23 or 25)
8 sour plums
1 tablespoon plus 2 teaspoons lemon juice
1¼ cups sugar
2 envelopes unflavored gelatin
3 large egg whites
Powdered sugar for dusting

Prepare a 9-inch pie shell as directed and prebake according to the directions on page 25.

Wash the plums and cut each into 8 wedges. Cut each wedge in half crosswise. Put them in the top of a double boiler with 2 teaspoons of lemon juice and ½ cup of sugar. Stir to coat the fruit. Cook over simmering water, stirring occasionally, until the plums are soft, about 15 minutes. To test for doneness, lift a plum on a spoon and pierce it with a fork. Some of the plums will have broken up, but most should be intact, with their skin beginning to peel. The juice should be cloudy and slightly thickened.

Sprinkle 1½ envelopes of gelatin over 2 tablespoons of cold water in a small bowl. Stir to soften the gelatin. Add 2 tablespoons of juice from the cooking fruit and stir until the gelatin is completely dissolved. Stir the gelatin mixture into the fruit and remove it from the heat. Set the pan on a wire rack to cool. When the fruit is cool, pour it into the prebaked pie shell. Chill it well before making the meringue.

To make the meringue, preheat the oven to 425°. Sprinkle ½ teaspoon of gelatin over 1 tablespoon of cold water; set aside.

Bring the remaining ¾ cup of sugar and ¼ cup of water to a boil in a small, heavy pot. Continue cooking until the syrup registers 238° on a candy thermometer. Remove from the heat, add the gelatin, and stir until it dissolves. When you lift the spoon, the syrup should run off.

Beat the egg whites with an electric mixer at high speed until they form stiff peaks. With the mixer running, add the sugar syrup in a slow, steady stream. Add the remaining 1 tablespoon of lemon juice, and beat to soft peaks. Spread about ½ cup of the meringue over the chilled pie, bringing it all the way to the edges. Draw a rubber scraper lightly over the perimeter of the shell to seal the meringue. Then spoon on the rest of the meringue, dropping it from the spoon to form blunt peaks (sharp tips will burn in the oven).

Dust the meringue lightly with powdered sugar and bake until the top is lightly browned, about 10 minutes. Cool on a wire rack, then return it to the refrigerator to chill well before serving.

Nectarine Meringue Pie

In this colorful summer pie, tender but still-firm chunks of nectarine are surrounded by a slightly tart lemon-orange curd. The touch of citrus in the curd makes the flavor of the nectarines sparkle, yet it is subtle enough not to draw attention away from the fruit. The juice from the nectarines is absorbed by the curd as the pie cools; don't cut into it while it is hot.

SERVES 10

½ recipe pie dough (page 23 or 25)
2 large eggs
1½ cups sugar
3 tablespoons cornstarch
¼ cup plus 2 tablespoons lemon juice
¼ cup orange juice
1 cup boiling water
3 medium nectarines, ripe and firm
½ teaspoon unflavored gelatin
3 large egg whites
Powdered sugar for dusting

Prepare a 9-inch pie shell as directed and prebake according to the directions on page 25.

While it bakes, make a lemon-orange curd, as follows. Beat the eggs and put them in the top of a double boiler. Combine ¾ cup of sugar and the cornstarch and beat them into the eggs. Add ¼ cup of lemon juice, the orange juice, and the boiling water. Place the mixture over simmering water and cook, stirring occasionally, until thick. Transfer the curd to a clean bowl and set it aside to cool.

Wash the nectarines and cut each into 8 wedges; cut each wedge crosswise into thirds. (*Note:* If your nectarines are not fully ripe, sauté the pieces in 2 tablespoons of butter until they begin to soften.) Put the fruit in a bowl and sprinkle it with 1 tablespoon of lemon juice. Let it stand about 5 minutes, then fold it into the curd.

When the pie shell is fully baked, remove it from the oven and fill it with the nectarine filling. Put it back in the oven until the curd starts to set, about 20 minutes. Set it aside to cool completely.

To make the meringue, raise the oven temperature to 425°. Sprinkle the gelatin over 1 tablespoon of cold water; set aside.

Bring the remaining ¾ cup of sugar and ¼ cup of water to a boil in a small, heavy pot. Continue cooking until the syrup registers 238° on a candy thermometer. Remove from the heat, add the gelatin, and stir until it dissolves. When you lift the spoon, the syrup should run off.

Beat the egg whites with an electric mixer at high speed until they form stiff peaks. With the mixer running, add the sugar syrup in a slow, steady stream. Add the remaining 1 tablespoon of lemon juice and beat to soft peaks. Spread about ½ cup of the meringue over the cooled pie, bringing it all the way to the edges. Draw a rubber scraper lightly over the perimeter of the shell to seal the meringue. Then spoon on the rest of the meringue, dropping it from the spoon to form blunt peaks (sharp tips will burn in the oven).

Dust the meringue lightly with powdered sugar and bake the pie until the top is lightly browned, about 10 minutes.

Chocolate Cream Pie

This pie is lighter than many versions of chocolate cream pie because it uses whole eggs instead of just yolks and has no butter in the filling. If you cannot find bittersweet chocolate, use semisweet; the result will be a little sweeter, but still not overly sweet.

SERVES 8

½ recipe pie dough (page 23 or 25)
½ cup sugar
1 tablespoon cornstarch
3 large eggs
½ teaspoon vanilla extract
2 cups milk
2 ounces bittersweet chocolate
1 cup whipping cream

Prepare a 9-inch pie shell as directed and prebake according to the directions on page 25.

Preheat the oven to 350°. Combine the sugar and cornstarch and whisk them into the eggs. Whisk in the vanilla.

Warm the milk in a saucepan. Cut the chocolate into pieces and stir it into the milk until it melts. Pour the milk into the egg mixture and whisk until well mixed. Transfer the mixture to the top of a double boiler and cook over simmering water, whisking frequently, until it starts to thicken. Pour it into the prebaked pie shell. Bake until the filling begins to set, 10 to 15 minutes.

Cool the pie completely on a wire rack. Whip the cream to soft peaks and either spoon it onto the pie or pipe it on with a pastry bag. Refrigerate until ready to serve.

Key Lime Chiffon Pie

The traditional Key lime pie is made with real Key limes and condensed milk. I have replaced the condensed milk with unsweetened whipped cream to produce a pie that is lighter and less sweet. Since small, yellowish Key limes, grown in the Florida Keys, are not generally available in other parts of the United States, I use Mexican limes, which look and taste the same. If you can't find either, a mixture of lemon and lime juice is a good substitute.

SERVES 10

½ recipe Tart Dough (page 50)
3 cups whipping cream
1 teaspoon unflavored gelatin
6 tablespoons Key lime or Mexican lime juice
    or 3 tablespoons lime juice plus 3 ta-
    blespoons lemon juice
3 large eggs, separated
⅔ cup sugar

Prepare the tart dough as directed and form it into a 9-inch pie shell (see page 50). Prebake according to the directions on page 51. Set aside.

Whip 1 cup of cream to soft peaks and refrigerate until needed. Sprinkle the gelatin over the lime juice and set aside.

Combine the egg yolks with ⅓ cup of sugar and beat until light

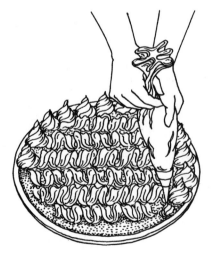

and smooth. Stir in the lime juice and gelatin mixture. Cook in the top of a double boiler over medium-high heat, stirring occasionally, until thick. Transfer to a bowl and set aside to cool.

Combine the egg whites with the remaining ⅓ cup of sugar and whip them to soft peaks. Fold in the cooled egg yolk mixture and then the 1 cup whipped cream. Spoon the filling into the cooled pie shell and chill until set, about 1 hour.

Whip the remaining 2 cups of cream to soft peaks. Spoon the cream into a pastry bag with a #7 star tip. Leaving about an inch around the edge of the pie, pipe out tight zigzag lines, the first from left to right, the next from right to left, until the center of the pie is covered in a herringbone pattern. (See illustration.) Then decorate the perimeter with a border of large rosettes. Refrigerate until ready to serve.

Kiwi-Lime Satin Cream Pie

Satin pies are light and cooling, the perfect end to a heavy or spicy meal. This one combines slightly tart kiwis with lime juice for a refreshing, tropical flavor.

SERVES 8

½ recipe pie dough (page 23 or 25)
3 large kiwis
2 teaspoons unflavored gelatin
3 tablespoons lime juice
3 large eggs
⅔ cup sugar
1 cup whipping cream

Prepare a 9-inch pie shell as directed and prebake according to the directions on page 25. Set aside.

Peel and purée the kiwis; you should have about 1 cup of purée. Set it aside.

Stir the gelatin into the lime juice and let it stand until softened.

Separate the eggs. Whisk the yolks. Stir in the kiwi purée, lime juice and gelatin, and ⅓ cup of sugar. Transfer the mixture to the top of a double boiler and cook over simmering water, stirring occasionally, until thickened. Set aside to cool.

Beat the cream until soft peaks form and refrigerate it.

Beat the egg whites and the remaining ⅓ cup of sugar until soft peaks form. Fold in the kiwi mixture and then the whipped cream. Spoon the filling into the prebaked, cooled shell. Refrigerate until ready to serve.

Lemon-Rum Ice Cream Pie with Strawberry Sauce

Ice cream pie is always a special treat. This one has a distinctly adult flavor, although the alcohol is completely burned off before the rum is added. Because both the crust and the filling need to be frozen, you'll need to start at least a day ahead.

SERVES 10

1 recipe Graham Cracker Crust (page 26)
4 large eggs
1½ cups plus 2 tablespoons sugar
⅔ cup lemon juice
1 cup dark rum
2 cups whipping cream
2 pints fresh strawberries

Prepare the graham cracker crust a day ahead and freeze it overnight. (You may freeze it for up to a week.)

Whisk the eggs and 1½ cups of sugar in the top of a double boiler until smooth. Stir in the lemon juice. Place over boiling water and cook, stirring occasionally, until thick. Set aside.

Pour the rum into a 6-cup frying pan; have a cover close by. Warm the rum for 30 seconds over low heat, then turn off the heat and ignite the rum by holding a lit match close to the edge of the pan. Allow the alcohol to burn off. If the flame gets too big, smother it by covering the pan. When the burning stops, shake the pan gently to be sure the flame is out. Stir in the lemon mixture, then transfer the mixture to a clean bowl and set it over ice water to cool.

When it is cool, stir in the cream. Freeze in an ice cream machine according to the manufacturer's instructions. Notice when the ice cream becomes firm. Continue freezing for about 10 minutes to incorporate air.

Spoon the ice cream into the frozen crust. Smooth the top, shaping it into a dome. Cover the pie with plastic wrap and a layer of foil, and freeze it until 10 minutes before serving.

Two hours before serving the pie, wash and drain the strawberries and remove the leaves. Cut the berries into ¼-inch slices. Toss them in a bowl with the remaining 2 tablespoons of sugar. Cover and chill. Serve the sauce with the pie.

Boston Cream Pie

No one knows why this cream-filled layer cake is called a pie. Perhaps the New England colonists who created it baked it in a pie pan, as I do. The cake was originally topped with a simple dusting of powdered sugar. The chocolate glaze was added by Boston's Parker House restaurant in the 1850s. Many Boston cream pies are glazed just on the top. This one, glazed top and sides, is based on the version I loved as a child in New Hampshire.

SERVES 12

PASTRY CREAM

½ cup sugar
2 tablespoons all-purpose flour
4 teaspoons cornstarch
2 large eggs
2 cups milk
6 tablespoons unsalted butter
½ teaspoon vanilla extract

CAKE

6 tablespoons unsalted butter (soft)
1 cup sugar
1⅓ cups all-purpose flour
1 teaspoon baking powder
1 large egg
½ cup milk
1 teaspoon vanilla extract

CHOCOLATE GLAZE

6 ounces bittersweet chocolate
6 tablespoons unsalted butter

PASTRY CREAM   Sift the sugar, flour, and cornstarch into a mixing bowl. Add the eggs and beat until light. Bring the milk to a boil in a heavy-bottomed saucepan. Stir half the milk into the egg mixture, then pour the whole mixture back into the saucepan. Cook over medium-high heat, stirring vigorously with a wire whisk, until the cream thickens and the center bubbles. Continue cooking and stirring another 30 seconds. Remove from the heat and stir in the butter and vanilla. Transfer to a bowl and cool to room temperature, stirring occasionally, then cover with plastic wrap and refrigerate at least 1 hour.

CAKE   Preheat the oven to 350°. Grease and flour a 9-inch pie pan. Cream the butter until soft and smooth. Sift the sugar, flour, and baking powder together.

Add the egg to the butter and mix until blended; they will not blend completely. Add half the dry ingredients and mix until smooth. The batter will be very thick. Scrape the sides and bottom of the bowl and add the milk. Mix gently until blended. Add the remaining dry ingredients and the vanilla and mix until light and smooth. Spoon the batter into the prepared pan and smooth the top. Bake until the top is golden brown, the sides have pulled away from the pan, and the center springs back when lightly touched, about 40 minutes. Cool in the pan on a wire rack.

When the cake has cooled completely, remove it from the pan, turn it upside down, and split it into two layers. Use a long-bladed slicer or serrated knife, and be sure to keep the knife level as you draw it through the cake. Center the wider, bottom layer on a cake plate, cut side up. Spread the chilled pastry cream over the layer. Add the second layer and press it down gently. Refrigerate the cake while you prepare the glaze.

CHOCOLATE
GLAZE

Cut the chocolate into small pieces. Put it and the butter in the top of a double boiler over boiled (not boiling) water. When most of the chocolate has melted, stir until smooth. Spread the glaze evenly over the top and sides of the cake. Refrigerate until 15 minutes before serving. The glaze will become quite hard. For clean slices, cut the cake with a thin-bladed knife rinsed with hot water before each cut.

Cherry-Coconut Pie

This pie recipe is a variation of a recipe given to me by a good friend and outstanding home cook, Joyce Lignelli from Clarion, Pennsylvania.

SERVES 8

3 cups fresh bing cherries
2 teaspoons lemon juice
3 tablespoons quick-cooking tapioca
¾ cup sugar
9-inch Tart Shell (page 50), prebaked
2 large eggs, beaten
¼ cup unsalted butter (melted)
¼ teaspoon vanilla extract
½ cup fresh grated coconut

Remove the stems from the berries. Wash them in cold water and drain until dry. Remove the pits from the cherries using a pitter or a small knife. In the top of a double boiler, combine the cherries, lemon juice, tapioca, and ¼ cup sugar. Cook over medium heat, stirring occasionally, until the tapioca dissolves and the juices thicken, 15 to 20 minutes. Remove from the heat. Spoon into a bowl and chill over ice water. Preheat the oven to 375°.

Spoon the cherry filling into the shell and spread it evenly. Blend together ½ cup sugar and the eggs. Stir in the remaining ingredients. Pour over the cherries and bake 45 to 50 minutes or until the top center is golden brown. Remove from the oven and cool on a wire rack. The pie may be served after 30 minutes or covered and chilled when completely cooled.

3

Tarts

TARTS ORIGINATED in Europe but have been enthusiastically adopted by American bakers. They are simpler for many home cooks to make than pies, because they have no top crust; if pie crusts are difficult for you to manage, tarts may be the answer.

I find tarts among the most beautiful of desserts. The gleaming berries or slices of fruit, whether carefully laid in concentric circles or scattered with abandon, are a glorious celebration of the fruits of the season. I especially like to pair the fruits with spices or other flavorings that highlight them and give them new dimension. Among my current favorite flavor combinations are cinnamon with quince and orange with caramel. I like pairing strawberries with peppermint, with anise, or with orange. Sometimes in creating a new tart I put a second flavor in the tart shell, sometimes with the fruit, and sometimes in a pastry cream layer under the fruit. I follow my whims and my instincts for compatible flavors.

If you want to try some of your own combinations, first taste the raw fruit you intend to put in the tart. Then taste the spice or flavoring or second fruit you think would go well with it. Let the two flavors mingle in your mouth. If they create a pleasant effect on your tongue, they will probably create a pleasant effect in the tart.

Fruits that are already soft when ripe need little or no baking. Berries and other tender fruits can simply be arranged in a prebaked tart shell and glazed to a shine. Fruits that need some baking, but not enough to bake the tart shell, I put into a partially baked (blind baked) shell, so that fruit and shell can bake together to perfection. Fruits that need long baking should go into an unbaked shell and the two should be baked together.

Tarts are complete and richly satisfying in themselves. I almost never serve them with ice cream or even whipped cream. An exception is the Brown Sugar Walnut Tart on page 70. I like that best with maple ice cream.

Tart Dough

I use this light, flaky dough for pies, tarts, and even cheesecake (see page 116). It can be made equally well by hand, in a mixer, or in a food processor. Just remember to use cold butter and to stop mixing as soon as the dough comes together. Overmixing will make your crust tough. The recipe can be doubled, but it will not work well if you increase it more than that.

MAKES 2 TART SHELLS OR 1 DOUBLE-CRUST PIE

8 tablespoons (¼ pound) unsalted butter
  (cold)
2 teaspoons sugar
¼ teaspoon kosher salt
1½ cups all-purpose flour
6 tablespoons whipping cream

MIXER METHOD

Cut the butter into 1-inch cubes. Place it in the mixer bowl with the sugar, salt, and flour. Using the paddle attachment, blend at low speed until the mixture resembles coarse meal. Add the cream and mix until the dough comes together.

*FOOD
PROCESSOR
METHOD*

Cut the butter into 1-inch cubes. Place it in the work bowl with the sugar, salt, and flour. Pulse until the butter is all cut in and the flour takes on a golden tone. Add the cream and pulse just until the dough starts to come together. Turn the dough out onto a lightly floured table and gently press it into the table until it comes together.

HAND METHOD

Combine the sugar, salt, and flour in a bowl and chill in the freezer for half an hour. Cut the butter into 1-inch cubes. Add it to the bowl and toss the ingredients together until the butter is coated with flour. Pinch the flour and butter together until all the butter is in thin flakes. Then begin rubbing small amounts of the mixture between your thumb and fingers, lifting it and letting it drop back into the bowl, until it resembles coarse meal. Pour in the cream. Turn it in with a rubber spatula, turning the flour over repeatedly in the bowl. When all the cream is absorbed, press the dough together against the bottom of the bowl.

Roll out immediately, or shape the dough into a 5-inch round patty. Wrap it well in plastic wrap and chill until needed.

*TO SHAPE
A TART SHELL*

Use a half-recipe of dough for each tart shell. On a lightly floured surface roll the dough into a 13-inch circle. Fold the dough into quarters and lift it into a 9- or 10-inch tart pan. Unfold the circle carefully and settle it into the pan, being sure it reaches into the corners. Gently press the dough against the sides of the pan.

Fold the overlapping dough into the pan just to where the sides and bottom meet, to form double-thick sides. Gently press the dough against the sides of the pan, being careful not to press against the bottom. (If the dough is too thin where the sides meet the bottom, it will split during baking.) Trim off the extra dough by running a cutting pin (see page 19) around the top edge. Chill until firm, about 20 minutes.

TO BLIND BAKE A TART SHELL   Preheat the oven to 400°. Line the tart shell with heavy aluminum foil, covering the edges as well as the bottom. Take a fork and poke holes all over the bottom of the shell, piercing both foil and dough. It is important to hold the fork straight down so that the tines will not tear large holes in the dough. Bake until the inside of the shell no longer looks raw (lift the foil and look at it), 15 to 20 minutes. It will still look pale. Remove the foil.

TO PREBAKE A TART SHELL   Blind bake as directed above. After 20 minutes of baking, remove the foil and continue baking until the shell is golden brown and has pulled away from the sides of the pan, about 15 minutes more.

Warm Pear Tart

This is a very simple tart. Its flavor is fresh and delicate, and being filled with only orange-scented pears, it is very light. When I want a somewhat richer dessert, I serve it with scoops of Anisette Ice Cream (page 167).

SERVES 8

½ recipe Tart Dough (page 50)
2 teaspoons all-purpose flour
2 teaspoons orange zest
4 ripe pears (see note below)
2 tablespoons orange juice
1 tablespoon sugar

Preheat the oven to 400°.

Prepare the tart dough and roll into an 11-inch circle. Fold the dough into quarters and lift it into a 9-inch tart pan. Unfold the circle carefully and settle it into the pan, being sure it reaches into the corners. Gently press the dough against the sides of the pan, being careful not to press against the bottom. Trim the edge of the dough, allowing it to extend ¼ inch above the pan.

Sprinkle the flour and then the orange zest inside the tart shell. Set aside. Peel, halve, and core the pears. Cut each half lengthwise into 8 slices. Set aside 2 of the prettiest halves, cut in slices but with the slices still formed into the half. Arrange the slices from the other 6 halves in a circle around the outer edge of the shell, with the wider ends touching the sides of the shell. The slices should overlap. Fan the slices

 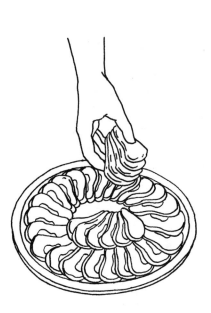

of the 2 remaining halves and fill in the center of the tart with them; they will overlap the outer circle.

Brush the pears with the orange juice and sprinkle the sugar over them. Work your way around the outside edge of the tart pushing the dough down with one finger so that it touches the fruit at 1-inch intervals; this will produce a wavy, decorative effect. Bake the tart on the lowest shelf in the oven until the shell is brown and the pear juice thickens and becomes glossy like a syrup, about 40 minutes. Cool 10 minutes on a wire rack; serve warm.

NOTE   If you cannot find fully ripe pears, you can achieve the same effect by poaching underripe pears. Peel, halve, and core the underripe pears. Combine 3 cups of water, 2 cups of sugar, and a vanilla bean in a saucepan and bring it to a boil. Add the pears, reduce to a simmer, and cook until tender. When the tip of a sharp knife easily pierces the pears, they are done. Remove the pan from the heat and let the pears cool in the syrup.

Cinnamon-Quince Tart

Spicy cinnamon and delicate quince are a wonderful combination. Here the cinnamon scents a pastry cream filling that is crowned with slices of the poached and glazed fruit.

SERVES 10

½ recipe Tart Dough (page 50)
2 large quinces
2 cups plus 1 tablespoon water
1¼ cups sugar
1 tablespoon all-purpose flour
2 teaspoons cornstarch
1 large egg
1 cup milk
¼ cinnamon stick
3 tablespoons unsalted butter (soft)
¼ teaspoon vanilla extract
¼ teaspoon gelatin

Prepare a 9-inch tart shell and prebake according to the directions on page 51. Set aside.

Peel the quinces, cut them into quarters, and remove their cores. (A melon baller does the coring very well.) Bring 2 cups of water and 1 cup of sugar to a boil in a medium saucepan. Add the quince and bring the water to a boil again; reduce the heat to maintain a simmer, cover the pan, and cook until the quince is glossy and can easily be pierced with a knife, about 15 minutes. Let the fruit cool in the syrup.

PASTRY CREAM   Sift the remaining ¼ cup of sugar, the flour, and the cornstarch together into a mixing bowl. Add the egg and beat until light. Put the milk and the cinnamon stick in a heavy-bottomed saucepan and bring it to a boil. Stir half the milk into the egg mixture, then pour the whole mixture back into the saucepan. Cook over high heat, stirring continuously and vigorously with a wire whisk, until the center bubbles and the mixture is very thick. Remove from the heat, discard the cinnamon stick, and stir in the butter and vanilla. Pour the pastry cream into a bowl, cover with plastic wrap, and refrigerate.

When the pastry cream is completely cooled, spread it evenly in the prebaked, cooled tart shell. Remove the quince from its syrup; set the syrup aside. Cut each quince quarter crosswise into ¼-inch-thick slices. Arrange the slices on the tart in rows. Start at the outer edge and make one row reaching to the center; each slice should slightly overlap the slice before. Start again at the edge and make a second row slightly overlapping the first. Continue until the entire tart is covered; place 2 slices in the center to fill the hole there. You should have some fruit left over.

Put 1 tablespoon of water in a small bowl and sprinkle the gelatin over it. Stir to dissolve the gelatin and set the bowl aside.

Purée the leftover slices of quince with the reserved syrup in a food processor. Transfer the purée to a saucepan and bring it to a simmer. Cook until it registers 230° on a candy thermometer. Strain the liquid into a bowl and stir in the softened gelatin. Brush the liquid generously over the tart to glaze it; don't get any on the crust. Use all the glaze. Set the tart aside until ready to serve.

Strawberry Tart with Peppermint Cream

Here's a new approach to an old favorite, the strawberry tart. Ripe strawberries lie on a bed of peppermint cream; its slight sharpness provides an unexpected counterpoint to the sweet-tart berries. The essence of peppermint adds enough flavor to the cream to bring it into the foreground, but not so that it competes with the berries. Dried peppermint, used to make peppermint tea, is available in bulk in health food stores.

SERVES 12

½ recipe Tart Dough (page 50)
1 teaspoon dried peppermint
1 cup milk
¼ cup sugar
1 tablespoon all-purpose flour
2 teaspoons cornstarch
1 large egg
3 tablespoons unsalted butter
½ cup whipping cream
2 pints strawberries
½ cup strawberry jelly (made with strawberries, not artificially flavored)

Prepare a 10-inch tart shell as directed and prebake according to the directions on page 51. Set aside.

Bring the peppermint and milk to a simmer in a heavy-bottomed saucepan. Remove the pan from the heat and let it stand for 2 minutes. Strain the milk into a bowl; press the peppermint against the sieve to extract all its flavor. Pour the milk back into the saucepan.

Rub the sugar, flour, and cornstarch together in a bowl. (This will prevent lumping when the egg is added.) Add the egg and mix until completely smooth. Meanwhile, bring the milk to a boil. Pour the milk into the egg mixture while mixing. Pour the mixture back into the saucepan and cook over medium-high heat, stirring constantly, until thick. Remove from the heat and stir in the butter. Transfer to a bowl and let cool completely, stirring occasionally.

Whip the cream to soft peaks and fold it into the cooked peppermint cream. Spread it evenly inside the prebaked, cooled tart shell. Chill for 30 minutes.

Wash and towel dry the berries. Discard the tops and cut the berries in half. Starting at the center, arrange the halves on the tart in concentric circles, points toward the center, covering it completely.

Melt the jelly over low heat, being careful not to let it get too hot. A hot glaze will draw juice out of the fruit. Brush a light coating of jelly over the berries. Serve at room temperature.

Anise and Strawberry Tart

I like to add spark to traditional tarts by flavoring the crust. Ground anise seeds make this tart shell taste toasty, with tiny bursts of licorice-like anise flavor. The filling is a smooth, vanilla-scented pastry cream topped with fresh strawberries.

SERVES 12

CRUST

1 tablespoon anise seeds
1¼ cups cake flour
½ cup powdered sugar
6 tablespoons unsalted butter (cold)
1 large egg yolk
2 teaspoons milk

FILLING

2 tablespoons all-purpose flour
1 teaspoon cornstarch
½ cup sugar
2 large eggs
2 cups milk
6 tablespoons unsalted butter
¼ teaspoon vanilla extract
2 pints strawberries
Powdered sugar for dusting

Preheat the oven to 350°. Spread the anise seeds in a pie pan and toast them in the oven until fragrant, about 30 seconds. Set them aside to cool and turn off the oven.

CRUST

To make the crust, blend the cake flour, powdered sugar, and anise seeds in a food processor until the anise is finely chopped. Cut the butter into 1-inch cubes and add them. Process until the mixture resembles coarse meal. Scrape the sides of the bowl. Add the egg yolk and milk and mix until the dough comes together. This is a very soft dough; if it is too soft to roll out, wrap it in plastic wrap and refrigerate for 30 minutes.

On a well-floured table, gently roll the dough into a 13-inch circle. Fold it into quarters and lift it into a 10-inch tart pan. Unfold the circle carefully and settle it into the pan, being sure it reaches into the corners. Gently press the dough against the sides of the pan.

Fold the overlapping dough into the pan just to where the sides and bottom meet, to form double-thick sides. Gently press the sides against the pan, being careful not to press against the bottom. Trim off the extra dough by running a cutting pin (see page 19) around the top edge. Chill until firm, about 20 minutes.

Preheat the oven to 400°. Line the tart shell with heavy aluminum foil, covering the edges as well as the bottom. Take a fork and poke holes all over the bottom of the shell, piercing both foil and dough. It is important to hold the fork straight down so that the tines will not tear large holes in the dough. Bake for 15 minutes, then remove the foil and continue baking until golden brown, about 5 minutes more. Set the shell aside to cool.

PASTRY CREAM   Sift the all-pupose flour, cornstarch, and sugar together. Beat the eggs and add the sifted ingredients to them. Beat until smooth and free of lumps. Bring the milk to a boil in a heavy saucepan. Pour half of the hot milk into the eggs and stir well. Pour the egg mixture back into the milk pan. Cook over medium-high heat, stirring constantly with a whisk, until the center bubbles and the cream thickens. Remove from the heat and stir in the butter and vanilla. Stir until the butter is completely incorporated. Pour the pastry cream into a clean bowl and refrigerate until it sets; keep it chilled until you are ready to use it.

Spread the pastry cream evenly in the cooled tart shell. Wash and towel dry the strawberries, cut off the tops, and cut the berries in half. Arrange the berry halves over the pastry cream in concentric circles. Start at the center and work outward, placing each berry with its point toward the center. Keep the tart refrigerated until ready to serve. Just before serving, dust the strawberries lightly with a tablespoon or two of powdered sugar.

Orange and Strawberry Tart for Elaine

I created this tart for Elaine Ratner's birthday. It was April and we were having a backyard dinner party. The fresh strawberries were beautiful that day, so I combined them with some sweet, seedless oranges to make a sort of sun design that celebrated the change of seasons as well as Elaine's birthday.

SERVES 8

CRUST

1 cup all-purpose flour
2 teaspoons sugar
Pinch of kosher salt
6 tablespoons unsalted butter (cold)
3 tablespoons half-and-half

FILLING

2 large eggs
½ cup sugar
⅓ cup orange juice (about 1 juice orange)
4 tablespoons unsalted butter
½ teaspoon vanilla extract
4 seedless oranges
1 pint strawberries

CRUST

Combine the flour, sugar, and salt in a large bowl. Cut the butter into ½-inch cubes and toss them with the flour until coated. Keeping the butter coated with flour, squeeze the lumps between your fingers and thumb to break it into flakes. Gently rub the flour and butter between open hands to produce a coarse meal. Add the half-and-half. Toss with a rubber spatula until the liquid is absorbed. Press the dough against the bottom of the bowl, then turn it out onto a lightly floured table and shape it into a patty. If the dough does not begin to come together, work it gently against the table until it does.

Dust the table and the dough lightly with flour. Roll the dough into a 13-inch circle. With a soft brush, brush any remaining flour off the dough. Lift the dough by winding it around the rolling pin and unroll it over a 9-inch tart pan so that it overlaps on all sides. Work your way around the pan, gently lifting the dough and letting it settle into the pan. Fold the overlapping dough into the pan just to where the sides and bottom meet, to form double-thick sides. Gently press the dough against the sides of the pan, being careful not to press against the bottom. Trim off the extra dough by running a cutting pin around the top edge (see page 19). Chill 30 minutes.

Preheat the oven to 400°. Line the tart shell with heavy aluminum foil, covering the edges as well as the bottom. Take a fork and poke holes all over the bottom of the shell, piercing both foil and dough. Hold the fork straight down so that the tines do not tear large holes in the dough. Bake until the bottom is very light brown, about 30 minutes. Remove the foil and cool the shell on a wire rack.

ORANGE CREAM

Reduce the oven temperature to 375°.

Beat the eggs with the sugar until light and smooth. Stir in the orange juice. Pour the mixture into the top of a double boiler. Cook it over simmering water, stirring occasionally, until it thickens. Stir in the butter and the vanilla. Pour this curd into the tart shell and bake until the filling sets, like a custard, about 12 minutes. Cool on a wire rack.

Cut the skin and white pith from the oranges. With a sharp knife, cut out the individual sections, leaving the dividing membranes behind. Arrange the orange sections on the tart in concentric circles, completely covering the top.

Wash and gently towel dry the strawberries. Remove the leaves and cut the berries in half vertically. Arrange them in concentric circles over the oranges, starting at the edge of the tart and leaving the center open. Cover the tart with plastic wrap and chill until 30 minutes before serving.

Lemon and Cointreau Tart

Adding white chocolate to a lemon cream reduces its acidity. The chocolate and lemon flavors balance each other, allowing a third flavor to shine through. In this case that flavor is the lovely orange liqueur Cointreau.

SERVES 10

½ recipe Tart Dough (page 50)
3 ounces white chocolate
2 large eggs
½ cup sugar
⅓ cup lemon juice
2 tablespoons Cointreau
1 cup whipping cream

Prepare a 9-inch tart shell and prebake according to the directions on page 51. Set aside. Cut the white chocolate into small pieces and set aside.

Beat the eggs until light. Beat in the sugar, then stir in the lemon juice. Transfer the mixture to the top of a double boiler and cook it over simmering water, stirring continuously, until it thickens enough to coat the back of a spoon. Remove the pot from the heat and stir in the chocolate until it is completely incorporated. Stir in the Cointreau. Set the lemon cream aside to cool; stir occasionally as it cools.

Whip the cream to just beyond soft peaks. Fold it into the cooled lemon cream and spoon it into the prebaked, cooled tart shell. Spread the filling evenly in the shell with the back of a spoon, doming it slightly in the center. Chill the tart at least 3 hours before serving. Serve chilled.

Nectarine and Walnut Tart

The walnuts in this tart are not in the filling but in the crust. They give it a subtly rich flavor that is not noticeably nutty; it provides a perfect background for ripe nectarines. The dough has to chill for an hour before baking, so be sure to allow yourself enough time.

SERVES 8

CRUST

⅓ cup walnuts
1 cup all-purpose flour
4 teaspoons sugar
⅛ teaspoon kosher salt
6 tablespoons unsalted butter (cold)
2 tablespoons milk

FILLING

1 teaspoon all-purpose flour
1 teaspoon cornstarch
3 tablespoons plus 1 teaspoon sugar
1 large egg
1 cup milk
1 tablespoon unsalted butter
3 drops vanilla extract
3 medium nectarines, ripe and firm

CRUST

Put the walnuts, flour, sugar, and salt in the work bowl of a food processor. Process until you stop hearing the nuts ping. Cut the butter into 1-inch cubes and add them to the bowl. Mix until the processor starts to hum. Add the milk and process until the dough comes together. Remove it from the bowl, wrap it in plastic wrap, and chill it for 40 minutes.

On a lightly floured surface roll the dough into a 12-inch circle. Fold the dough into quarters and lift it into a 9-inch tart pan. Unfold the circle carefully and settle it into the pan, being sure it reaches into the corners. Gently press the dough against the sides of the pan.

Fold the overlapping dough into the pan just to where the sides and bottom meet, to form double-thick sides. Gently press the dough against the sides of the pan, being careful not to press against the bottom. (If the dough is too thin where the sides meet the bottom, it will split during baking.) Trim off the extra dough by running a cutting pin around the top edge (see page 19). Chill the tart shell until firm, about 20 minutes.

Preheat the oven to 375°. Line the tart shell with heavy aluminum foil. Take a fork and poke holes all over the bottom of the shell, piercing both foil and dough. Hold the fork straight down so that the tines do not tear large holes in the dough. Bake for 30 minutes, then remove the foil. Continue baking until the shell is brown, about 5 minutes more.

PASTRY CREAM

While the shell is baking, make the pastry cream for the filling by sifting the flour with the cornstarch and 3 tablespoons of sugar. Beat the egg and add the sifted ingredients; beat until smooth and free of lumps. Bring the milk to a boil in a heavy saucepan. Pour half of the hot milk into the egg mixture, mix well, then pour the whole mixture back into the milk pan. Cook over medium heat, stirring constantly with a whisk, until the center bubbles and the cream thickens. Remove the pan from the heat and stir in the butter and the vanilla. Continue stirring until all the butter melts. Transfer the pastry cream to a clean bowl and set aside until the tart shell is done.

Spread the pastry cream evenly in the bottom of the hot tart shell. Wash and towel dry the nectarines and cut them into quarters. Cut each quarter lengthwise into 6 slices. Arrange the slices over the pastry cream in concentric circles. The slices from two of the nectarines will make the outer circle. Place each slice with one point toward the edge. Overlap them, making sure the skin is down against the cream (so it won't burn). Once you have laid down the entire circle, you can go back and straighten individual slices with the tip of a knife.

Three-quarters of the remaining nectarine will make the next circle. Place the slices facing the same way as those in the outer circle, slightly overlapping them. With the last ¼ nectarine, fill in the center. The entire top of the tart should be covered. Sprinkle the remaining teaspoon of sugar over the fruit. Bake until the pastry cream puffs up and the fruit begins to release its juices, about 30 minutes.

Remove the tart from the oven and set it on a wire rack to cool. Dip a pastry brush in the juice on top and very gently brush it over the fruit to moisten and glaze it. Serve at room temperature.

Pistachio and Peach Crumb Tart

Pistachios offer a pleasant flavor and texture contrast to the peaches in this tart without overwhelming them. The dry crumb topping absorbs much of the juice released by the peaches during baking. In baking, always use natural, unsalted pistachios.

SERVES 12

CRUST

¼ cup shelled pistachios
1 cup all-purpose flour
2 tablespoons sugar
1 teaspoon kosher salt
8 tablespoons (¼ pound) unsalted butter
    (cold)
¼ cup cold water

FILLING

8 tablespoons (¼ pound) unsalted butter
    (cold)
1 cup all-purpose flour
1 cup plus 2 tablespoons sugar
½ cup shelled pistachios
8 medium peaches
½ cup orange juice

CRUST

To make the crust, finely chop the pistachios. Combine them with the flour, sugar, and salt. Cut the butter into ½-inch cubes. Mix it into the flour mixture in a food processor or with the paddle attachment of an electric mixer until the mixture resembles coarse meal. Add the water and mix until the dough comes together.

Turn the dough out onto a lightly floured surface, dust the top with flour, and roll it out into a 13-inch circle. Lift the dough by rolling it around the rolling pin. Unroll it over a 10-inch tart pan so that the dough is draped over the pan with a 1-inch overlap all around. Work your way around the pan, gently lifting the edge of the dough so that it slips down into the pan. Press the dough against the sides of the pan; trim off any overlap by running a cutting pin the along the top edge (see page 19). Chill until firm, about 20 minutes.

Heat the oven to 375°. Line the tart shell with heavy aluminum foil, being sure to press it against the sides and all the way into the corner where the sides meet the bottom. Fill the foil with pie weights or dry beans. Bake 30 minutes. Carefully remove the foil and beans. Cool on a wire rack.

FILLING

To make the crumb topping for the filling, cut the butter into ½-inch cubes. Mix it with the flour and 1 cup of sugar until the mixture forms large, tender clumps that crumble when pinched; this is the stage beyond a fine meal. If when you pinch you feel solid butter, continue mixing until you reach the right consistency, but be careful not to overmix. Slightly overmixed topping will be tough; greatly overmixed topping will turn into a dough.

Coarsely chop the pistachios and add them to the topping; toss to distribute them.

Wash the peaches; cut them in half and discard the pits. Cut each half into 4 wedges, then cut the wedges in half crosswise. You should have about 6 cups. Toss the peaches in the orange juice, drain them, then toss them with the remaining 2 tablespoons sugar. Spoon the peaches into the tart shell and cover them evenly with the crumb topping. Do not press the topping into the fruit.

Bake until the top is golden brown, about 50 minutes. Cool on a wire rack. Serve at room temperature.

Cranberry Crumb Tart

I love the bright taste of cranberries. Here they are crowned with a golden crumb topping, which adds a pleasing contrast in texture and flavor. This is a wonderful holiday dessert.

SERVES 10

½ recipe Tart Dough (page 50)
6 cups cranberries (24 ounces)
12 tablespoons unsalted butter (cold)
1¼ cups bread flour
2½ cups sugar
½ teaspoon kosher salt

Prepare a 10-inch tart shell as directed and prebake according to the directions on page 50. Preheat the oven to 375°. Wash and towel dry the cranberries. Discard any bad ones. Set aside.

To make the crumb topping, cut the butter into 1-inch cubes. Using the paddle attachment on an electric mixer, mix the butter, flour, and 1¾ cups of sugar at medium-low speed until the mixture forms large clumps. The clumps should crumble when pinched; if you pinch into solid butter, keep mixing but be careful not to overmix to the dough stage. Set aside.

Combine the remaining ¾ cup sugar with the salt and toss it with the cranberries to coat them. Spoon the cranberries into the prebaked tart shell, mounding them slightly in the center. Spoon the crumb topping over the berries. Do not press the topping into the fruit.

Bake until the topping is golden brown and the fruit bubbles a little around the edge, about 40 minutes. Serve at room temperature.

Blueberry and Cream Tart

Adding a few ounces of white chocolate to whipped cream imparts a subtle flavor that goes extremely well with blueberries. The chocolate also binds the cream, making it more stable and preventing the liquid from separating out to make the crust soggy.

SERVES 12

CRUST

1 cup all-purpose flour
1 cup sliced almonds
9 tablespoons unsalted butter (cold)
3 tablespoons sugar

FILLING

2 ounces white chocolate
1 cup whipping cream, chilled
2½ pints blueberries, washed and towel dried

CRUST

To make the crust, mix the flour, almonds, butter, and sugar in a food processor or with the paddle attachment of an electric mixer. Mix beyond the crumb stage until the dough comes together. Turn the dough out onto a lightly floured surface and dust the top with flour. Roll the dough out into a 13-inch circle. Dust the dough and the table with more flour as needed to keep the dough from sticking.

Lift the dough by rolling it around the rolling pin. Unroll it over a 10-inch tart pan, so that it is loosely draped over the pan with at least a 1-inch overlap all around. Work your way around the pan, gently lifting the edge of the dough so that it settles to the bottom of the pan and against the sides without stretching. Fold in the overlapping dough to make double-thick sides; press the dough gently against the sides of the pan. Trim off any excess by running a cutting pin around the top edge (see page 19). Chill 20 minutes.

Preheat the oven to 375°. Line the shell with heavy aluminum foil and fill it with pie weights or dried beans. Bake 25 to 30 minutes, until the edges are golden brown and have begun to pull away from the sides of the pan. Remove the foil and beans. If the bottom of the shell is very pale, return it to the oven for a few minutes to brown. Cool on a wire rack.

FILLING　　　Melt the chocolate in the top of a double boiler over low heat. Remove the top from the pot and stir half the cream into the chocolate with a wire whisk. Stir in the remaining cream, which should cool the mixture down. Whip it to soft peaks. Spread the cream in the cooled tart shell, mounding it higher around the edge to form a ¼-inch-wide outer ring. Fill the center with the blueberries. Serve at room temperature.

Coconut Cream Tart

Fresh coconut, far superior to processed coconut in both flavor and texture, is used here in both the crust and the filling. As the crust bakes, it toasts the coconut, intensifying its flavor. The untoasted coconut in the filling maintains its moist chewiness. The brown inner skin, left attached to the meat, adds a nice color effect and subtly calls attention to the fact that the coconut is fresh.

SERVES 12

CRUST

1 medium coconut (1 to 2 pounds)
8 tablespoons (¼ pound) unsalted butter
　　　(cold)
1¼ cups all-purpose flour
2 tablespoons sugar
2 tablespoons water

FILLING

2 cups milk
½ cup sugar
2 tablespoons all-purpose flour
4 teaspoons cornstarch
2 large eggs
6 tablespoons unsalted butter
1 teaspoon vanilla extract
1½ cups whipping cream

With an ice pick, poke through the eyes of the coconut. Open them as much as you can, then pour out and discard the juice. The easiest way to open a coconut is simply to throw it against a hard surface, such as a cement floor. If you'd rather, you can bake the coconut for 30 minutes in a 400° oven then hit the brittle shell with a hammer. Once you have the coconut open, pull the meat away from the outer shell, leaving the dark skin attached to the meat. Cut the meat into 1-inch cubes, then chop it in a food processor until the pieces are the size of grains of rice. You should have about 6 cups.

CRUST

To make the crust, cut the butter into 1-inch cubes. Combine the butter with 1 cup of the coconut, the flour, and the sugar in a food processor or with the paddle attachment of an electric mixer. Mix to the consistency of coarse meal. Add the water and mix until the dough comes together.

Turn the dough out onto a lightly floured surface and dust the top with flour. Roll it out into a 13-inch circle. Sprinkle the table and dough with more flour as needed to prevent sticking. Lift the dough by rolling it up onto the rolling pin. Unroll it over a 10-inch tart pan so that the dough is loosely draped over the pan with at least 1 inch of overlap all the way around. Work your way around the pan, gently lifting the edge of the dough so that it settles into the bottom and against the sides of the pan without stretching or having to be pushed. Stretching and pushing cause uneven edges. Press the dough gently against the sides of the pan and trim off any excess by running a cutting pin around the top edge (see page 19). Chill for 20 minutes.

Preheat the oven to 375°. Line the tart shell with heavy aluminum foil and fill it with pie weights or dried beans. Bake until the sides and bottom are golden brown, 25 to 30 minutes. Remove the foil and beans. Cool on a wire rack.

FILLING

Set aside 1 cup of coconut and combine the remaining coconut with the milk; bring it to a boil. Remove it from the heat and let it stand for 1 hour. Strain the milk, pressing all the liquid you can from the coconut. Discard the coconut; all of its flavor is now in the milk.

Combine the sugar, flour, and cornstarch in a bowl. Add the eggs and mix until smooth. Bring the milk back to a boil. Stir half the milk into the egg mixture, then pour the mixture back into the milk pan and cook over medium-high heat, stirring constantly, until the center bubbles and the mixture thickens. Pour the mixture back into the bowl and stir in the butter. When the butter is fully incorporated, stir in the vanilla and the reserved cup of coconut. Set the filling aside to cool, stirring occasionally to prevent lumps and to keep a skin from forming on the surface.

Spread the cooled filling evenly in the prebaked tart shell. Whip the cream to soft peaks and decorate the top with it. Chill the tart until ready to serve.

Plum Tart with Lemon Curd

Sweet plums make a marvelous tart, but concentrating their flavor by baking them can make them too sweet. Here, a layer of lemon curd under the plums cuts the sweetness. The lemon curd also absorbs excess juices released by the plums during baking, and takes on a beautiful purple color from their skins.

SERVES 12

½ recipe Tart Dough (page 50)
13 medium-size sweet plums
½ cup lemon juice
2 large eggs
½ cup plus 2 tablespoons sugar
2 tablespoons unsalted butter
½ cup plum jelly

Prepare a 10-inch tart shell as directed and prebake according to the directions on page 50. Set aside.

Wash the plums, cut them in quarters, and discard the pits. Toss the plums in the lemon juice to keep them from turning brown. Drain, reserving the plums and juice.

To make the lemon curd, beat the eggs with ½ cup of sugar at high speed until double in volume. Stir in the reserved juice. Transfer the mixture to the top of a double boiler and cook, stirring occasionally, until thick. Stir in the butter. Cool to room temperature.

Preheat the oven to 350°. Spread the lemon curd evenly inside the prebaked tart shell. Starting at the outside edge and working in, arrange the plums on top, skin side down, in concentric circles, points toward the center. For a more even pattern, be sure the plums are facing the same way, with either all the stem ends or all the tips pointing to the center. Gently press the plums into the curd. Sprinkle on the remaining sugar. Bake until the lemon curd is lightly browned and the plums are tender, about 30 minutes. Cool on a wire rack.

Remove the tart from the pan. Slowly melt the jelly over low heat, being careful not to let it get too hot. Brush a thin coating of jelly over the plums. Serve at room temperature.

Orange-Zested Blackberry Tart

Tangy orange zest adds a pleasant zip to both the crust and the pastry cream in this bright-tasting tart. The naturally sweet berries are scattered on top, providing contrasts in texture and color as well as taste.

SERVES 12

FILLING

¼ cup sugar
1 tablespoon all-purpose flour
2 teaspoons cornstarch
1 large egg
1 cup milk
1 teaspoon orange zest, finely chopped
3 tablespoons unsalted butter (soft)
¼ teaspoon vanilla extract

CRUST

8 tablespoons (¼ pound) unsalted butter
*   (cold)*
1¼ cups all-purpose flour
1 tablespoon orange zest
2 teaspoons sugar
½ teaspoon kosher salt
¼ cup cold water

2 baskets (1 pint) blackberries

PASTRY CREAM   To make the orange pastry cream for the filling, sift the sugar, flour, and cornstarch together. Add the egg and beat until light. Bring the milk and 1 teaspoon of orange zest to a boil in a heavy-bottomed saucepan. Stir half the milk into the egg mixture, then pour the mixture back into the saucepan. Cook over high heat, stirring continuously with a wire whisk, until the mixture thickens and bubbles in the center. (Stir vigorously or the egg will scramble.)

Remove from the heat and stir in the butter and vanilla. Pour the pastry cream into a bowl; cover it with plastic wrap and refrigerate.

CRUST   To make the crust, cut the butter into 1-inch cubes and mix it with the flour and orange zest in a food processor or with the paddle attachment of an electric mixer until it resembles coarse meal. Dissolve the sugar and the salt in the water. Add them to the flour mixture, stop to scrape the bowl and paddle, then continue mixing until the dough comes together.

Turn the dough out onto a lightly floured surface and sprinkle a little flour on top. Roll the dough out into a 13-inch circle. Lift it by rolling it up onto the rolling pin. Unroll it over a 10-inch tart pan so that it is loosely draped over the pan with at least 1 inch of overlap all around. Work your way around the pan gently lifting the edge of the dough so that it settles into the bottom of the pan and against the sides without stretching. Fold in the excess to make double-thick sides. Gently press the dough against the sides of the pan. Trim off any overlap by running a cutting pin around the top edge (see page 19). Chill until firm, about 20 minutes.

Preheat the oven to 400°. Line the tart shell with heavy aluminum foil and fill it with pie weights or dried beans. Push the beans all the way to the edges to keep the shell from shrinking during baking. Bake 20 minutes. Remove the foil and beans and continue baking until the crust is golden brown and has pulled away from the sides of the pan, about 15 minutes. Cool on a wire rack.

Spread the chilled pastry cream evenly inside the cooled tart shell. Top with the berries. Serve cold.

Warm Cheese Tart with Blackberry Purée

From time to time I am asked to create a dessert to go with a particular wine. I enjoy the challenge. I developed this tart to accompany a 1987 Sanford Pinot Noir. Though not a perfect match it was certainly an enjoyable one. Any good young pinot will probably harmonize as well. If using frozen blackberries, be sure they are IQF (individually quick frozen). They should be loose in the bag when you buy them, like marbles.

SERVES 10

Crust

1 rounded tablespoon hazelnuts
1 cup bread flour
8 tablespoons (¼ pound) unsalted butter (cold)
¼ teaspoon kosher salt
2 tablespoons cold water
3 tablespoons seedless raspberry preserves

Filling and Sauce

2 large eggs
2 tablespoons sugar plus more to taste
1 pound cream cheese (cold)
3 tablespoons bittersweet chocolate, finely grated
12 ounces fresh or frozen blackberries

CRUST

Preheat the oven to 300°. Place the hazelnuts on a cookie sheet and toast them in the oven until golden brown, about 7 minutes. Transfer the nuts to a clean kitchen towel and rub them inside the towel to remove their skins. Set them aside to cool.

Set aside 1 tablespoon of flour. Place the remaining flour and the hazelnuts in a food processor. Process until the nuts are ground very fine. Cut the butter into ½-inch cubes. Add it and the salt to the work bowl. Process until the mixture resembles coarse meal. Add the water and process just until the dough forms a ball.

Remove the dough from the processor and dust it with the reserved tablespoon of flour. Roll it out into a 12-inch circle. Gently fold it in half, lift it, and unfold it over a 9-inch tart pan. Work your way around the pan, gently lifting the edge of the dough so that it settles into the bottom and against the sides of the pan. Fold the overlapping dough in just to where the sides and bottom meet, making double-thick sides. Press the sides gently against the pan and trim off any overlapping dough by running a cutting pin along the top edge (see page 19). Chill for 30 minutes.

Preheat the oven to 375°. Line the inside of the shell with heavy foil. Poke holes through the foil and dough with a fork, piercing it every half inch over the entire bottom. Hold the fork straight down so the tines do not tear large holes in the dough. Bake on the lower oven shelf until the edge is golden brown, about 25 minutes. Remove the foil and continue baking until the bottom is light brown, about 5 minutes. Remove the tart pan to a cooling rack and immediately spread the preserves on the inside bottom of the shell. Allow the shell to cool completely. Lower the oven temperature to 350°.

FILLING

Blend the eggs in a food processor until smooth. Add 2 tablespoons of sugar and process until mixed. Add the cream cheese and pulse 4 times to help break it up, then process until the mixture is completely smooth. Pour it into the cooled shell. Bake in the lower third of the oven until the top of the filling is set, about 30 minutes. Remove the tart to a cooling rack and immediately sprinkle the grated chocolate over the filling.

SAUCE

To make a sauce, defrost the berries and purée them in a food processor. Strain the purée through a sieve to remove the seeds. Add just enough sugar to balance the tartness of the berries (don't make it sweet).

While the tart is still warm, remove it from the pan and cut it into 10 slices. Place each slice on a plate and pour a small pool of blackberry purée beside it.

Caramel-Pecan Tart

Pecan pies and tarts, beloved throughout the American South, are richly flavorful, but often too sweet for my taste. This one is made with a slightly bitter caramel, which cuts down considerably on the sweetness.

SERVES 12

½ recipe Tart Dough (page 50)
3 cups pecan halves
1½ cups sugar
¾ cup whipping cream
1 tablespoon corn syrup

Prepare a 10-inch tart shell as directed and prebake according to the directions on page 50. Set aside.

When you take the prebaked tart shell from the oven, place it, in the pan, on a wire rack. Spread the pecans evenly inside it.

Put the sugar in a large, heavy saucepan and set it over medium-high heat. Watch it carefully, but do not stir it. The sugar will melt and then begin to turn brown. If it colors unevenly, swirl the pan to distribute the color. When the caramel reaches a mahogany color, turn off the heat.

While the caramel cooks, combine the cream and corn syrup in another pan and heat them until hot to the touch. As soon as the caramel is done, pour the hot cream into it and stir with a wooden spoon. It will probably bubble up, so be careful—caramel is very hot. Keep stirring, dragging the spoon around the edge of the pan to dislodge lumps, until the caramel is completely smooth. Pour it over the pecans. Allow the tart to cool. Serve at room temperature.

Do not refrigerate this tart. If you have leftovers, cover them with plastic wrap and keep them at room temperature.

Orange-Caramel-Walnut Tart

Nut tarts are wonderfully crunchy and full flavored. This one combines toasty walnuts with a caramel perfumed with orange zest and a bit of orange liqueur.

SERVES 10

CRUST

6 tablespoons unsalted butter (cold)
1 teaspoon sugar
Pinch of kosher salt
1 cup all-purpose flour
3 tablespoons whipping cream

FILLING

¾ cup whipping cream
1 tablespoon light corn syrup
1 tablespoon grated orange zest
1 tablespoon Cointreau
1½ cups sugar
3 cups walnut halves

CRUST

Cut the butter into 1-inch cubes. Place it in a mixer or food processor bowl with the sugar, salt, and flour. Blend (using the paddle attachment if using a mixer) until the mixture resembles coarse meal. Add the cream and mix until the dough comes together.

Lightly dust your work surface with flour. Shape the dough into a patty, handling it as little as possible. Center the patty on the floured surface and lightly dust the top with floor. Roll the dough into a 13-inch circle. Slide the dough around on the floured surface from time to time to prevent it from sticking, and keep the top lightly dusted with flour.

Brush the flour from the top of the dough. Lift the dough by rolling it around your rolling pin, brushing the flour from the bottom as you go. Unroll the dough over a 9-inch tart pan, draping it evenly over the pan. Work your way around the pan, gently lifting the edges of the dough so that it settles into the bottom of the pan without stretching. Fold the overlapping dough back into the pan, just to where the sides and bottom meet, making double-thick sides. Press the sides against the pan. Trim off any dough still overlapping the top of the pan by running a cutting pin across the top edge (see page 19). Chill the shell for 30 minutes.

Preheat the oven to 375°. Line the inside of the shell with heavy foil. With a fork, poke holes through the foil and dough every inch or so all over the bottom. Hold the fork straight down so the tines do not tear large holes in the dough. Bake the shell until the sides are light brown and the bottom is dry and no longer doughy, about 35 minutes (lift the foil and peek under it). Remove the foil and continue baking until the shell is golden brown, about 5 minutes more.

FILLING

Combine the cream with the corn syrup, orange zest, and Cointreau in a saucepan. Heat until warm to the touch. Set aside and keep warm without simmering or boiling.

Spread the sugar evenly in the bottom of a 6-cup frying pan. Cook the sugar over medium-high heat, watching it carefully. When you begin to see puffs of smoke or you see dark caramel breaking through the sugar, stir the caramel into the sugar with a metal spoon. Continue cooking until most of the sugar has melted, stirring only when the caramel seems to become overly dark in spots. When only a little sugar remains, stir to dissolve the remaining crystals and any lumps that have formed.

Remove the caramel from the heat. Stirring continuously, slowly pour in the warm cream mixture. Scrape the bottom of the pan, making sure that all the caramel is blended in.

Fill the prebaked tart shell with the walnuts. Pour the hot caramel over the nuts starting at the outside edge and finishing in the center. Set the tart aside to cool before serving.

Brown Sugar– Walnut Tart

This tart is sweeter than most of my desserts, but it is delicious. The vinegar cuts what might otherwise be a cloying sweetness. The walnut filling is crusty on top and soft and rich inside. I serve it with freshly made Orange Ice Cream (page 164).

SERVES 10

½ recipe Tart Dough (page 50)
½ cup corn syrup
1½ cups dark brown sugar, firmly packed
3 tablespoons unsalted butter (soft)
1 teaspoon vanilla extract
1 tablespoon apple cider vinegar
3 large eggs
3 cups walnut halves or pieces

Prepare a 10-inch tart shell as directed and blind bake according to the directions on page 50. After blind baking the tart shell, lower the oven temperature to 350°.

Combine the corn syrup, brown sugar, and butter in a heavy-bottomed saucepan. Heat gently until the butter melts. Add the vanilla and vinegar. Remove from the heat and stir until smooth.

In a medium bowl, beat the eggs with a whisk until all the specks of egg white disappear. Stir the sugar mixture into the eggs until fully combined.

Spread the walnuts evenly over the bottom of the tart shell. Pour the egg mixture over them. Bake until the shell is brown and the filling has formed a brittle top, about 45 minutes. The top may crack during baking, but that's okay.

Serve at room temperature with orange ice cream.

4

Cobblers, Crisps, Bettys, and Puddings

THERE'S SOMETHING very satisfying about sinking a spoon into a deep, deep dessert. I think it makes us all feel like children again, digging into a warm pudding or cobbler and feeling that at last we have found the dessert that will go on forever.

Cobblers, crisps, and bettys are very American desserts, desserts that could have developed only in a land of plenty. They are great favorites among cooks who are blessed with fruit trees or berry bushes in the yard and, as a result, more fresh fruit than they know what to do with. What other single dessert will use up eight cups of boysenberries all at once?

Even if you don't have a huge supply of free fresh fruit in the yard, you and your family will love the exuberant goodness of a fresh-baked cobbler, crisp, or betty. Keep in mind that when fruit is at its best—that is, ripe and at the peak of its season—it is also at its most abundant and cheapest. Watch for the moment when berries or peaches or figs are ripe and plentiful, and have your baking dish ready.

Fall and winter fruits also make wonderful cobblers, crisps, and bettys. I especially like cranberries in crisps, either by themselves or combined with apples. Being a New Englander, I am partial to their bright tartness, but you don't have to be a New Englander to appreciate the way a cranberry crisp can make holiday entertaining colorful and simple. If you freeze a few bags of cranberries in October, you can enjoy them in the middle of summer as well.

One dessert in this chapter is so different from the rest, I feel it deserves special mention. It is the Tiramisu on page 84. Tiramisu is a rich and flavorful Italian pudding that brings together some of my favorite flavors—espresso, rum, and bittersweet chocolate. It is a welcome foreign visitor in an otherwise very American chapter. This is a dessert for special occasions. To make it you must first make lady fingers and either find Italian mascarpone cheese or make your own (the recipe is included). If you have the time and the occasion, it is an unforgettable dessert.

Peach and Cherry Cobbler

A warm, fragrant cobbler is one of the best ways to celebrate the abundance of summer fruit. When peaches and cherries are both at the height of their seasons, I bake them together, and add a touch of spice by scenting the traditional biscuit topping with nutmeg.

SERVES 12

3 cups cherries
5 large peaches
⅓ cup plus 1 teaspoon sugar
2 tablespoons tapioca
2 tablespoons dark brown sugar, firmly
    packed
1 cup all-purpose flour
1 teaspoon baking powder
¼ teaspoon grated nutmeg
6 tablespoons unsalted butter (cold)
¼ cup whipping cream

Preheat the oven to 375°. Wash the fruit. Pit the cherries and cut them in half. Cut each peach into 8 wedges, then cut each wedge in half crosswise.

Put the fruit in a 2½-quart shallow earthenware baking dish. Sprinkle on ⅓ cup of sugar. Grind the tapioca in a food processor until fine, then sprinkle it over the cherries. Toss to coat the fruit. Set aside.

Put the brown sugar, flour, baking powder, and nutmeg in a food processor. Cut the butter into 6 pieces and add it on top of the dry ingredients. Process until the butter is in pea-size pieces. Add the cream and process until the dough is soft and crumbly. Take the dough out and press it together with your hands.

If you prefer, you can mix the dough in an electric mixer. Use the paddle attachment. Cut the butter into 1-inch chunks and mix it into the flour, baking powder, and salt until they are the consistency of coarse meal. Add the cream and mix just until the dough comes together.

On a lightly floured surface roll the dough out to the inside dimension of your baking dish. Lift it with your fingers spread wide underneath and place it over the fruit. Tuck in any edges that stick out; the dough doesn't have to lie smooth. Brush the top with water and sprinkle on the remaining 1 teaspoon of sugar. Make 4 slashes in the dough to allow steam to escape. Bake until the top is firm and lightly browned and the fruit is bubbling around the edges, about 50 minutes.

Serve warm or at room temperature, plain or with lightly whipped unsweetened cream or vanilla ice cream.

Plum and Apricot Cobbler

The subtle sweetness of apricots contrasts perfectly with the slight tartness of the plums in this simple and delicious cobbler. The sweeter the plums you use, the sweeter your cobbler will be. I prefer to use slightly sour plums.

SERVES 12

8 plums
8 apricots
½ cup plus 2 teaspoons sugar
2 tablespoons tapioca
1 cup all-purpose flour
1 teaspoon baking powder
Pinch of kosher salt
6 tablespoons unsalted butter (cold)
¼ cup whipping cream

Preheat the oven to 400°. Wash the fruit. Cut the plums into quarters, then cut each quarter in half crosswise. Cut the apricots the same way. Put the fruit in a 2½-quart shallow earthenware baking dish. Sprinkle on ½ cup of sugar. Grind the tapioca in a food processor until fine, then sprinkle it over the plums. Toss to coat the fruit. Set aside.

Put the flour, baking powder, and salt in a food processor. Cut the butter into 6 pieces and add it on top of the dry ingredients. Process until the butter is in pea-size pieces. Add the cream and process until the dough is soft and crumbly. Take the dough out and press it together with your hands. (For mixer method, see page 73.)

On a lightly floured surface roll the dough out to the inside dimension of your baking dish. Lift it with your fingers spread wide underneath and place it over the fruit. Tuck in any edges that stick out; the dough doesn't have to lie smooth. Brush the top with water and sprinkle on the remaining 2 teaspoons of sugar. Make 4 slashes in the dough to allow steam to escape.

Put the cobbler in the oven and immediately turn the temperature down to 350°. Bake until the top is firm and lightly browned and the fruit is bubbling around the edges, about 35 minutes.

Serve warm or at room temperature, plain or with lightly whipped unsweetened cream or vanilla ice cream.

Boysenberry and Cinnamon Cobbler

This is a wonderful dessert for anyone who has boysenberries growing in the yard or has access to them in quantity. Boysenberries have a slightly spicy flavor that is accented beautifully by a touch of cinnamon.

SERVES 12

7 to 8 cups boysenberries
⅓ cup plus 1 tablespoon sugar
2 tablespoons tapioca
1 cup all-purpose flour
1 teaspoon baking powder
Pinch of kosher salt
6 tablespoons unsalted butter (cold)
¼ cup whipping cream
1 teaspoon cinnamon

Preheat the oven to 375°. Wash the fruit. Put the berries in a 2½-quart shallow earthenware baking dish. Sprinkle on ⅓ cup of sugar. Grind the tapioca in a food processor until fine, then sprinkle it over the berries. Toss the berries gently to coat them with sugar and tapioca. Set aside.

Put the flour, baking powder, and salt in a food processor. Cut the butter into 6 pieces and add it on top of the dry ingredients. Process until the butter is in pea-size pieces. Add the cream and process until the dough is soft and crumbly. Take the dough out and press it together with your hands. (For mixer method, see page 73.)

On a lightly floured surface roll the dough out to the inside dimension of your baking dish. Lift it with your fingers spread wide underneath and place it over the fruit. Tuck in any edges that stick out; the dough doesn't have to lie smooth. Brush the top with water. Mix the remaining tablespoon of sugar with the cinnamon and sprinkle it over the dough. Make 4 slashes to allow steam to escape. Bake until the top is firm and lightly browned and the fruit is bubbling around the edges, about 40 minutes.

Serve warm or at room temperature, plain or with lightly whipped unsweetened cream or vanilla ice cream.

Fig, Peach, and Raspberry Cobbler

The rich taste and meltingly smooth texture of fresh figs add a delightful new dimension to the classic combination of peaches and raspberries. I like to serve this cobbler with Vanilla or Raspberry Swirl Ice Cream (page 158 or 162).

SERVES 8

1 cup fresh calimyrna figs
2 pints raspberries
3 cups sliced peaches (3 or 4 peaches)
½ cup plus 1 tablespoon sugar
¼ cup water
8 tablespoons (¼ pound) unsalted butter
    (cold)
1½ cups all-purpose flour
2 teaspoons baking powder
6 tablespoons milk
½ teaspoon ground cinnamon

Preheat the oven to 400°.

Remove the stems from the figs and cut the figs into quarters. Combine them with the raspberries, peach slices, ¼ cup of sugar, and the water. Spoon the fruit mixture into a 6-cup shallow earthenware baking dish. Cut 2 tablespoons of butter into small pieces and distribute them over the top. Set aside.

In a medium bowl blend together the flour, baking powder, and ¼ cup of sugar. Cut the remaining 6 tablespoons of butter into 8 small pieces and toss it with the flour. Using both hands, press the butter between your index fingers and thumbs to form it into thin flakes. Be sure each piece of butter remains coated with flour to prevent it from becoming warm and soft. When all the butter is in flakes, gently rub the mixture between your hands to blend it into a crumble. Add the milk and toss with a rubber spatula or spoon until absorbed. Press the mixture into a dough.

Dust the dough lightly with flour and roll it into a shape to fit the top of the baking dish. Place it over the fruit covering it completely. Cut 4 small holes in the center with a knife. Brush the top lightly with water; blend the remaining 1 tablespoon of sugar with the cinnamon and sprinkle it evenly over the top.

Place the cobbler in the middle of the oven and reduce the temperature to 375°. Bake until the top is nicely browned, 35 to 45 minutes. To be certain the top is fully baked, make a small cut with a knife and look to see that no wet batter is left. Set the cobbler aside to cool for 30 minutes before serving. Serve with vanilla or raspberry swirl ice cream.

Blueberry Crisp

When blueberries are at the height of their season, they are plump and spicy, and so sweet they need hardly any sugar when baked. This crisp is full of blueberries—six cups' worth; it is delicious plain, or you can top it with a dollop of unsweetened whipped cream or a scoop of Vanilla Ice Cream (page 158).

SERVES 12

6 cups fresh blueberries
1¼ cups sugar
1 cup all-purpose flour
8 tablespoons (¼ pound) unsalted butter
    (cold)
1 tablespoon lemon zest (about 1 lemon)

Preheat the oven to 375°. Wash and drain the berries and gently pat them dry in a kitchen towel. Spread them evenly in a 2½-quart shallow earthenware baking dish. Sprinkle on ¼ cup of sugar and toss the berries lightly with a spoon. Set aside.

Combine the remaining cup of sugar and the flour in a bowl. Cut the butter into ½-inch cubes. Toss the butter in the flour to coat it, then press the butter between your thumbs and fingers, repeatedly moving the thumbs from little finger to index finger, to form thin flakes.

When all the butter is in flakes, gently rub the flour and butter between your hands until the mixture is golden and has the texture of coarse meal. Toss in the lemon zest.

Squeeze the topping gently in your hands to form tender clumps. Spread the clumps evenly over the blueberries; do not press the topping into the fruit. Bake on the lowest shelf in the oven until the top is golden brown and the fruit bubbles, 35 to 40 minutes. Once the topping has started to brown, turn the pan once for more even baking. Cool the crisp on a wire rack; serve warm.

Peach and Brown Sugar Crisp

Graham crackers hold a special place in the American dessert repertoire. For generations home and professional bakers have crushed them and combined them with butter to make a quick and richly satisfying sweet pie crust. Here their nut-like crunchiness makes a fine topping for a fresh peach crisp.

SERVES 12

2½ pounds peaches (about 8 medium
    peaches)
¼ cup sugar
1 tablespoon tapioca
1½ packets (8 ounces) graham crackers
¾ cup light brown sugar, firmly packed
8 tablespoons (¼ pound) unsalted butter
    (cold)

Preheat the oven to 375°. Wash and towel dry the peaches. Cut each peach into 8 wedges, then cut each wedge in half crosswise. Put the fruit in a bowl and sprinkle on the sugar. Grind the tapioca in a food processor until fine, then sprinkle it over the fruit; toss gently. Transfer the peaches to a 2½-quart shallow earthenware baking dish. Set aside.

Finely chop the graham crackers in a food processor. Add the brown sugar and blend. Cut the butter into ½-inch chunks and add it. Mix until small tender clumps form. Stop the machine and remove the blade. Gently squeeze the topping with your hand to form larger clumps.

Cover the fruit evenly with the topping by dropping it gently from your hand. Bake the crisp on the lowest shelf in the oven until the top is brown and the fruit bubbles, about 40 minutes. Cool slightly before serving.

Pineapple Crisp with Rum Sauce

Pineapple and brown sugar are wonderful together. In this somewhat unusual crisp, a crunchy brown sugar topping provides just the right contrast to the natural juicy sweetness of ripe pineapple. Note that the fruit is unsweetened; all the sweetness in the filling comes from the pineapple itself, so be sure the one you buy is ripe and fragrant.

SERVES 12

12 tablespoons unsalted butter (cold)
1¼ cups all-purpose flour
1½ cups brown sugar
1 large pineapple
6 ounces white chocolate
⅓ cup whipping cream
⅓ cup rum

Preheat the oven to 375°. Cut the butter into 2-inch cubes. Blend the flour and sugar together. Using the paddle attachment on a counter-top electric mixer or a hand-held mixer, mix the butter into the dry ingredients until it is completely incorporated. Continue mixing until large, tender clumps begin to form.

Peel and core the pineapple and cut it into 1½-inch cubes. Spread the fruit evenly in a 2½-quart shallow earthenware baking dish. Press the fruit gently into the pan, then spread the clumps of topping evenly over it. Bake until the top is golden brown, about 40 minutes. Cool to room temperature.

Just before serving, melt the white chocolate in the top of a double boiler over boiled, not boiling, water. Warm the cream, and stir it and the rum into the chocolate. Top each serving of crisp with sauce, or pass the sauce separately.

Brown Sugar–Pineapple Crisp

The tanginess of pineapple is balanced by a richly flavorful brown sugar topping in this popular warm wintertime dessert. Serve it topped with either Vanilla or Coconut Ice Cream (page 158 or 170).

SERVES 8 TO 10

1 large pineapple
1¼ cups all-purpose flour
1¼ cups brown sugar, firmly packed
12 tablespoons unsalted butter (cold)

Preheat the oven to 375°. Butter a 1½-quart shallow baking dish.

Twist the top off the pineapple. With a large knife trim the top and bottom and stand it upright. Cutting from top to bottom, trim the skin off in strips about 1½ inches wide. Slice the pineapple in half vertically, then into quarters. Remove the core and cut the fruit into 1-inch chunks. Spread the chunks evenly in the prepared baking dish. Set aside.

Blend the flour and sugar with the paddle attachment on an electric mixer. Cut the butter into 1-inch chunks and mix it into the flour until the mixture resembles coarse meal. Continue mixing until large, tender clumps begin to form. These should crumble when squeezed between your fingers. Drop the topping evenly over the fruit from cupped hands. If some of the topping is still loose, squeeze it into clumps in your hand before dropping it on the fruit.

Bake the crisp in the lower middle of the oven until the juices that bubble up are clear and shiny, about 40 minutes. The topping should be golden brown outside and dry throughout (cut into it with the tip of a knife to check). Set the crisp aside to cool 15 minutes before serving.

Plum Crisp with Pecans and Oats

Although unusual, baked plums make a wonderful warm dessert. Here their bright, smooth flavor contrasts with and is enhanced by a fragrant toasted pecan-and-oat topping.

SERVES 12

⅓ cup pecans
2½ pounds plums
¼ cup sugar
1 tablespoon tapioca
1 cup all-purpose flour
½ cup light brown sugar, firmly packed
8 tablespoons (¼ pound) unsalted butter (cold)
½ cup rolled oats (not quick-cooking)

Preheat the oven to 375°. Spread the pecans on a cookie sheet and toast them in the oven until fragrant, about 5 minutes. Set aside.

Wash and towel dry the plums. Cut each plum into quarters, then cut each quarter in half crosswise. Put the pieces in a bowl and sprinkle on the sugar. Grind the tapioca in a food processor until fine, then sprinkle it over the fruit; toss gently. Transfer the fruit to a 2½-quart shallow earthenware baking dish. Press the pieces down lightly with your hands.

Combine the flour and brown sugar with the paddle attachment of an electric mixer. Cut the butter into ½-inch chunks and add it. Mix until crumbly. Coarsely chop the pecans (to pieces about the size of corn kernels). Add the pecans and the rolled oats and continue mixing until large clumps form.

Cover the fruit evenly with the topping. Bake on the lowest shelf of the oven until the top is brown and the fruit bubbles slightly, 35 to 40 minutes. Cool slightly before serving.

Cranberry Crisp

I'm from New England, and I love cranberries. But I think most people sweeten them too much. I like my cranberries still slightly tart and sparkling with flavor. Sweetened with a moderate amount of sugar they make a wonderful autumn or winter crisp, especially with a nutty oat-and-almond topping.

SERVES 12

2 bags (24 ounces) fresh cranberries
¾ cup sugar
8 tablespoons (¼ pound) unsalted butter (cold)
1 cup rolled oats (not quick-cooking)
1 cup light brown sugar, firmly packed
½ cup all-purpose flour
½ cup sliced almonds

Preheat the oven to 375°. Spread the cranberries evenly in a 2½-quart shallow earthenware baking dish. Sprinkle the sugar over them and toss lightly. Set aside.

Cut the butter into ¾-inch cubes. With the paddle attachment on a countertop mixer or with a hand-held electric mixer, cream the butter to remove the lumps. At first the beaters will hold the butter and you'll have to poke it out. Mix until the butter is nearly smooth (a few small lumps are okay), but not light. The butter should still be cold. Add the oats, brown sugar, and flour and blend with your fingers to combine the ingredients. Use a rubber spatula to scrape the sides of the bowl from time to time. Rub the mixture lightly between your hands until it has a mealy texture. Add the almonds and continue mixing with your hands until the topping is in small, soft, doughy clumps. Spread it evenly over the cranberries.

Bake in the middle of the oven until the topping is brown and crisp and the fruit is bubbling, about 50 minutes. Cool on a wire rack. Serve warm or at room temperature, plain or with Vanilla Ice Cream (page 158).

Cranberry-Apple-Almond Crisp

Cranberries and apples are a traditional fall and winter combination. Almonds in the crisp topping add a pleasant new dimension. Natural (skin on) almonds will give you the fullest, toastiest flavor.

SERVES 12

1 bag (12 ounces) fresh cranberries
3 apples
⅔ cup plus ¾ cup sugar
10 tablespoons unsalted butter (cold)
1 cup all-purpose flour
1¼ cups sliced almonds

Preheat the oven to 375°. Spread the cranberries evenly in a 2½-quart shallow earthenware baking dish. Set aside.

Peel, quarter, and core the apples. Cut each quarter in half lengthwise then cut each wedge crosswise into quarters. Add the apples to the baking dish and toss the fruit together. Sprinkle on ⅔ cup of sugar; turn the fruit gently with a spoon to coat it with sugar. Set aside.

Cut the butter into 1-inch cubes. Place in a food processor with the flour, ¾ cup of sugar, and ¼ cup of almonds. Process until the dough starts to clump. Transfer the dough to a bowl and add the remaining cup of almonds. Toss the dough lightly with your hands to distribute the almonds, then press it into the bottom of the bowl. Squeeze small handfuls of dough into clumps and cover the top of the fruit with them.

Bake in the middle of the oven until the topping is brown and crisp and the fruit is bubbling, about 50 minutes. Cool on a wire rack. Serve warm or at room temperature, plain or with Vanilla Ice Cream (page 158).

Boysenberry Cream Brown Betty

A twentieth-century American botanist named Boysen crossed a blackberry with a raspberry and came up with the delightful sweet-tart berry that bears his name. In this moist and fruity brown betty, boysenberries are surrounded by a not-too-rich pastry cream and crowned with a crunchy graham cracker topping.

SERVES 12

2 large eggs
4 tablespoons all-purpose flour
2 teaspoons cornstarch
1 cup sugar
4 cups milk
14 tablespoons unsalted butter
½ teaspoon vanilla extract
4 baskets (2 pints) fresh boysenberries
1 packet (5⅓ ounces) graham crackers

Make the pastry cream as follows: Beat the eggs. Sift together the flour, cornstarch, and sugar, and add them to the eggs. Whisk until the mixture is smooth and free of lumps. Bring the milk to a boil in a heavy saucepan. Pour half the hot milk into the eggs, stirring constantly until well blended. Pour the egg mixture back into the saucepan of milk. Cook over medium heat, stirring constantly with the whisk, until the center bubbles and the cream thickens. Remove from the heat and stir in 6 tablespoons of butter and the vanilla. Continue stirring until all the butter melts. Pour the pastry cream into a clean bowl, cover it, and refrigerate until it sets.

Preheat the oven to 350°. Wash and drain the berries well. Spread the pastry cream in the bottom of a 2½-quart shallow earthenware baking dish. Pour the berries over the pastry cream and turn the cream with a spoon to lightly mix in the berries.

Crush the graham crackers with a rolling pin or chop them to crumbs in a food processor. Melt the remaining 8 tablespoons of butter and stir it into the crumbs. Spread the crumb mixture evenly over the berry cream. Bake until the topping is browned, about 20 minutes. Serve at room temperature.

Blackberry Cream Brown Betty

These homey, satisfying, individual-serving brown bettys are served right in their baking dishes. On the bottom is a smooth layer of vanilla-scented pastry cream. In the middle, fresh, plump blackberries, just beginning to release their gleaming juices. On top, a crumbly, crisp brown sugar topping, made almost instantly with a food processor and graham crackers.

SERVES 8

2 large eggs
2 tablespoons all-purpose flour
1 teaspoon cornstarch
½ cup sugar
2 cups milk
26 tablespoons unsalted butter
¼ teaspoon vanilla extract
3 pints fresh blackberries
4 packets (21⅓ ounces) graham crackers
1 cup dark brown sugar, firmly packed

Make the pastry cream as follows: Beat the eggs. Sift together the flour, cornstarch, and sugar, and add them to the eggs. Whisk until the mixture is smooth and free of lumps. Bring the milk to a boil in a heavy saucepan. Pour half the hot milk into the eggs, stirring constantly until well blended. Pour the egg mixture back into the saucepan of milk. Cook over medium heat, stirring constantly with the whisk, until the center bubbles and the cream thickens. Remove from the heat and stir in 6 tablespoons of butter and the vanilla. Continue stirring until all the butter melts. Pour the pastry cream into a clean bowl, cover it, and refrigerate until it sets. Keep it chilled until you are ready to use it.

Preheat the oven to 350°. Fill 8 individual oval baking dishes or ramekins one-third full of pastry cream. Wash and thoroughly drain the berries and divide them among the dishes.

Chop the graham crackers one package at a time to very fine crumbs in a food processor. Cut the remaining 20 tablespoons of butter into 1-inch chunks. Add them and the brown sugar to the crumbs and process until the mixture goes beyond the coarse meal stage to form large, tender clumps. Cover the berries with the crumb topping. Bake on a cookie sheet until the topping has browned and the berries bleed a little, about 10 minutes. Serve at room temperature.

Banana Brown Betty

In the summer I like to make my brown bettys with berries. In winter, when no fresh berries are available, I use bananas. The filling is very much like that in a banana cream pie (one of my favorite pies). The topping is buttery, crunchy, and extremely easy to make.

SERVES 12

2 large eggs
4 tablespoons all-purpose flour
2 teaspoons cornstarch

1 cup sugar
4 cups milk
14 tablespoons unsalted butter
½ teaspoon vanilla
6 bananas, ripe and firm
1 packet (5⅓ ounces) graham crackers

Make the pastry cream as follows: Beat the eggs. Sift together the flour, cornstarch, and sugar, and add them to the eggs. Whisk until the mixture is smooth and free of lumps. Bring the milk to a boil in a heavy saucepan. Pour half the hot milk into the eggs, stirring constantly until well blended. Pour the egg mixture back into the saucepan of milk. Cook over medium heat, stirring constantly with the whisk, until the center bubbles and the cream thickens. Remove from the heat and stir in 6 tablespoons of butter and the vanilla. Continue stirring until all the butter melts. Pour the pastry cream into a clean bowl, cover it, and refrigerate until it sets.

Preheat the oven to 350°. Spread the pastry cream in the bottom of a 2½-quart shallow earthenware baking dish. Peel the bananas and cut them into ½-inch slices. Scatter the slices over the pastry cream and turn the cream with a spoon to lightly mix them in.

Crush the graham crackers with a rolling pin or chop them to crumbs in a food processor. Melt the remaining 8 tablespoons of butter and stir it into the crumbs. Spread the crumb mixture evenly over the banana cream. Bake until the topping is browned, about 25 minutes. Serve at room temperature.

Tiramisu

Tiramisu is a luscious Italian pudding-like dessert based on rich, smooth mascarpone cheese. The creamy cheese filling, layered with homemade lady fingers, is a perfect canvas for showcasing the assertive flavors of espresso, rum, and bittersweet chocolate. Tiramisu can be prepared one day ahead and stored covered in the refrigerator.

SERVES 8 TO 10

LADY FINGERS

1½ cups cake flour
6 large eggs, separated
½ cup plus 2 tablespoons sugar

FILLING

4 large eggs
½ cup sugar

¼ cup dark rum
1 pound mascarpone cheese (recipe below)
1 tablespoon lemon juice
1 teaspoon vanilla extract
1 cup whipping cream
¾ cup espresso
4 to 6 ounces bittersweet chocolate

LADY FINGERS

To make the lady fingers, preheat the oven to 350°. Line 2 cookie sheets with parchment. Sift the flour 4 times. Whip the 6 egg whites until foamy. Slowly add ¼ cup of sugar and continue whipping to soft peaks. Set the whites aside.

Whip the yolks with the remaining ¼ cup plus 2 tablespoons of sugar until light in color and slightly thick. Fold them into the whites. Sift the flour over the eggs and fold it in. Spoon the batter into a pastry bag with a #4 plain tip. Pipe sixty 1½-inch-long fingers onto the lined cookie sheets. Bake until light brown, 15 to 20 minutes. Cool on the cookie sheet.

FILLING

To make the filling, beat the eggs with the sugar until smooth. Cook in the top of a double boiler over boiling water, stirring continuously, until ivory in color. Add the rum and continue cooking until thick enough to heavily coat the back of a spoon. Set aside to cool.

Soften the cheese with a spoon or by mixing it at low speed with an electric mixer. Blend in the lemon juice and vanilla. Fold the cheese mixture into the cooled egg mixture. Whip the cream to soft peaks and fold it in.

Line the bottom of a large, 2-inch-deep baking dish with lady fingers. Brush them with espresso until they stop absorbing it, then cover them with half of the filling. Add another layer of lady fingers. Brush them with espresso and cover them with the remaining filling. Grate the chocolate on top and chill for 1 hour before serving. Spoon onto plates to serve.

Mascarpone

Mascarpone is a creamy, sweet-tart cheese used in many Italian desserts, the best known of which is Tiramisu. Tartaric acid may be hard to find; it is sold in some health food stores and some pharmacies. It is necessary for this recipe.

MAKES 1 POUND (2 CUPS)

2 cups whipping cream
⅛ teaspoon tartaric acid

Heat the cream in a medium stainless-steel saucepan over moderately high heat until it registers 180° on a candy or instant-read thermometer. Turn off the heat and stir in the tartaric acid. Continue stirring for 2 minutes. Pour the cream into a clean 3-cup container. Cover and chill overnight before using. The resulting cheese will be quite soft.

5

Cakes

THERE ARE SIMPLE CAKES and there are elaborate cakes, and there are lots of cakes in between. The right cake for any meal depends on the occasion, the menu, and the cook's inclination.

Lately I've been leaning more toward simple cakes. I think simple cakes are as appropriate for special, fancy dinners as they are for small family suppers. A tender, moist butter sponge cake served with fresh fruit and a dollop of whipped cream can be the perfect ending for an otherwise complicated multicourse dinner. Straightforward and unassuming, it invites people to relax, and its fresh flavor restores a weary palate.

This chapter contains a number of unfrosted cakes that are appealing because of the wonderful flavors of their ingredients—ripe fruit, toasted nuts, the finest-quality chocolate. They don't require a lot of preparation or decoration, yet they leave everyone at the table with a warm glow of satisfaction. These are the cakes I serve to my friends at home. They begin in my mind as a combination of compatible ingredients, such as hazelnuts and persimmons or plums and pecans. I try to bring the flavors and textures of those ingredients together in a cake that carries them but doesn't upstage them. I cut the cake in wedges and top each serving with a dollop of unsweetened whipped cream and perhaps a few slices of the fruit on which the cake is based.

I like inviting people for afternoon tea, and these simple cakes are just right for a refreshing and not-too-sweet midday break. I believe afternoon tea is making a comeback—if it isn't, it should. If you haven't tried this very civilized approach to afternoon socializing, the Cranberry-Walnut Tea Cake on page 119 may give you an excuse to start.

Of course, there are times that call for an all-out, knock-'em-dead, great-looking cake. I save such lavish cakes for occasions where dessert is the highlight of the meal and for days when I have the time to enjoy assembling one. Nothing is more fun than creating a spectacular cake for a special occasion. And every cook loves to hear the appreciative oohs and aahs when a truly gorgeous cake is presented at the table. The

Chocolate-Almond Meringue Cake on page 103 is a guaranteed winner in the dramatic entrance category. If chocolate is not your passion, try the Nectarine-Walnut Cake with Rum Sauce on page 111. Alternating layers of tender cake, crisp wafers, and lush buttercream interspersed with nectarines, walnuts, and rum create a delightful melange of flavors and textures in an unusual, nontraditional cake for a birthday, anniversary, or any other celebration.

Butter Sponge Cake

Sometimes I serve this fine, moist sponge cake very simply—accompanied by sliced fruit and topped with a dollop of whipped cream. Sometimes I split it into layers and use it as the foundation for a more elaborate cake.

SERVES 8

4 large eggs
½ cup sugar
¼ teaspoon vanilla extract
1 cup cake flour, sifted
2 tablespoons butter

Preheat the oven to 350°. Cut a circle of parchment to fit inside a 9-inch round cake pan. Butter the pan and line the bottom with the parchment circle, then flour the sides.

Warm the eggs by cracking them into the top of a double boiler set over simmered water. Add the sugar and beat with a hand-held electric mixer until the eggs are light in color and have doubled in volume. Remove the top from the double boiler and stir in the vanilla. Beat at high speed until the eggs look satiny; reduce the mixer speed to medium and continue beating until the eggs are cool. The beating should take about 10 minutes in all.

If it is a rainy day or you live in a damp or humid area, sift the flour 4 times instead of once. Transfer the egg mixture to a large bowl and sprinkle the flour over it. Fold it in with a rubber spatula. Melt the butter and fold it in while still hot. Pour the batter into the prepared pan and bake until the sides begin to pull away from the pan, about 30 minutes; the top should be brown and should spring back when lightly touched. Cool the cake completely on a wire rack before removing it from the pan.

Pound Cake

Pound cake has been an American favorite since colonial days. It is simple, moist, tasty, and versatile. Its name refers to the measurement of ingredients: it was traditionally made with a pound each of butter, sugar, eggs, and flour. I guess I should really call this a half-pound cake. I like to serve it topped with fresh or poached fruit and some softly whipped cream.

SERVES 8 TO 10

16 tablespoons (½ pound) butter (soft)
1 cup plus 2 tablespoons sugar
⅛ teaspoon ground mace
¼ teaspoon grated lemon zest
6 large eggs
1⅔ cups all-purpose flour

Preheat the oven to 300°. Butter a 9¼- × 5¼-inch loaf pan and line the bottom and sides with parchment.

Cream the butter, sugar, mace, and lemon zest until fluffy. Beat the eggs with a whisk or a hand-held electric mixer. Add them to the butter mixture in 4 stages, beating well after each addition. If it is a very cool day, beat the eggs and incorporate them on top of the stove, or set the mixing bowl over simmered water. If the eggs curdle from the heat, just keep mixing and they will be all right. After measuring the flour, sift it twice, then stir it into the mixture in 2 stages.

Spoon the batter into the prepared pan and smooth the top. Bake until the top is golden brown and firm to the touch and a toothpick inserted in the center comes out clean, about 1¾ hours. Cool in the pan on a wire rack. To serve, cut the cake into slices.

Apple and Butter Pound Cake

Pound cakes are traditionally very simple. This version is lighter than most, moist, delicate, and not too sweet. Sweet-tart apple chunks give it a lively spirit.

SERVES 6 TO 8

1 large apple, peeled, cored, and cut into
*   ½-inch chunks (about 1⅔ cups)*
6 to 8 tablespoons unsalted butter (soft)
1 cup sugar
1 teaspoon vanilla extract
1⅓ cups all-purpose flour
1 teaspoon baking powder
1 large egg
½ cup milk

If you are using a firm green apple, such as a Pippin, a Fuji, or an underripe Granny Smith, lightly sauté the chunks in 2 tablespoons of butter. Set aside to cool.

Preheat the oven to 350°. Butter and flour a tube or loaf pan.

Cream 6 tablespoons of butter with the sugar and vanilla until light and smooth. Sift together the flour and baking powder. Add half the flour and the egg to the butter mixture; mix well. Add the rest of the flour and the milk. Mix until smooth and light. Fold in the apple chunks with a rubber scraper. (If you have sautéed the apple, drain off any butter before adding the chunks to the batter.)

Spoon the batter into the prepared pan. Bake until the top of the cake is golden brown and a knife blade inserted in the center comes out clean, about 45 minutes. Cool in the pan on a wire rack for 10 minutes. Then turn the cake out onto a plate and let it cool upside down. When the cake is completely cool, invert it onto a serving plate.

Nectarine-Pecan Cake

This is a festive cake, perfect for birthday parties and other special occasions. It is a medley of flavors and textures: crisp, light wafers; a pecan layer cake; rich vanilla buttercream; fresh, juicy nectarines; and toasted pecans. Each slice is picture-pretty, and very rich.

SERVES 10

WAFERS

6 tablespoons unsalted butter (cold)
¾ cup all-purpose flour
2 tablespoons cold water

CAKE

8 tablespoons (¼ pound) unsalted butter
3 large eggs
¾ cup sugar
½ teaspoon vanilla extract
1 cup all-purpose flour
1 teaspoon baking powder
⅓ cup finely chopped pecans

BUTTERCREAM

*24 tablespoons (¾ pound) unsalted butter
    (soft)*
1¼ cups powdered sugar, sifted
½ teaspoon vanilla extract

FRUIT AND NUTS

2 medium nectarines
1 cup lightly toasted pecans

WAFERS   Preheat the oven to 375°. Line two cookie sheets with parchment. Cut the cold butter into small pieces. Toss it in a bowl with the flour. Gently rub the flour and butter together with your fingers until the butter is in thin flakes and the flour has taken on a golden color. Add the cold water and blend only until the dough comes together.

Divide the dough in half. On a floured surface roll each half into a 9½-inch circle. Lift each circle by rolling it around the rolling pin, then unroll it onto one of the lined cookie sheets. Chill the circles for 30 minutes, then bake them until firm to the touch and golden brown, about 20 minutes. Set aside to cool.

CAKE

While the wafers bake, cut a circle of parchment to fit the bottom of a 9-inch round cake pan. Butter the pan and line it with the parchment, then flour the sides.

Melt the butter and set it aside to cool. Beat the eggs. Beat in the sugar. Add the melted butter and vanilla and beat with an electric mixer at medium-high speed until the batter is thick, smooth, and noticeably lighter in color. Add the flour, baking powder, and chopped pecans and beat until smooth.

Spoon the batter into the prepared pan and smooth the top. Bake in the middle of the 375° oven until the center springs back when lightly touched, about 20 minutes. Cool in the pan on a wire rack.

BUTTERCREAM

Whip the soft butter, powdered sugar, and vanilla with an electric mixer at high speed until it is white and very light in texture, 10 to 15 minutes.

To assemble, be sure both the cake and the wafers are completely cooled. Cut each nectarine into 8 wedges. Line a cookie sheet with waxed paper or parchment. Using a long-bladed slicer or serrated knife, split the cake into two equal layers. If the cake is domed, trim off the domed part. If the wafers and cake are not the same diameter, trim the cake to the size of the wafers.

Lay one of the wafers on the cookie sheet. Spread it with about ½ cup of the buttercream. Add one cake layer. Arrange the nectarine wedges on top of the cake. Start at the outer edge and lay the wedges tip to tip around the perimeter. Work toward the center, making overlapping concentric circles until all of the wedges are used. Slip in any leftover wedges wherever they will fit. Spoon ½ cup of buttercream over the nectarines and gently smooth the top.

Add the second cake layer, and spread it with ½ cup of buttercream. Then add the second wafer and press it down gently. Cover the sides and top of the cake with the remaining buttercream.

Coarsely chop the toasted pecans. Holding them in an open hand, press them gently onto the sides of the cake. Leave the top undecorated. Refrigerate the cake until firm (otherwise it will be hard to cut). Once it is firm, lift it with 2 large spatulas and place it on a serving plate.

Orange-Pecan Cake

This is a moist cake that is excellent served plain with afternoon tea. For after lunch I like to serve it with peaches that have been marinated in Cointreau.

SERVES 10

1 cup pecans
8 tablespoons (¼ pound) unsalted butter (soft)
1 cup sugar
1 tablespoon grated orange zest
¼ teaspoon vanilla extract
1 large egg
1⅓ cups cake flour
4 teaspoons baking powder
¼ teaspoon kosher salt
1 cup milk

Preheat the oven to 375°. Butter and flour a 9-inch springform pan. Spread ¾ cup of pecans on a cookie sheet and toast them lightly in the oven for about 10 minutes. Set them aside to cool completely.

Cream the butter, sugar, orange zest, and vanilla until smooth and light in color. Mix in the egg. Scrape the sides and bottom of the bowl.

Combine the toasted pecans and flour in a food processor. Process until the pecans are ground into a very fine powder. Add the baking powder and salt; pulse to blend.

Add half the flour mixture to the butter mixture, just to blend. Then add the remaining flour and then the milk. Mix with a rubber spatula until the batter comes together. Spoon the batter into the prepared pan. Slice the remaining ¼ cup pecans and sprinkle them over the top. Bake in the middle of the oven until the center springs back when lightly touched, about 45 minutes. Cool in the pan on a wire rack for 10 to 15 minutes. Remove from pan and serve.

Peach and Hazelnut Cake

This is a light and pretty cake, perfect for a summer afternoon. Because so much of the flavor comes from the peaches, it is important that they be ripe and flavorful. Peaches go especially well with toasted hazelnuts; the combination is enhanced here by adding a bit of Frangelico, a hazelnut liqueur.

SERVES 10

3 medium peaches (ripe and firm)
1 teaspoon lemon juice
¾ cup plus 2 tablespoons sugar
½ cup hazelnuts

8 tablespoons (¼ pound) unsalted butter
3 large eggs
¾ teaspoon vanilla extract
1 cup all-purpose flour
1 teaspoon baking powder
2 tablespoons Frangelico
1½ cups whipping cream
¼ teaspoon unflavored gelatin
1 tablespoon powdered sugar

Wash the peaches and cut each into 8 wedges; cut each wedge crosswise into quarters. Put the peaches in a bowl and sprinkle them with the lemon juice and 2 tablespoons of sugar. Set aside for 1 hour, turning the fruit over with a spoon every 15 minutes.

Preheat the oven to 350°. Cut a circle of parchment to fit the bottom of a 9-inch round cake pan. Butter the pan and line it with the parchment, then flour the sides.

Spread the hazelnuts on a cookie sheet and toast them in the oven. After 5 minutes, spray enough water on the nuts to dampen them lightly. The water will help to loosen the skins. Toast about 7 minutes longer, until the skins get quite dark. Remove the nuts from the oven and let them cool a little, then put them in a terry cloth kitchen towel and rub them to remove the skins. If some of the skins refuse to come off, leave them on.

Crush the nuts. The easiest way is to use the blade of a Chinese cleaver. Put the nuts on a table, fairly close to the corner. Lay the flat side of the cleaver blade on them; have the handle off the side of the table and the cutting edge away from you. Lay a flat hand on the blade, lay your other hand on top, and lean all your weight on it. Repeat until all nuts are crushed to a texture somewhat like coarsely chopped. Set aside.

Increase the oven temperature to 375°. Melt the butter and set it aside to cool. Beat the eggs. Beat in the remaining ¾ cup of sugar. Add the melted butter and ½ teaspoon of vanilla and beat with an electric mixer at medium-high speed until the batter is thick, smooth, and noticeably lighter in color. Add the flour and baking powder and beat until smooth.

Spoon the batter into the prepared pan and smooth the top. Bake in the middle of the oven until the center springs back when lightly touched, about 20 minutes. Cool in the pan on a wire rack.

Put the peaches in a colander over a bowl and let them drain for 5 minutes. Add the Frangelico to the liquid. You should have about ¼ cup of syrup.

Remove the cooled cake from the pan and discard the parchment. If the top is domed, trim the domed part off with a serrated knife. With a long-bladed slicer or serrated knife, cut the cake into two equal layers.

Put ¼ cup of cream in a small bowl and sprinkle the gelatin over it. Let it sit until the gelatin softens and the cream swells, about 5 minutes. Transfer the mixture to a heatproof measuring cup and sit it in a little simmering water until the gelatin dissolves. Set aside.

Add the powdered sugar and the remaining ¼ teaspoon of vanilla to the rest of the cream and whip it to soft peaks. With the mixer running on low, hold the cup of dissolved gelatin mixture high over the bowl and pour it slowly into the cream (it will cool a little as it pours). Continue whipping the cream to stiff peaks.

To assemble, place the bottom cake layer on a serving plate. Sprinkle 2 tablespoons of syrup over it. Spread the peaches evenly on top. Spoon on enough whipped cream to cover the peaches; smooth the surface with an icing spatula. Add the second cake layer and sprinkle the remaining syrup over it. Spread the remaining cream evenly over the top and sides of the cake. Holding the crushed hazelnuts in an open hand, press them gently onto the sides of the cake. Refrigerate until ready to serve.

Hazelnut and Persimmon Cake

This is a light cake, studded with brightly colored fruit. It is especially nice at afternoon tea. Fuyu persimmons are the squat, sort of tomato-shaped variety that can be eaten while still crisp. Some have large seeds, others have none. It is impossible to tell when buying a Fuyu whether a seed lurks inside or not, so it is difficult to know how much flesh a given persimmon will yield. Buy more than you think you'll need so there's enough to yield one cup.

SERVES 12

½ cup hazelnuts
Fuyu persimmons to yield 1 cup chunks
1⅓ cups all-purpose flour
1 teaspoon baking powder
¾ cup sugar
6 tablespoons unsalted butter, melted
¼ teaspoon vanilla extract
2 large eggs (cold)
1 tablespoon unsalted butter for greasing the
*   pan*
1 cup whipping cream
½ tablespoon fresh mint leaves, cut into
*   strips*
Fresh persimmon slices

Preheat the oven to 350°. Spread the hazelnuts on a cookie sheet and toast them in the oven until fragrant, about 10 minutes. Roll the nuts in a towel to remove the skins and set them aside to cool. Peel and quarter the persimmons, remove any seeds, and cut the flesh into ¼-inch chunks.

Place the toasted nuts, flour, and baking powder in a food processor. Process until the pieces of nut are the size of sunflower seeds. (If you prefer, you can chop the nuts by hand, then mix them thoroughly with the flour and baking powder.)

Beat the sugar and butter together with an electric mixer. Add the vanilla. Add 1 egg and beat until smooth and light in color. Add the second egg and beat until smooth. Mix in the flour until it is completely incorporated. Fold in the persimmon chunks.

Butter a tube cake pan very well (use the entire tablespoon of butter) and dust it with flour. Spoon the batter into the pan and smooth the top. Bake until the top is browned, it springs back when lightly touched, and a knife inserted in the thickest part comes out clean, about 35 minutes. Let the cake cool, then remove it from the pan and set it on a serving plate.

Just before serving, whip the cream to soft peaks. Top each slice of cake with a dollop of cream and garnish with fresh mint strips. Serve with slices of fresh persimmon.

Plum and Pecan Cake

Chopped dates add a smooth, sweet richness to this moist, tender cake, and contrast beautifully with the sour plums. Although the cake holds its own very well served plain, it is wonderful with softly whipped unsweetened cream or Vanilla Ice Cream (page 158).

SERVES 8

3 sour plums
½ cup dates
½ cup pecans
8 tablespoons (¼ pound) unsalted butter
2 large eggs
1 cup sugar
1⅓ cups all-purpose flour
1 teaspoon baking powder

Cut a circle of parchment to fit the bottom of a 9-inch round cake pan. Butter the pan and line it with the parchment, then flour the sides. Preheat the oven to 350°.

Wash the plums and cut each into 8 wedges. Cut each wedge crosswise into quarters. If the dates are fresh and moist, pit them and cut them into quarters. If they are older and firm to the touch, pit them and chop them coarsely. Coarsely chop the pecans. Set the fruits and nuts aside.

Melt the butter. Whisk the eggs and sugar together. Whisk in the melted butter. Beat with an electric mixer until the batter thickens slightly; it should be smooth and light in color. Add the flour and baking powder and beat until thick and smooth. Beat in the dates and pecans. Add the plums and mix on low until incorporated.

Spoon the batter into the prepared pan and spread it smooth with a rubber spatula, mounding higher around the edges. Bake until a toothpick inserted in the center comes out clean, about 45 minutes. Set the pan on a wire rack and immediately run a sharp knife around the edge. Cool completely in the pan.

Mocha-Fig Cake

Combine chocolate and coffee and you have mocha, one of the most delicious flavors I know. Here, fresh figs add a new dimension, a lush fruitiness that underscores both the smoothness of the chocolate and the slight bitterness of the coffee. Be sure your figs are ripe enough to be full flavored; otherwise they will get lost.

SERVES 10

CHOCOLATE CAKE

¼ pound bittersweet chocolate
2 tablespoons unsalted butter
2 large eggs
½ cup milk
⅓ cup unsweetened cocoa powder
¾ cup sugar
1 cup all-purpose flour
½ teaspoon baking soda
¼ teaspoon kosher salt

CHOCOLATE GLAZE

6 ounces semisweet chocolate
6 tablespoons unsweetened butter

COFFEE BUTTERCREAM

16 tablespoons (½ pound) unsalted butter
      (soft)
¾ cup powdered sugar
2 teaspoons instant freeze-dried coffee
      crystals
1 teaspoon hot water

6 large or 8 small fresh figs

CHOCOLATE
CAKE

Cut a parchment circle to fit the bottom of a 9-inch round cake pan. Butter the pan and line it with the parchment, then flour the sides. Preheat the oven to 350°.

Melt the chocolate and butter in the top of a double boiler over boiled (not boiling) water. Stir until smooth. Transfer the chocolate to a bowl and add the eggs one at a time, mixing with an electric mixer at high speed until thick. The batter will look like frosting.

Bring the milk to a simmer. Turn off the heat and stir in the cocoa until no lumps remain. Set aside to cool a bit.

Beat the sugar into the chocolate batter. Add ½ cup of the flour, the baking soda, and the salt and mix well. Add the cocoa milk, then the remaining ½ cup of flour. Mix until smooth.

Pour the batter into the prepared pan and bake until a toothpick inserted in the center comes out clean, 25 to 30 minutes. Set the pan on a wire rack and immediately run a sharp knife around the edge. Cool the cake completely in the pan.

CHOCOLATE GLAZE

Melt the chocolate and butter together in the top of a double boiler over boiled (not boiling) water. When they are almost completely melted, remove the bowl from the heat and stir until smooth. Cool to room temperature.

BUTTERCREAM

While the glaze is cooling, make the coffee buttercream. Whip the soft butter and powdered sugar together at high speed until light in both color and texture. Dissolve the coffee in the hot water. Stir the coffee into the whipped butter and continue whipping until the buttercream is light and smooth.

To assemble: Wash and drain the figs. Cut off the stems. Cut each fig into 8 wedges.

Remove the cooled cake from the pan and discard the parchment. Using a long-bladed slicer or serrated knife, split the cake into two layers. Set the bottom layer on a plate; set the top layer aside.

Spread ½ cup of buttercream evenly over the bottom cake layer. Arrange the figs in concentric circles on top of the butter cream, starting at the edge and working toward the center. Lay the figs with one cut side down, tips pointing toward the center. Spoon a few dollops of buttercream over the figs, and spread it smooth with an icing spatula.

If the top cake layer is domed, trim off the domed part with a long-bladed slicer or serrated knife. Set the layer on top of the buttercream and press it down gently. Spread the remaining buttercream evenly over the top and sides of the cake. This forms a "crumb layer" that fills any holes and prepares a smooth surface to receive the glaze.

Pour enough glaze around the top edge of the cake so that it drips down and almost entirely covers the sides; pour the rest on top. Spread the glaze evenly over the top and sides with an icing spatula; it should look smooth and glossy. Use the tip of the spatula to clean any drips from the plate. Refrigerate the cake until ready to serve.

Chocolate Cake with Rum-Spiked Figs

Rum is a happy companion to both chocolate and figs. In this rich, exotic flourless cake it pulls the two flavors together into sumptuous harmony.

SERVES 10 TO 12

1½ cups dried mission figs or 1 cup prunes
⅓ cup rum (Myers's or Mount Gay Eclipse)
⅓ cup water
8 ounces semisweet chocolate
16 tablespoons (½ pound) unsalted butter
6 large eggs
1 cup unsweetened cocoa powder
1½ cups sugar
1 cup whipping cream, softly whipped

With a small knife, remove the hard bit of stem at the tip of each fig. Place the figs in a small saucepan with the rum and water; bring it to a boil, reduce it to a simmer, and continue cooking until the figs are tender, 15 to 20 minutes. Set aside.

Preheat the oven to 350°. Grease the bottom and sides of a 9-inch round cake pan with vegetable oil or shortening. Line the bottom with a circle of parchment or foil. Set aside.

Cut the chocolate into small pieces and melt it with the butter in the top of a double boiler. Remove from the heat and stir until smooth.

Crack the eggs into a large bowl. Add the cocoa and sugar to the eggs and beat until blended evenly. Drain the figs, discarding the liquid. Stir them and the chocolate into the egg mixture and mix well. Spoon the batter into the prepared pan.

Bake until the cake rises to the top of the pan and feels set in the center, 35 to 45 minutes. Let it cool in the pan on a wire rack. When cool, turn it out onto a plate or cake circle. Remove the parchment or foil, invert the cake back onto a plate, cover it, and chill until ready to serve. Serve with softly whipped cream.

Rhubarb and White Chocolate Cake

Rhubarb and strawberries are a traditional, and delicious, combination. Here a slightly tart rhubarb-strawberry compote is the filling for a white layer cake. Instead of frosting, I use lightly sweetened whipped cream, which complements rather than obscures the fresh taste of the fruit. The only decoration is grated white chocolate pressed onto the sides of the cake. Be sure to use a high-quality white chocolate; I use Tobler Narcisse.

SERVES 10

8 tablespoons (¼ pound) unsalted butter
3 large eggs
¾ cup sugar
½ teaspoon vanilla extract
1 cup all-purpose flour
1 teaspoon baking powder
1 cup whipping cream
1 tablespoon powdered sugar
2 cups (½ recipe) Strawberry-Rhubarb Com-
      pote (page 200)
3 ounces white chocolate

Cut a circle of parchment to fit the bottom of a 9-inch round cake pan. Butter the pan and line it with the parchment, then flour the sides. Preheat the oven to 375°.

Melt the butter and set it aside to cool. Beat the eggs. Beat in the sugar. Add the melted butter and the vanilla and beat with an electric mixer at medium-high speed until the batter is thick, smooth, and noticeably lighter in color. Add the flour and baking powder and beat until smooth.

Spoon the batter into the prepared pan and smooth the top. Bake in the middle of the oven until the center springs back when lightly touched, about 20 minutes. Cool in the pan on a wire rack.

To assemble, remove the cooled cake from the pan and set it upside down on a serving plate. If the top is domed and doesn't sit flat, trim the domed part off with a serrated knife. Discard the parchment. With a long-bladed slicer or serrated knife, cut the cake into 2 equal layers. Set the top layer aside.

Whip the cream and powdered sugar to stiff peaks. Spread the rhubarb-strawberry compote over the bottom cake layer. (Be sure the compote is cold; if it is warm the liquid will soak into the cake.) Place the second cake layer on top, cut side down, and cover the top and sides of the cake with whipped cream.

Coarsely grate the white chocolate. If using bar chocolate, break the bar into 4 pieces; hold the pieces together in your hand, broken ends outward, and grate them all at once on a box grater. Hold the grated chocolate in an open hand and press it gently against the sides of the cake to coat them. Refrigerate until 15 minutes before serving.

Blackberry Cake with Chocolate Cream

This cake really shows off the bright color and flavor of fresh blackberries. On the outside, it looks like a chocolate cake. But as soon as you cut it, the purple ribbon of berries between white cake layers delights the eye. The flavor combination of chocolate and blackberries is one of my favorites.

SERVES 10

CAKE

8 tablespoons (¼ pound) unsalted butter
3 large eggs
¾ cup sugar
½ teaspoon vanilla extract
1 cup all-purpose flour
1 teaspoon baking powder

BERRIES AND FROSTING

2 cups blackberries
10 ounces bittersweet chocolate
8 tablespoons (¼ pound) unsalted butter
3 tablespoons corn syrup
¾ cup whipping cream

CAKE

Cut a circle of parchment to fit the bottom of a 9-inch round cake pan. Butter the pan and line it with the parchment, then flour the sides. Preheat the oven to 375°.

Melt the butter and set it aside to cool. Beat the eggs. Beat in the sugar. Add the melted butter and the vanilla and beat with an electric mixer at medium-high speed until the batter is thick, smooth, and noticeably lighter in color. Add the flour and baking powder and beat until smooth.

Spoon the batter into the prepared pan and smooth the top. Bake in the middle of the oven until the center springs back when lightly touched, about 20 minutes. Cool in the pan on a wire rack.

Wash and drain the blackberries; set them aside in a paper towel–lined bowl. Rake 2 ounces of the chocolate for decorating the cake (see illustration below). Set aside.

FROSTING

Cut the remaining 8 ounces of chocolate into chunks and melt it in the top of a double boiler over boiled (not boiling) water. Cut the butter

RAKING CHOCOLATE.

into 1-inch cubes. Add the butter and corn syrup to the chocolate and stir until all the butter is melted. Stir in the cream. Transfer to a bowl and beat with an electric mixer at high speed, stopping occasionally to scrape the sides and bottom of the bowl. Beat until the frosting is light and smooth and has almost doubled in volume.

To assemble, remove the cooled cake from the pan and set it upside down on a serving plate. If the top is domed and doesn't sit flat, trim the domed part off with a serrated knife. Discard the parchment. With a long-bladed slicer or serrated knife, cut the cake into 2 equal layers. Set the top layer aside.

Spread ¾ cup of frosting over the bottom cake layer. Arrange the blackberries on top in concentric circles, starting at the outside edge and working toward the center. Don't lay the berries on their sides; stand them up, close together.

Spoon another ¾ cup of frosting over the berries and gently spread it smooth. Add the top cake layer; press it down lightly. Using an icing spatula, smooth any frosting that has oozed from between the layers over the sides of the cake. Cover the top and sides of the cake with the remaining frosting. (If the frosting in the bowl starts to separate before you are done, mix it a little more to restore its texture.)

Spread the raked chocolate evenly over the top of the cake. Refrigerate until 15 minutes before serving.

Chocolate Angel Food Cake with Hot Fudge and Toasted Hazelnuts

Many food historians believe that Pennsylvania Dutch cooks started baking angel food cakes to use up the egg whites they had left over from noodle making. Angel food cakes, which contain neither egg yolks nor butter, are extremely light and airy. This chocolate version tastes surprisingly rich and fudgy. I like to top it with a devilishly creamy hot fudge.

SERVES 12

1¼ cups sugar
¾ cup cake flour
¼ cup unsweetened cocoa powder
10 large egg whites
½ teaspoon cream of tartar
½ teaspoon kosher salt
1 teaspoon vanilla extract
1 cup hazelnuts
8 ounces bittersweet chocolate
2 tablespoons corn syrup
¾ cup heavy cream

Preheat the oven to 275°. Sift ¼ cup of sugar with the flour and cocoa six times (they must be blended very well).

Beat the egg whites with the cream of tartar and salt until frothy. Add the remaining cup of sugar slowly while beating. Add the vanilla and beat just until the whites form stiff peaks; do not overbeat. Add the flour mixture in 4 stages, folding it in completely after each addition. Spoon the batter into a clean, dry tube pan. Bake 30 minutes, then raise the oven temperature to 300° and continue baking until the top of the cake springs back when lightly touched, about 30 minutes more. Turn the cake over on a rack and let it cool upside down in the pan for 40 minutes. Remove it from the pan and set it on a serving plate right side up.

When the cake is done baking, raise the oven temperature to 325°. Spread the hazelnuts on a cookie sheet and toast them in the oven until fragrant, 10 to 15 minutes. Cool them slightly and wrap them in a kitchen towel. Rub them inside the towel to remove their skins. Chop them coarsely and set them aside.

Just before serving the cake, cut the chocolate into chunks and melt it in the top of a double boiler over boiled (not boiling) water. With the bowl still over the hot water, stir in the corn syrup and cream. Continue stirring until smooth. (If you prefer to make the hot fudge ahead, keep it refrigerated, then heat it in the top of a double boiler just before serving.) You should have about 1⅔ cups of hot fudge.

To serve, cut the cake into slices; a serrated knife is best for angel food cakes. Pour hot fudge over one corner of each slice and sprinkle chopped hazelnuts on top.

Chocolate–Almond Meringue Cake

This is an elegant cake, made with crisp almond meringues on the top and bottom, and a moist chocolate almond cake in between. A smooth buttercream holds it all together, and it is served in a pool of raspberry sauce. Be sure to use almond paste, not marzipan, in the cake; marzipan is way too sweet.

SERVES 12

ALMOND MERINGUE

½ cup sliced almonds
2 tablespoons cornstarch
¾ cup sugar
4 large egg whites

CHOCOLATE-ALMOND CAKE

6 tablespoons unsalted butter (soft)
6 tablespoons sugar
4 ounces almond paste
¼ cup unsweetened cocoa powder
2 large eggs

BUTTERCREAM

24 tablespoons (¾ pound) unsalted butter
(soft)
¾ cup powdered sugar plus more for dusting
¼ teaspoon vanilla extract
4 ounces bittersweet chocolate

RASPBERRY SAUCE

2 pints raspberries
1 tablespoon sugar

Preheat the oven to 225°. Place one oven shelf in the center of the oven and another at the lowest level.

ALMOND MERINGUE

Combine the almonds with the cornstarch and chop them very fine. Stir in 1 tablespoon of sugar and set aside.

Half fill a medium saucepan with water; bring it to a boil and turn off the heat. Combine the egg whites with the remaining ½ cup plus 3 tablespoons of sugar in a medium stainless-steel bowl; beat until smooth. Set the bowl over the pan of boiled water and stir, scraping the bottom of the bowl so the eggs won't cook and to distribute the heat, until the eggs are warm. Remove the bowl from the pan and whip with a hand-held electric mixer at high speed until stiff peaks form. Fold in the almond mixture.

Line 2 cookie sheets with parchment. Draw a 9-inch circle on each sheet of parchment, then turn it over so the circle is against the pan. Spoon the meringue into a large pastry bag with a #3 plain tip. Pipe out two 9-inch circles of meringue on the parchment-lined cookie sheets as follows: Hold the tip about an inch above the center of one of the circles. Starting with a dot of meringue, pipe out a continuous spiral, with each circle touching but not overlapping the one before, until you have filled the entire 9-inch circle. If there are large gaps, go back when the circle is finished and fill them in; if there are lumps, smooth them with a fingertip.

Bake one circle on each oven shelf until they are golden brown and firm to the touch in the center, 60 to 90 minutes. Rotate the cookie sheets and reverse their positions halfway through baking to assure even browning. Set them aside to cool.

CHOCOLATE-ALMOND CAKE

Raise the oven temperature to 350°. Cut a parchment circle to fit inside a 9-inch round cake pan. Butter the sides and bottom of the pan. Line the bottom with the parchment circle, then butter the parchment. Dust the pan with flour.

Cream the butter and sugar until smooth. Add the almond paste and mix until completely blended. Mix in the cocoa. Beat the eggs lightly and slowly add them to the batter. Mix until smooth.

Spoon the batter into the prepared pan and smooth the top. Bake in the lower middle of the oven until the sides pull away from the pan and the center is set, about 25 to 30 minutes. Cool in the pan on a wire rack.

BUTTERCREAM — Whip the butter with the powdered sugar and vanilla until light and fluffy.

To assemble the cake, set one of the meringue circles on a serving plate and spread ⅓ of the buttercream evenly over it. Set the chocolate almond cake over the buttercream and spread another ⅓ of the buttercream on it. Set the second meringue on top. Use the remaining buttercream to cover the sides of the cake; the top remains uncovered.

Coarsely grate the chocolate and gently press it onto the sides with your open hand. Cover with plastic wrap; refrigerate.

RASPBERRY SAUCE — Wash the raspberries by dropping them into a bowl of cold water. Remove them from the water and let them drain and dry on a towel. Purée them with the sugar in a food processor, blender, or food mill. Strain the purée through a sieve to remove the seeds. Chill the sauce until ready to use.

The cake is best cut while cold. After cutting, dust the top lightly with powdered sugar. Spoon a pool of raspberry sauce onto each dessert plate and set a slice of cake on it. Serve cold.

Chocolate Cake with Brandied Cherries

Brandied cherries and chocolate are a great combination, in a candy box or a festive cake. Although this recipe has several steps, all of them are easy—so long as you own a cherry pitter. If you don't, I recommend that you get one. They are relatively inexpensive, and they make an otherwise difficult job simple. If you wish, you can make this cake a day ahead; chill it until the buttercream is firm, about ½ hour, then wrap it in plastic wrap and refrigerate until 15 minutes before serving.

SERVES 8 TO 10

BRANDIED CHERRIES

1 pound bing cherries
1 tablespoon lemon juice
3 tablespoons sugar
2 tablespoons brandy

CHOCOLATE CAKE

¼ pound bittersweet chocolate
2 tablespoons unsalted butter
2 large eggs
½ cup milk
⅓ cup unsweetened cocoa powder
¾ cup sugar
1 cup all-purpose flour
½ teaspoon baking soda
¼ teaspoon kosher salt

CHOCOLATE BUTTERCREAM

8 ounces semisweet chocolate
16 tablespoons (½ pound) unsalted butter

BRANDIED CHERRIES

Select the 12 most beautiful cherries. Remove the pits, but leave the stems attached (align the pitter so it goes through the cherry sideways or at an angle, not through the stem end). Set aside.

Remove the stems from the rest of the cherries and pit them. Place them in a bowl and sprinkle on the lemon juice, sugar, and brandy. Mix gently with a spoon to dissolve the sugar and coat the cherries. Cover the bowl with plastic wrap and set it aside while you prepare the cake. Uncover the bowl and stir the cherries every half hour or so. The alcoholic harshness of the brandy will disappear as the cherries stand.

CHOCOLATE CAKE

Cut a parchment circle to fit the bottom of a 9-inch round cake pan. Butter the pan and line it with the parchment, then flour the sides. Preheat the oven to 350°.

Melt the chocolate and butter in the top of a double boiler over boiled (not boiling) water. Stir until smooth. Transfer to a bowl and add the eggs one at a time, mixing with an electric mixer at high speed until thick. The batter will look like frosting.

Bring the milk to a simmer. Turn off the heat and stir in the cocoa until no lumps remain. Set aside to cool a bit.

Beat the sugar into the chocolate batter. Add ½ cup flour, the baking soda, and the salt and mix well. Add the cocoa milk, then the remaining ½ cup of flour. Mix until smooth.

Pour the batter into the prepared pan and bake until a toothpick inserted in the center comes out clean, 25 to 30 minutes. Set the pan on a wire rack and immediately run a sharp knife around the edge. Cool the cake completely in the pan.

CHOCOLATE BUTTERCREAM

Melt the chocolate in the top of a double boiler over boiled (not boiling) water. Remove from the heat and stir the chocolate to help it cool a little. Cut the butter into 1-inch pieces and stir it in. When the butter is incorporated, beat with an electric mixer until the buttercream turns thick and light in color and increases noticeably in volume.

To assemble the cake, turn the cooled cake out onto a cake plate and discard the parchment. Leave the cake upside down. Using a long-bladed slicer or serrated knife, split the cake into 2 layers. Set the top layer aside.

Drain the brandied cherries, reserving the liquid. Drizzle half of the liquid over the bottom cake layer. Cut the cherries in half and arrange them in a single layer on the cake. Cover the cherries with half of the chocolate buttercream. Smooth the surface. Place the second cake layer on top and drizzle the remaining cherry liquid over it. Using an icing spatula, spread the remaining buttercream smoothly over the top and sides of the cake. Arrange the 12 cherries with stems in a circle on top, about a half inch in from the edge.

Bourbon– Chocolate Pecan Cake

This is a flourless chocolate cake made without ground nuts. It is lighter than most flourless cakes and less sweet, but it would be hard to find a more intense chocolate flavor. Make the cake a day ahead and refrigerate it overnight.

SERVES 12

CAKE

2 cups pecans
16 tablespoons (½ pound) unsalted butter
8 ounces bittersweet or semisweet chocolate
1½ cups sugar
1 cup unsweetened cocoa powder
6 large eggs
⅓ cup good-quality bourbon

GLAZE

4 ounces bittersweet or semisweet chocolate
8 tablespoons (¼ pound) unsalted butter

To make the cake, preheat the oven to 350°. Spread the pecans on a cookie sheet and toast them in the oven until fragrant, about 10 minutes. Set them aside to cool.

Cut a circle of parchment to fit the bottom of a 9-inch round cake pan. Butter the pan well and line it with the parchment circle; be sure it lies flat.

Melt the butter and chocolate together in the top of a double boiler over simmering water. Stir until very smooth. Set aside to cool.

Mix the sugar, cocoa, and eggs together just until well combined. Add the melted chocolate and stir to combine. Coarsely chop the pecans and stir in 1½ cups. Stir in the bourbon.

Pour the batter into the prepared pan. Place the pan inside a larger pan and pour hot water to the level of an inch in the outer pan. Bake until the cake is firm to the touch, about 45 minutes. Don't worry if the surface cracks a little. Cool the cake on a wire rack, then remove it from the pan, leaving the parchment paper attached. Wrap the cake in plastic wrap and refrigerate it overnight.

The following day, make the glaze by melting the chocolate and butter in the top of a double boiler over simmering water. Stir until completely smooth. Cool about 5 minutes. Place the cake upside down on a wire rack with a sheet of waxed paper underneath to catch drips. Peel off the parchment circle, then drizzle spoonfuls of glaze along the edges of the cake so that it drips down and coats the sides. When the sides are completely covered, spoon the rest of the glaze on top of the cake and smooth it with an icing spatula. Cover the sides of the cake with the remaining ½ cup of pecans by pressing them gently against the glaze with your open hand. Refrigerate the cake until ½ hour before serving.

Lemon and White Chocolate Cake

In the course of experimenting with white chocolate, I discovered that adding it to a cream frosting makes the frosting exceptionally smooth and stable. The chocolate also smooths the flavor, in this case beautifully rounding out the tartness of fresh lemon.

SERVES 12

1 Butter Sponge Cake (page 89), with ½ teaspoon grated lemon zest added to the batter before baking
4 large eggs
1 cup sugar
¾ cup lemon juice
4 ounces white chocolate
2 cups whipping cream
4 ounces coarsely grated white chocolate (optional)

Bake the cake as directed and set it aside to cool on a wire rack.
Whisk the eggs and sugar together in a large saucepan. Whisk in the lemon juice. Set the pan over medium heat and continue whisking until the mixture thickens and becomes lighter in color. Turn off the heat. Chop the white chocolate into chunks and stir it in with the whisk until it melts completely. Transfer the mixture to a stainless-steel bowl and set it in a larger bowl of ice water to cool it quickly.

Using a long-bladed slicer or serrated knife, trim the top of the cake to make it level and split the cake horizontally into 2 equal layers. Set the bottom layer on a serving plate. Whip the cream to soft peaks. Spoon the cooled chocolate-lemon mixture into the cream and fold it in.

Spoon about 2 cups of the chocolate-lemon cream onto the bottom cake layer and spread it smooth with an icing spatula. Add the top cake layer and press it gently into the cream. Spoon 2 cups of cream on top of the cake and spread it smoothly over the top and sides. Put the remaining cream into a pastry bag with a #4 star tip.

Decorate the top of the cake by piping out 12 lines of crisscrossing shells, radiating from the center of the cake like spokes on a wheel (see illustration). Make a rosette in the middle. If you wish, decorate the sides of the cake with grated white chocolate, gently pressing it on with your open hand. Refrigerate the cake until ready to serve.

Walnut Cake with Strawberry Sauce

This is a simple, homey cake. It is moist and light and it tastes like walnuts. I serve it heaped with whipped cream and pass a little pitcher of strawberry sauce for dribbling over it.

SERVES 8

WALNUT CAKE

6 tablespoons unsalted butter
1 cup walnuts
1⅓ cups all-purpose flour
1 large egg
1 cup sugar
½ teaspoon vanilla
1 teaspoon baking powder
½ cup milk

STRAWBERRY SAUCE AND WHIPPED CREAM

2 pints fresh strawberries
2 tablespoons sugar
1½ cups whipping cream
2 teaspoons powdered sugar

Preheat the oven to 350°. Cut a circle of parchment to fit the bottom of a 9-inch round (2-inch-deep) cake pan. Butter and flour the pan and line it with the parchment circle.

To make the cake, melt the butter and set it aside. Chop the walnuts with ⅓ cup of flour in a food processor until the nuts are finely ground.

Beat the egg with an electric mixer. While beating, slowly add the melted butter and then the sugar. Mix until smooth and light. Add the vanilla, baking powder, and ground nut mixture; mix. Add half the milk and mix until it is completely incorporated and has thinned the batter. Scrape the bowl and beaters, then mix in ½ cup of flour. Mix in the rest of the milk then scrape again. Add the remaining ½ cup of flour and mix until smooth.

Scrape the batter into the prepared pan. Smooth the top with a rubber spatula. Bake in the middle of the oven until the top springs back when lightly touched, about 40 minutes. Cool the cake in the pan on a wire rack. When completely cool, turn it out of the pan, peel off the parchment circle, and set it on a serving plate.

Two hours before serving the cake, wash and drain the strawberries and remove the leaves. Cut the berries into ¼-inch slices. Toss them in a bowl with the granulated sugar. Cover and chill.

Just before serving, whip the cream and powdered sugar to stiff peaks. Spoon dollops of cream all over the top of the cake. Serve with the strawberry sauce.

Date and Walnut Cake with Lemon Buttercream

Dates have been grown in California for more than eighty years now, and their once-exotic sweetness has come to be taken for granted by American bakers. In cakes and quick breads dates are most often paired with walnuts, a match that's hard to beat for contrast and natural compatibility. In this fine-crumbed cake the heavier, moist dates tend to sink to the bottom, while the walnuts provide crunchiness throughout. A light lemon buttercream adds elegance and tang.

SERVES 8 TO 10

CAKE

1 cup walnuts
6 tablespoons unsalted butter (soft)
¾ cup sugar
3 large eggs, slightly beaten
1 cup all-purpose flour
1 teaspoon baking powder
½ cup chopped dates

LEMON BUTTERCREAM

2 medium lemons
2 large eggs
¾ cup sugar
24 tablespoons (¾ pound) unsalted butter
   (soft)

CAKE   Cut a parchment circle to fit the bottom of a 9-inch round cake pan. Butter the pan and line it with the parchment, then flour the sides. Preheat the oven to 350°.

Chop the walnuts into ¼-inch pieces. Beat the butter and sugar together until light and smooth (about 3 minutes at high speed with a hand-held electric mixer). Beat in the eggs one at a time. Sift the flour and baking powder together twice. Beat them into the batter at moderate speed. Fold in the dates and ½ cup walnuts.

Spoon the batter into the prepared pan and bake in the lower-middle part of the oven until the top is golden brown, the edges have begun to pull away from the pan, and the center springs back when lightly touched, about 30 minutes. The cake will be about 1½ inches high. Cool it in the pan on a wire rack. If you are not ready to assemble the cake when it is completely cool, wrap it in plastic wrap to keep it from drying out. You may refrigerate it for up to 2 days or freeze it for up to 2 weeks.

BUTTERCREAM   Wash the lemons well with hot water and dishwashing liquid; rinse and dry them. Grate 2 tablespoons of zest and set it aside. Squeeze ½ cup of lemon juice.

Beat the eggs, sugar, and zest until well blended. Stir in the juice. Cook in the top of a double boiler over boiling water, stirring occasionally, until the mixture thickens enough to coat the back of a spoon, 10 to 15 minutes. Set it aside to cool; stir occasionally.

Whip the butter until light, about 2 minutes with a hand-held electric mixer. Add the lemon mixture and continue whipping until light and fluffy, 5 to 7 minutes.

Set the cake upside down on a serving plate. Using a long-bladed slicer or serrated knife, cut it into 2 equal layers. Set the top layer aside.

Spoon 1 cup of buttercream onto the bottom layer and spread it smooth with an icing spatula. Be sure it comes all the way to the edges. Add the top layer, brown side up. Cover the top and sides of the cake evenly with the remaining buttercream. Cover the sides of the cake with the remaining ½ cup of chopped walnuts by pressing them gently onto the buttercream with your open hand. Refrigerate the cake until 15 minutes before serving.

Nectarine-Walnut Cake with Rum Sauce

I am especially fond of this style of cake. I like the contrast between crisp wafers and tender cake, between juicy fresh fruit and smooth buttercream. In structure, this is very much like the Nectarine-Pecan Cake on page 91. And yet each element is different. Here the cake is less rich, and has nuts ground into the flour; it is used whole, not cut into layers. There is twice as much fruit as in the Nectarine-Pecan Cake, plus more in a separate sauce. Both cakes are beautiful and delicious; they are variations on a favorite theme. Either would also be good with ripe, firm peaches substituted for the nectarines.

SERVES 10

CAKE

¼ *cup walnuts*
3 *tablespoons unsalted butter*
⅓ *cup cake flour*
¼ *cup sugar*
2 *large eggs plus 2 large yolks*

WAFERS

8 *tablespoons (¼ pound) unsalted butter*
    (cold)
1 *cup bread flour*
3 *tablespoons cold water*

BUTTERCREAM

32 *tablespoons (1 pound) unsalted butter*
    (soft)
1¾ *cups powdered sugar, sifted*
½ *teaspoon vanilla extract*

FRUIT AND NUTS

4 *medium nectarines*
1 *cup walnuts*

SAUCE

4 *medium nectarines*
¼ *cup sugar*
3 *tablespoons dark rum*

CAKE

Preheat the oven to 325°. Spread the walnuts on a cookie sheet and toast them in the oven until fragrant, about 10 minutes. Set them aside to cool. Butter and flour a 9-inch round cake pan. Melt the butter and set it aside.

Grind the flour and walnuts in a food processor until fine. Fill the bottom of a double boiler one-third full of water and bring it to a simmer. Combine the sugar, eggs, and yolks in the top of the double boiler. Cook them over the simmering water, whipping continuously with a hand-held electric mixer, until the batter forms a ribbon and will hold a crease when you draw your finger through it. This step will take 7 to 10 minutes. Remove the batter from the heat.

Pour the flour evenly over the batter and fold it in; be sure not to leave any flour clinging to the sides or bottom of the pan. Pour ¼ of the batter into a small bowl. Quickly fold the butter into it, then fold it back into the rest of the batter. Stop as soon as everything is combined; if you overfold, the cake may fall during baking.

*THE BATTER FORMS A RIBBON
AS IT FALLS FROM THE BEATER.*

Pour the batter into the prepared pan and bake in the middle of the oven until the sides begin to pull away from the pan and the center springs back when lightly touched, about 45 minutes. Cool the cake in the pan on a wire rack for 15 minutes, then turn it out onto a plate and set it aside.

WAFERS Line 2 cookie sheets with parchment. Cut the butter into small pieces and put it in a bowl with the flour. Gently rub the butter into the flour with your fingers until the butter is in thin flakes and the flour has taken on a golden color. Add the water and blend only until the dough comes together.

Divide the dough in half. On a lightly floured surface, roll each half into a 9½-inch circle. Lift the circles one at a time by rolling them gently around the rolling pin. Unroll them onto the cookie sheets. Refrigerate for 45 minutes. Preheat the oven to 375°. Bake the wafers until firm to the touch and golden brown, about 20 minutes. Set them aside to cool.

BUTTERCREAM Whip the butter, sugar, and vanilla until white and light tasting, 10 to 15 minutes.

To assemble the cake, wash the nectarines and cut each one into 8 wedges. Line a cookie sheet with waxed paper or parchment. Place one of the wafers on the sheet and spread ¼ of the buttercream evenly over it. Using a long-bladed slicer or serrated knife, trim the browned surface from the top and bottom of the cake, and set it on the buttercream. Arrange the nectarine wedges on the cake layer, leaving ½ inch around the edge. Spread enough buttercream over the fruit to cover it.

Set the second wafer over the fruit, bottom side up. Press on it gently to fuse the layers. Cover the top and sides of the cake evenly with the remaining buttercream. Chop the nuts coarsely and press them onto the sides of the cake with your open hand. Refrigerate the cake until 15 minutes before serving.

SAUCE   Wash the nectarines and cut them into ½-inch chunks. Combine them with the sugar and rum in a blender or food processor. Blend until smooth. Serve with the cake.

Caramel-Walnut Roll

A roulade is a traditional European rolled cake. In America the roulade is best known as a jelly roll, or a chocolate cream roll. There are endless possibilities for rolled cakes, however; I prefer those that are not too sweet and are subtle in their flavoring. Here is one that combines a light vanilla cake with caramel and walnuts.

SERVES 8

CAKE

4 large eggs
¾ cup sugar
½ teaspoon vanilla extract
¾ cup cake flour

CARAMEL CREAM AND WALNUT FILLING

½ cup sugar
¼ cup water
½ cup whipping cream
8 tablespoons (¼ pound) unsalted butter
       (soft)
½ cup powdered sugar
½ cup chopped walnuts

CAKE   Preheat the oven to 350°. Combine the eggs and sugar in the top of a double boiler. Warm them over boiling water, stirring constantly, until hot to the touch. Remove from the heat and stir in the vanilla. Transfer the mixture to the bowl of an electric mixer and whip it to soft peaks; the whipping will take 15 to 20 minutes.

Meanwhile, line an 11- × 17-inch cookie sheet with parchment; butter and flour it.

When the eggs are fully whipped, sift the flour over them and fold it in until the batter is smooth. Spoon the batter onto the sheet pan and smooth the surface with the edge of a rubber spatula. Bake until the center springs back when lightly touched, about 10 minutes.

Cool the cake in the pan for 5 minutes. Spread a clean kitchen towel on a counter and turn the cake out onto it. With the parchment still attached, roll the cake and the towel together into a 17-inch-long log. Let the log stand for 10 minutes, then unroll it and remove the towel. Reroll it without the towel and wrap it in plastic wrap.

CARAMEL
CREAM

Combine the sugar and water in a heavy saucepan. Make a caramel by cooking the mixture over medium heat until the sugar dissolves and turns a mahogany color. If the caramel colors unevenly, swirl the pan to distribute the color; do not stir.

Warm the cream in a separate saucepan until it is hot to the touch. When the caramel is done, turn off the heat, place a colander or strainer over the saucepan to prevent spatters (caramel is very hot), and pour in the cream. Stir until smooth, then set aside to cool.

Whip the butter and powdered sugar until light and smooth. Beat the caramel into the butter-sugar mixture; whip again until light and smooth.

To assemble, unroll the cake and remove the parchment. Spread the top of the cake with the caramel cream. Sprinkle the walnuts over the cream. Roll the cake back into a log, wrap it with plastic wrap, and chill it until set. To serve, unwrap the log and cut it into slices.

Fruit Cake

Fruit cake tastes a lot better when you candy the fruit yourself. And you know it's free of artificial colors and preservatives. I like to brush the syrup left over from candying the fruit onto the finished cake to give it even more flavor and moisture.

SERVES 8

8 tablespoons (¼ pound) unsalted butter
     (soft)
⅓ cup sugar
¼ teaspoon kosher salt
¼ teaspoon vanilla extract
2 large eggs plus 1 large egg yolk
¾ cup all-purpose flour
¼ teaspoon baking powder
1 cup Candied Cranberries (page 211)
⅓ cup candied lemon peel (page 211)
¼ cup candied orange peel (page 211)
¼ cup candied grapefruit peel (page 211)
1½ cups pecan halves

Preheat the oven to 325°. Butter a 9- × 5- × 2-inch loaf pan and line it with parchment.

Cream the butter, sugar, salt, and vanilla until light, about 2 minutes at high speed on an electric mixer. Beat the eggs and egg yolk with a fork until blended, then beat them into the butter in 4 stages. Sift the flour and baking powder together 3 times; beat them into the batter at low speed.

Strain the syrup from all of the candied fruit; press the fruit against the strainer with the back of a spoon to extract as much of the syrup as possible. Save the syrup. Fold the fruit and nuts into the batter and spoon it into the prepared loaf pan. Place the pan on a cookie sheet and bake in the lower third of the oven until the center of the cake is set, 50 to 55 minutes. Cool the cake on a wire rack for 5 minutes, then turn it out of the pan and cool it completely on the rack.

Bring the syrup from the fruit to a boil in a small saucepan. Allow it to cool for 10 minutes, then brush it over the top and sides of the cake. Keep the cake covered until served.

Ricotta and Vanilla Cheesecake with Lemon Sauce

Cheesecake can be moist or slightly dry, plain or adorned with fruit or sauce, set in a traditional pie crust or a graham cracker crust. One of my favorites, included in *The American Baker*, has chopped almonds on the bottom instead of a crust. The cheesecake I make most often now has a flaky tart-like shell and a smooth, moist filling of ricotta cheese enriched with whipping cream. I serve it with a tangy lemon sauce.

SERVES 8 TO 10

½ recipe Tart Dough (page 50)

FILLING

2 large eggs
1 tablespoon all-purpose flour
½ cup sugar
1 package (15 ounces) unsalted whole milk ricotta cheese
⅓ cup whipping cream
½ teaspoon vanilla extract

LEMON SAUCE

2 large eggs
½ cup sugar
⅓ cup lemon juice
4 tablespoons unsalted butter
½ cup whipping cream

CRUST

Prepare the tart dough as directed. On a lightly floured surface, roll the dough into a 13-inch circle. Fold the circle into quarters and lift it gently into an 8-inch springform cake pan. Unfold the dough, settle it into the pan, press it gently against the sides, and trim off the excess. Chill until firm, about 20 minutes.

Preheat the oven to 350°. Line the unbaked shell with heavy aluminum foil, dull side up. Prick all over the bottom with a fork, piercing both foil and dough. Hold the fork straight down so the tines do not tear large holes in the dough. Bake 10 minutes. Carefully lift the foil and look at the bottom crust. If it is domed, gently press it flat. Bake 15 minutes more. Remove the foil and bake 5 minutes more. Set aside to cool on a wire rack.

FILLING

Using the paddle attachment on an electric mixer, cream the eggs, flour, and sugar at medium speed until well blended. (Beaters will beat too much air into the mixture.) Mix in the ricotta cheese, then the cream and vanilla. The mixture will be a little lumpy. Pour it into the prebaked shell. Trim the crust with a knife anywhere it overlaps the pan. Bake until the filling is just set and the top is golden brown, about 40 minutes. Cool on a wire rack.

When the cheesecake is cool, chill it for ½ hour. Then release the sides of the pan and lift the cake out on the pan bottom. Slide the blade of a large spatula under the cake, tilt the pan bottom slightly, and slide the cake onto a serving plate. If the crust is stuck in spots, gently loosen it with the spatula or a long knife blade, then slide it onto the serving plate.

LEMON SAUCE

Combine the eggs, sugar, and lemon juice and beat at high speed until foamy. Bring about 1½ inches of water to a boil in a pot or the bottom of a double boiler. Set the bowl of lemon mixture over the water and cook, whisking occasionally, until thick. Remove from the heat and stir in the butter until it is completely melted. Whisk in the cream. Refrigerate.

To serve, spoon some sauce atop each slice of cheesecake so that it cascades down one side.

Cranberry-Almond Cake

This is a simple loaf cake made fancy by a layer of crunchy almonds on the outside. Serve it in slices, with lightly whipped unsweetened cream or Vanilla Ice Cream (page 158).

SERVES 8 TO 10

½ cup sliced natural (skin on) almonds
1½ cups cranberries
¼ cup almond paste
4 tablespoons unsalted butter (soft)
¾ cup sugar
2 large eggs, separated
1½ cups plus 2 tablespoons all-purpose flour
2 teaspoons baking powder
½ cup milk (room temperature)

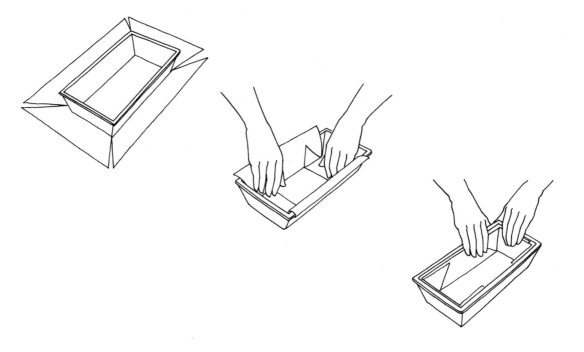

Butter a 9- × 5-inch loaf pan and line it with parchment (see illustration above); butter the parchment heavily. Press the almonds against the sides and bottom of the pan.

Wash the cranberries and put them in a colander to drain. Preheat the oven to 350°.

Cut the almond paste into 4 pieces. Put it in a 3-quart bowl with the butter, and cream them with an electric mixer at high speed for 3 minutes. Stop a few times to scrape the bowl. Slowly beat in ½ cup of sugar. Scrape the bowl. Beat in the egg yolks; continue mixing until the batter becomes lighter in color, about 2 minutes.

Sift 1½ cups of flour with the baking powder 3 times. Add half of the flour mixture to the batter and mix well. Add the milk and then the rest of the flour-baking powder, mixing well after each addition. Toss the cranberries with the remaining 2 tablespoons of flour and set them aside.

Whip the egg whites at high speed until frothy. With the mixer running, slowly add the remaining ¼ cup of sugar; continue whipping to stiff peaks. Fold the egg whites into the batter, scraping the bottom and sides of the bowl as you fold, until the batter is smooth and free of lumps. Fold in the cranberries.

Spoon the batter into the prepared pan and smooth the top. Bake in the middle of the oven. After 20 minutes rotate the pan. Continue baking until the center of the cake springs back when lightly touched and the edges have pulled away from the pan, 25 to 30 minutes more. Remove from the oven and turn the cake upside down on a wire cooling rack. Leave the parchment on the cake until it is completely cooled. Serve upside down.

NOTE

This cake can be frozen for up to 3 weeks. Cool completely, then wrap in plastic wrap. Cover the plastic wrap with a layer of foil. Do not remove the parchment until the cake is defrosted.

Cranberry-Walnut Tea Cake

Cranberries, of course, are at their peak at holiday time when most of us do a lot of entertaining. This is a simple, moist cake that goes very well with afternoon coffee or tea. It has plenty of cranberries, which give it a bright and refreshing tartness.

SERVES 8 TO 10

8 tablespoons (¼ pound) unsalted butter
2 large eggs
1 cup sugar
1 teaspoon vanilla extract
1⅓ cup all-purpose flour
1 teaspoon baking powder
2 cups cranberries (fresh or defrosted)
¾ cup chopped walnuts

Cut a piece of parchment to fit inside a 9- × 5-inch loaf pan. Butter the pan, then line it with the parchment as illustrated on page 118. Preheat the oven to 350°.

Melt the butter. Whisk the eggs and sugar together. Whisk in the melted butter and the vanilla. Beat with an electric mixer until the batter thickens slightly; it should be smooth and light in color. Add the flour and baking powder and beat until thick and smooth. Fold in the cranberries and nuts.

Spoon the batter into the prepared pan and bake until a toothpick inserted in the center comes out clean, about 55 minutes. Cool in the pan on a wire rack. When cool, remove from the pan and discard the parchment. Cut into slices and serve plain or with softly whipped unsweetened cream or vanilla ice cream.

6

Shortcakes, Filled Pastries, Brownies, and Bars

As CHILDREN we all fall in love with brownies and chewy bars; as adults, most of us are still in love with them. I've had a lot of fun over the years exploring countless variations on brownies, some chewy, some cakey, some intensely chocolatey, others less so. I've included two of my favorites here—one chewy and one cakey; both are intensely chocolate.

I've spent even more time on recipes for bars than on brownies, because there are so many possibilities. In developing a new bar recipe, I try to use just two main ingredients that harmonize and play off one another. Among my current favorite combinations are sesame with orange, apricot with almond, and cranberry with walnut. These take-them-anywhere desserts are great contributions to pot luck suppers and school cake sales, but mostly I like to keep them on hand for drop-in visitors. (Friends who know you have them tend to drop by often.)

In my first book, *The American Baker*, I explored a lot of traditional European pastries. Unfortunately, most home bakers don't often have the time to turn out trays of eclairs and napoleons. When you do have the time, they're wonderful. So, along with the simple shortcakes, brownies, and bars in this chapter, I've included a few European-inspired delicacies, and even a recipe for making your own puff pastry. As soon as there's puff pastry available, my mind turns to napoleons. Those I've included here are made with caramel and fresh strawberries. They're less sweet than traditional napoleons and a real treat when strawberries are at their peak of ripeness.

Like ripe strawberries, ripe cherries start my creative juices flowing. They find their way into all sorts of desserts, most recently—and happily—into a compote to serve with cannoli. I have a particular fondness for Italian food, especially Italian desserts. Cannoli, hollow pastry cylinders stuffed with a sweetened cheese filling, are among my favorites. One day I felt like making cannoli, bing cherries were plump and delicious, and the recipe for Cannoli and Bing Cherries (page 128) was born. Another day I combined lemon and pistachios and was pleased to discover another very good cannoli variation.

Pastries like cannoli, bars, tartlettes, and even brownies are easy to vary. It's fun to substitute one fruit for another, add nuts, or create a sauce or topping that turns a longtime favorite recipe into a sparkling new one. Let the fresh fruits in the market, your favorite nuts, or an intriguing taste or texture combination be the start of your own experiments.

Puff Pastry

A multilayered puff pastry can be the beginning of many a spectacular dessert. I especially like to use it for napoleons (see page 125) and turnovers (see page 206). The process for making all those delicate, buttery layers is time consuming, but not difficult.

MAKES 2 POUNDS

2½ cups bread flour
1 cup cake flour
2 teaspoons kosher salt
36 tablespoons unsalted butter (cold)
1 cup plus 2 tablespoons cold water

Combine 2 cups of bread flour, the cake flour, and the salt in a mixing bowl. Cut 4 tablespoons of butter into small pieces. Mix the butter into the flour with the paddle attachment of an electric mixer until completely combined. Add the water and mix just until a smooth dough forms; do not overmix. Wrap the dough in plastic wrap and refrigerate for 30 minutes.

While the dough is chilled, cut the remaining pound of butter into small chunks. Put it in a mixing bowl with the remaining ½ cup of bread flour and mix with a dough hook until the butter is free of lumps. Set aside.

On a lightly floured surface roll the chilled dough into a 10- × 20-inch rectangle; dust the surface of the dough with flour as needed to keep the pin from sticking, and brush away any excess when you are finished. Roll the butter mixture into a rectangle slightly less than two-thirds the size of the dough. Place the butter rectangle over the right two-thirds of the dough. Fold the left one-third of the dough over the butter, covering half of it. Fold the right half of the dough over the left half. Press the top and bottom edges together and fold them under the dough. Press the unsealed left edge together and fold it under the dough.

Roll the dough into a 30- × 12-inch rectangle, dusting with flour as necessary and brushing it away when done. With a long side toward you, fold the two ends in to meet at the center. Brush off any flour and fold the dough in half along the line where the sides meet. Wrap the dough in plastic wrap and refrigerate for 15 minutes.

Repeat the last rolling out, folding, and chilling steps three more times. After the third time, wrap the dough in plastic wrap and chill it for at least 1 hour. Puff pastry dough will keep up to 3 days in the refrigerator, or for up to 4 weeks in the freezer. Defrost frozen dough in the refrigerator.

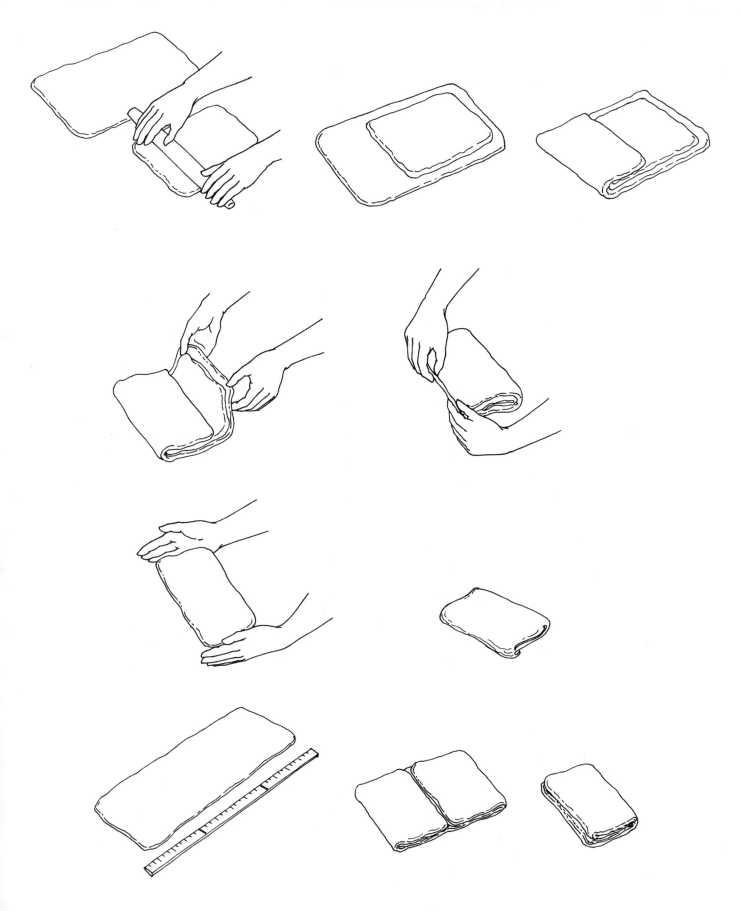

Old-Fashioned Shortcake

Strawberry shortcake is a centuries-old American tradition, and one that deserves a place in our history. But other fruits make fine shortcake too. Try any kind of fresh berries, cup-up peaches or nectarines, or a mixture of your favorite fruits.

SERVES 10

2 cups all-purpose flour
4 teaspoons baking powder
1 teaspoon kosher salt
2 tablespoons plus 2 teaspoons sugar
7 tablespoons unsalted butter (cold)
1 large egg
½ cup milk
4 cups berries or cut-up fruit
2 cups whipping cream

Preheat the oven to 400°. Butter a 9-inch round cake pan very well.

Mix together the flour, baking powder, salt, and 2 tablespoons of sugar. Cut 3 tablespoons of butter into 9 pieces. With the paddle attachment of an electric mixer, a food processor, or by pinching it between your fingers, combine the butter with the dry ingredients until the mixture resembles coarse meal.

In a separate bowl, beat the egg, then beat the milk into it. Fold the egg into the flour mixture one-quarter at a time, turning it with a rubber spatula after the last addition until all the flour is incorporated.

Spread half the dough in the cake pan. Cut the remaining 4 tablespoons of butter into small pieces and dot the dough all over with it. Spread the rest of the dough over the butter with your fingers. Sprinkle the remaining 2 teaspoons of sugar on top.

Bake until the top of the shortcake is golden and firm, about 30 minutes. Turn it out of the pan and cool it right side up on a wire rack. It will be about 1 inch high.

When the shortcake is cool, slice it with a long-bladed slicer or serrated knife into two layers. Set the bottom layer on a serving plate and cover it with fresh berries or cut-up fruit. Whip the cream to soft peaks and cover the fruit with it. Place the top layer of cake over the cream. Cut in wedges to serve.

Individual Shortcakes

These individual shortcakes are lighter than the old-fashioned kind, and they give you flexibility in serving. You can offer a variety of fruits to choose from, or use half the batch for strawberry shortcake today and the rest for peach (or blueberry, or blackberry) shortcake tomorrow.

MAKES 12

2 cups all-purpose flour
1 tablespoon baking powder
½ teaspoon kosher salt
1 tablespoon plus 1 teaspoon sugar
4 tablespoons unsalted butter (cold)
1 large egg
1 cup milk
3 cups berries or cut-up fruit, sweetened to taste
1½ cups whipping cream

Preheat the oven to 375°. Butter a muffin pan very well.

Mix together the flour, baking powder, salt, and 1 tablespoon of sugar. Cut the butter into 16 pieces. With the paddle attachment of an electric mixer, a food processor, or by pinching it between your fingers, combine the butter with the dry ingredients until the mixture resembles coarse meal.

In a separate bowl, beat the egg, then beat the milk into it. Fold the egg mixture into the flour mixture one-quarter at a time, turning it with a rubber spatula after the last addition until all the flour is incorporated.

Spoon about ¼ cup of batter into each muffin cup. Sprinkle the remaining teaspoon of sugar over the centers of the shortcakes (sugar on the edges will burn). Bake until the shortcakes are browned around the edges and domed in the center like muffins, about 15 minutes. Cool them for 5 minutes in the pan, then turn them out and finish cooling on a wire rack.

To serve, cut each shortcake in half crosswise. Spoon berries or cut-up fruit over each bottom and replace the top at a jaunty angle. Whip the cream to soft peaks and spoon on top of each serving.

Caramel-Glazed Strawberry Napoleon

This is a not-very-sweet napoleon that capitalizes on the bright flavor of fresh strawberries and the lightness of whipped cream. You might think of it as strawberry shortcake's more sophisticated and somewhat richer cousin.

SERVES 8

¼ cup all-purpose flour
8 ounces (¼ recipe) Puff Pastry (page 122)
¼ cup sugar
2 pints fresh strawberries
1 cup whipping cream
¼ teaspoon vanilla extract

Line a cookie sheet with parchment. Dust your work surface with half the flour and center the puff pastry on it. Dust the top of the dough with the rest of the flour. With a heavy rolling pin, roll the dough into a 9- × 10½-inch rectangle. Brush the flour from the top of the dough with a soft pastry brush.

Lift the dough by rolling it up onto the rolling pin, brushing any flour from the underside as you roll. Unroll the dough onto the lined cookie sheet. Cover and place in the freezer until firm to the touch, 15 to 20 minutes.

Preheat the oven to 400°. Using a pastry wheel or a thin, sharp knife, cut 8 diamond-shaped pieces from the dough, each about 5½ × 2½ inches. Remove the odd pieces of dough from the pan and spread out the diamonds so they don't touch each other. Brush the tops with water and sprinkle 1 teaspoon of sugar over each. Bake until golden brown, about 25 minutes. The sugared tops will caramelize. Set aside to cool.

Wash, drain, and gently towel dry the strawberries; remove the stems and leaves. Select the 16 choicest berries. Cut them into quarters from tip to stem. Place the quarters in a bowl, cover it, and put it in the refrigerator.

Purée the remaining strawberries with 1 tablespoon of sugar in a food processor, blender, or food mill. Set aside. Whip the cream with the vanilla and 1 teaspoon of sugar to soft peaks. Cover and refrigerate. Carefully slice the pastry diamonds in half horizontally.

To serve, spoon 3 tablespoons of strawberry purée onto the center of each dessert plate. Place the bottom half of a diamond on it, slightly off center. Arrange 8 strawberry quarters on top. Spoon on 2 heaping tablespoons of whipped cream, and cover with the top half of the diamond, caramel side up. Serve at once.

Cannoli Shells

Cannole (more than one cannoli) are light, fried Italian pastry rolls stuffed with sweetened cheese. You'll need twenty 5¾-inch cannoli forms to make these luscious pastry shells, but they are so good, I'm sure you'll want to make them often.

MAKES 20

1 large egg
8 tablespoons (¼ pound) unsalted butter
1½ cups all-purpose flour
2 tablespoons dry or sweet marsala
3 cups vegetable shortening, for frying

Lightly beat the egg. Melt the butter. Mix the egg, butter, flour, and marsala until a smooth dough forms; it will be soft and oily. Wrap the dough in plastic wrap and refrigerate it for 1 hour or overnight.

Cut the dough into 20 equal pieces; make each into a ball. On a lightly floured table flatten one ball into a 2-inch circle, then roll it into a 4½-inch circle. Brush a 2-inch section of the edge lightly with water. Place a cannoli form on the dough on the edge opposite the brushed section. Roll the form to the opposite edge, wrapping the dough around it as you go. Gently press the form against the table to seal the moistened edge of the dough. Repeat with the remaining dough. When all the dough is rolled on forms, cover it and refrigerate for at least 1 hour (you can chill it overnight if you wish).

Heat the shortening to 350° in a 5-cup frying pan; adjust the flame to maintain a constant temperature. Fry the dough, still wrapped around the forms, 3 at a time until they are golden brown on all sides. Use metal tongs to turn them as necessary. Remove the fried shells to drain and cool on paper towels. After cooling about 5 minutes, remove the forms.

Lemon-Pistachio Cannoli

The filling for these cannoli is dotted with toasted pistachios and candied lemon peel. Be sure to use natural, uncolored and unsalted, pistachios.

MAKES 20

20 Cannoli Shells (page 126)
½ cup pistachios
2 containers (15 ounces each) whole milk
    ricotta cheese
1 cup powdered sugar plus more for dusting
½ cup whipping cream
⅔ cup candied lemon peel (page 211)

Prepare the cannoli shells as directed and set aside to cool.

Preheat the oven to 325°. Spread the pistachios on a cookie sheet and toast them in the oven for 10 minutes. Chop the nuts in half and set them aside to cool.

Beat the cheese and sugar together until blended, about 30 seconds. Fold in the pistachios, cream, and lemon peel and mix until the nuts and lemon peel are evenly distributed. Put the cheese mixture into a pastry bag with a #6 plain tip. Pipe the filling into the cooled cannoli shells from both ends. Dust the tops of the cannoli lightly with powdered sugar. Serve within 2 hours or the shells become too soggy.

Cannoli with Bing Cherries

I've kept the filling for these cannole simple, to let the sparkling sweet-tart cherry compote that accompanies them shine. You'll need a cherry pitter to remove the pits without cutting the cherries open. I recommend the one that looks something like a paper punch; it's a handy tool to have in the kitchen (and it works on olives too).

MAKES 20

20 Cannoli Shells (page 126)

COMPOTE

2 pounds Bing cherries
⅔ cup sugar
2 tablespoons fruit pectin
3 tablespoons fresh lemon juice
¼ cup Amaretto liqueur

FILLING

2 containers (15 ounces each) whole milk
    ricotta cheese
2 tablespoons powdered sugar plus more for
    dusting
½ teaspoon vanilla extract

Fresh mint, for garnish

Make the cannoli shells as directed and set aside to cool.

COMPOTE

To make the cherry compote, stem, wash, and drain the cherries. Remove the pits with a cherry pitter. (If you do the pitting inside a paper bag, it reduces the spattering.) Combine the cherries, sugar, and pectin in a medium-size heavy stainless-steel saucepan. Stir gently and let stand for 20 minutes to allow the sugar to dissolve. Simmer until the cherries are just tender, about 5 minutes, stirring occasionally so the fruit cooks evenly. Remove the pan from the heat and stir in the lemon juice and Amaretto.

Pour the cherries and syrup into a stainless-steel bowl and set the bowl in a larger bowl of ice water to chill the fruit quickly. Stir occasionally during cooling. When cool, cover the compote and refrigerate until needed. If the syrup becomes overly thick, warm the compote slightly before using it.

FILLING

Place the cheese, powdered sugar, and vanilla in a food processor or blender and blend until smooth. Chill the mixture for 30 minutes, then put it in a pastry bag with a #6 plain tip. Pipe the filling into the cooled cannoli shells from both ends. Dust the tops of the cannoli lightly with powdered sugar. Serve each cannoli on a plate with cherry compote beside it. Garnish with a sprig of mint.

Peach and Cherry Cobbler
(*page 73*)

Individual Shortcakes (*page 124*)

Caramel-Glazed Strawberry Napoleons (*page 125*)

Lemon-Sesame Tartlettes (*page 129*)

Sour Plum Meringue Pie (*page 41*)

Pineapple Meringue Pie (*page 38*)

Lemon and Caramel Parfait (*page 173*)

Orange–Chocolate Chip Ice Cream (*page 164*)

Raspberry Sundae with Chocolate Swirl Ice Cream (*page 176*)

Gala Apple Pie (*page 27*)

Tropical Chocolate Sundae (*page 175*)
Rhubarb and White Chocolate Cake (*page 99*)
Plum Tart with Lemon Curd (*page 65*)

Lemon-Pistachio Cannoli
(*page 127*)

Cannoli with Bing Cherries
(*page 128*)

Lemon-Sesame Tartlettes

These are lemon tartlettes with a nice twist—sesame seeds in the shells. They are pretty and easy to make, but you will need small tartlette tins to bake them in.

MAKES 20 TO 22
(DEPENDING ON THE SIZE
OF THE TARTLETTE TINS)

DOUGH

8 tablespoons (¼ pound) unsalted butter
¼ cup sugar
¼ cup sesame seeds
¾ cup plus 2 tablespoons all-purpose flour

FILLING

1 large lemon
½ cup plus 4 teaspoons sugar
¼ cup water
2 large eggs
2 teaspoons unsalted butter

DOUGH

Preheat the oven to 350°. Gently heat the butter in a small saucepan until half melted. Remove the pan from the heat and stir until the butter is completely melted.

Blend the sugar, sesame seeds, and flour together in a bowl. Add the melted butter and mix until a smooth dough forms. Break the dough into 20 to 22 equal pieces, about 1 tablespoon each. Line each tartlette tin with a piece of dough, pressing it gently against the bottom and sides. Line up the tins on a cookie sheet and poke 4 holes in the center of each shell with the tines of a fork; the holes allow steam to escape and help the shells maintain their shape. Bake the shells for 10 minutes, then remove the cookie sheet from the oven and gently press down the center of each shell with a towel. Continue baking until the shells are golden brown, 8 to 10 minutes.

FILLING

Wash the lemon with soapy water; rinse well. Using a vegetable peeler, remove the outer yellow skin, moving the peeler from tip to tip. Cut the peel into long, thin strips. Combine ¼ cup of sugar, ¼ cup of water, and the strips of lemon peel in a small saucepan and bring it to a boil. Reduce the heat and simmer for 10 minutes. Set the pan aside to cool.

Juice the lemon; you will need ½ cup of juice. Blend the eggs with the remaining ⅓ cup of sugar. Stir in the lemon juice and cook in the top of a double boiler, stirring continuously, until thickened. Stir in the butter until it is completely incorporated. Spoon about a tablespoon of this lemon cream into each tartlette shell.

Drain the candied lemon peel. Place a bit of peel on top of each tartlette. Bake until the centers dome slightly without cracking, 10 to 12 minutes. Allow the tartlettes to cool completely before turning them out of the tins.

Cake Brownies

Brownies have been an American favorite for at least a hundred years. Some are dense and moist, almost like fudge; others are crisp like cookies. These moist, very chocolatey brownies have a cake-like texture.

MAKES 30

8 tablespoons (¼ pound) unsalted butter
8 ounces semisweet chocolate
4 large eggs
1 cup sugar
1 teaspoon vanilla extract
¼ teaspoon baking soda
½ cup unsweetened cocoa powder
½ cup all-purpose flour
1½ cups coarsely chopped walnuts

Preheat the oven to 350°. Butter a 9- × 13-inch oblong baking pan.

Melt the butter in a saucepan over low heat. Remove the pan from the heat. Cut the chocolate into chunks and add it to the butter. Stir continuously with a wooden spoon until smooth. (If you do not stir, the chocolate may overheat from contact with the bottom of the pan.) Set aside.

Beat the eggs and sugar with an electric mixer at medium speed until blended. Mix in the vanilla. Add the baking soda, cocoa, flour, and melted chocolate mixture and stir with a rubber spatula, occasionally scraping the sides of the bowl, until the batter is smooth. It will be somewhat bubbly.

Stir in the walnuts and pour the batter into the prepared pan. Bake in the middle of the oven until firm and glossy, about 25 minutes. Cool completely on a wire rack. Cut the cooled brownie lengthwise into six 1½-inch-wide strips. Cut the strips crosswise into 2½-inch lengths. Carefully remove the brownies from the pan with a spatula.

Becca Brownies

These are moist, slightly chewy brownies, named for my goddaughter, Rebecca Harlow, who rode her tricycle through the kitchen at least twenty times while I was making them. Becca doesn't like nuts, so the nuts are optional.

MAKES 35

6 tablespoons unsalted butter
8 ounces semisweet chocolate
3 large eggs
¾ cup all-purpose flour
¼ cup unsweetened cocoa powder

1 cup sugar
⅛ teaspoon baking soda
1½ cups coarsely chopped walnuts (optional)

Preheat the oven to 350°. Butter a 9- × 13-inch oblong baking pan.

Melt the butter in a saucepan over low heat. Remove the pan from the heat. Cut the chocolate into chunks and add it to the butter. Stir continuously with a wooden spoon until smooth. (If you do not stir, the chocolate may overheat from contact with the bottom of the pan.) Set aside.

Whisk the eggs in a large bowl. Add the flour, cocoa, sugar, and baking soda and mix. Stir in the melted chocolate. If you are using nuts, stir them in.

Pour the batter into the prepared pan and smooth the top with a rubber spatula. Bake in the middle of the oven until the sides start to pull away from the pan and a knife inserted in the center comes out clean, about 25 minutes. Cool completely on a wire rack. Cut the cooled brownie lengthwise into seven 1¼-inch-wide strips. Cut the strips crosswise into 2¾-inch lengths. Carefully remove the brownies from the pan with a spatula.

Wrap leftovers in plastic wrap and store in the refrigerator.

Toasted Sesame and Orange Bars

The tang of orange and the crunch of sesame combine to make these chewy bars almost irresistible. But try not to eat them all right away; they taste even better the second day. As always when using the skin of a fruit, remember to wash the oranges before zesting them.

MAKES 24

SESAME DOUGH

¼ cup sesame seeds
8 tablespoons (¼ pound) unsalted butter (cold)
¾ cup plus 2 tablespoons all-purpose flour
¼ cup sugar

FILLING

2 large eggs
1 cup sugar
2 tablespoons all-purpose flour
¼ teaspoon baking powder
Zest of 2 small juice oranges, finely grated (about 2 tablespoons)
¼ cup fresh orange juice

DOUGH

Preheat the oven to 350°. Spread the sesame seeds on a cookie sheet and toast them in the oven until they are lightly golden and mildly fragrant, about 5 minutes. A few seeds will have started to brown. Set the seeds aside to cool. Increase the oven temperature to 375°.

*TO MIX
THE DOUGH
BY HAND*

Cut the butter into ½-inch chunks. Rub the flour into the butter with your fingers until the butter is in flakes. Then rub it between your hands until the mixture resembles coarse meal. Toss in the cooled sesame seeds and sugar. Toss the dough lightly between your hands letting it sift through your fingers back into the bowl.

*TO MIX
THE DOUGH
IN A MIXER*

Using the paddle attachment on an electric mixer, mix the butter, flour, and sugar at low speed until it is the consistency of coarse meal. Add the cooled sesame seeds and toss together gently. Do not use a hand-held mixer; it does not have a speed that is low enough.

*TO MIX THE
DOUGH IN A
FOOD
PROCESSOR*

Put the flour and sugar in the work bowl first, then place the butter on top. Process about 30 seconds to the consistency of coarse meal. Transfer the dough to a bowl and add the cooled sesame seeds. Toss gently to combine.

Grease the sides and bottom of a cookie sheet or a 7½- × 10½-inch oblong pan. Line the pan with parchment or waxed paper, then grease the paper. Press the dough evenly into the bottom of the pan and a little bit up the sides. Sprinkle another teaspoon of flour over the dough to keep it from sticking to your hands, and pat it smooth. Bake until the crust is light brown, about 15 minutes.

FILLING

While the crust is baking, beat the eggs and sugar together until smooth. Add the remaining ingredients and mix until smooth. As soon as the crust is baked, pour the filling over it and return the pan to the oven. Bake until the filling is brown around the edges and lightly browned in the center, 15 to 20 minutes. The top will have a honey-combed appearance. Cool in the pan on a wire rack.

When cool, cut around the edges to loosen the crust. Then slide a spatula underneath and remove from the pan. Peel the paper off the sides (cut it away carefully with a knife if it is stuck). Cut into 3 long strips, then cut each strip crosswise into 8 bars. Lift the bars off the paper and onto a plate. Cover and refrigerate until ready to serve.

Apricot-Almond Bars

Dried apricots make at least one luscious summer fruit available all year round. Here they are combined with almonds, citrus peel, and rum in a chewy bar filling. Serve these bars with ice cream for dessert or alone for a tasty between-meals snack.

MAKES 36

DOUGH

2 cups all-purpose flour
½ cup sugar
12 tablespoons unsalted butter (cold)
2 teaspoons grated orange peel
1 large egg, beaten
2 tablespoons milk

FILLING

1¾ cups dried apricots
1¾ cups water
4 tablespoons unsalted butter
1 teaspoon grated lemon peel
2 tablespoons dark rum
¼ teaspoon vanilla extract
1 pinch cinnamon
¼ cup sugar plus more for sprinkling
½ cup sliced almonds plus more for sprin-
kling

DOUGH

Blend together the flour and sugar. Cut the butter into small pieces and blend them with the flour until the mixture resembles coarse meal. Add the orange peel and toss to combine. Blend the egg and milk; pour them into the flour and mix until the dough comes together. Divide the dough in half, wrap it, and chill until needed.

FILLING

Bring the apricots and water to a boil in a medium saucepan. Reduce the heat to maintain a simmer and cook until the apricots are tender, about 20 minutes. Pour the apricots and any remaining liquid into a food processor. Add the butter, lemon peel, rum, vanilla, cinnamon, ¼ cup sugar, and ½ cup almonds and purée. Cover and set aside to cool.

Preheat the oven to 375°. Lightly butter a 9- × 13-inch cake pan. Work the dough with your hand until it is pliable. Roll one half into a 10- × 14-inch rectangle. Lift it by rolling it up around the pin and unroll it over the prepared pan. Press it into the bottom of the pan and a little way up the sides; cover it with apricot filling.

Roll the second half of the dough into a 10- × 14-inch rectangle. Lift it by rolling it around the rolling pin and unroll it over the filling. Press gently with your hands to fuse the layers. Sprinkle the top lightly with sugar and almonds. Bake in the middle of the oven until the edges are golden brown and the center light brown, 25 to 30 minutes. Cut immediately into 36 bars, each measuring about 1 × 3 inches. Set aside to cool. Store covered in a cool, dry place. Remove the bars from the pan just before serving.

Cranberry and Walnut Bars

Cranberries contain enough natural pectin to thicken the filling in these bars without any added starch. A bit of butter helps to round out the somewhat sharp flavor of the berries, and a dash of Amaretto carries them to a new level of sophistication.

MAKES 36

DOUGH

2 cups all-purpose flour
½ cup sugar
12 tablespoons unsalted butter (cold)
1 large egg, beaten
2 tablespoons milk

FILLING

¾ cup walnuts
1 bag (12 ounces) cranberries
1 cup water
1¼ cups sugar plus more for sprinkling
2 tablespoons unsalted butter
1 tablespoon Amaretto liqueur

DOUGH

Combine the flour and sugar. Cut the butter into small pieces and blend it with flour until the mixture resembles coarse meal. Blend the egg and milk; pour them into the flour and mix until the dough comes together. Halve the dough, wrap in plastic, and refrigerate.

FILLING

Preheat the oven to 300°. Spread the walnuts on a cookie sheet and dry them in the oven for about 5 minutes. Bring the cranberries, water, and sugar to a boil in a medium saucepan. Reduce the heat to maintain a simmer and cook until the berries have broken down and thickened, about 15 minutes. Remove from the heat and stir in the remaining butter and the Amaretto. Cover the saucepan and set it aside to allow the berries to cool and thicken.

Chop the walnuts into ¼-inch chunks and stir them into the cranberries. Raise the oven temperature to 375°. Lightly butter a 9- × 13-inch cake pan.

Work the dough with your hands until it is pliable. Roll one half into a 10- × 14-inch rectangle. Lift it by rolling it around the rolling pin and unroll it over the prepared pan. Press the dough into the bottom of the pan and a little up the sides. Pour the cranberry filling over it. Roll the second half of the dough into a 10- × 14-inch rectangle. Roll it up onto the rolling pin, then unroll it over the filling. Press it down gently with your hands to fuse the layers. Sprinkle the top lightly with sugar.

Bake in the middle of the oven until the edges are golden brown and the center light brown, 25 to 30 minutes. Cut immediately into 36 bars, each measuring about 1 × 3 inches. Set aside to cool. Store covered in a cool, dry place.

7

Cookies

I PREFER SMALL COOKIES to large ones. When I want to serve afternoon tea or offer a tray of cookies for dessert after a nice dinner, I always bake bite-size cookies. An assortment of small cookies is an invitation to taste, savor, and compare. Presented with a tempting variety of flavors and textures, most people approach a cookie tray dessert as an adventure and happily sample every cookie on the tray.

With all my cookies I strive for intensity and clarity of flavor. If a cookie is only a bite or two, it must make an entire impression right away. There's no time for subtle flavors to slowly build on the palate. A chocolate cookie has to boldly assert its chocolateness. A crisp cookie has to snap. Of course, not all of my cookies are bite-size, but I demand small-cookie taste from all of them.

This chapter includes some of my longtime favorite cookies and some new ones I've only recently developed. Oatmeal and chocolate chip are on just about everyone's list of favorites, adult or child. As I've grown older I've refined my early recipes. My oatmeal cookies now have currants in place of the traditional raisins, and my chocolate chip cookies are studded with milk chocolate chips and pecans.

Had we been born in France, we all would no doubt have grown up eating moist, light madeleines as after-school snacks. Every cookie collection should include this French childhood classic, which is actually more a tiny sponge cake than a cookie. My version is on page 148.

As a child I loved to dunk my cookies in milk; as an adult I love to dunk Italian biscotti in a cup of espresso or a glass of sweet wine. Fragrant, nut-filled biscotti are baked twice to make them extremely hard and dry; when dunked, they absorb liquid without disintegrating. These are among the best cookies in the world, and part of the collection I consider cookies for grown-ups. Into that category I also put Chocolate-Dipped Ginger Cookies (page 151), because of their delicacy, and Amaretto Macaroons (page 149), because of their liqueur.

By and large, though, cookies are a dessert on which children and adults usually agree. What's more, because the recipes are uncomplicated, making them is a wonderful family project. I can think of no better way to introduce children to the pleasures of baking.

135

Crisp Oatmeal Cookies

Currants in place of the usual raisins make these oatmeal cookies a bit more sophisticated.

MAKES ABOUT 48

16 tablespoons (½ pound) unsalted butter (soft)
⅔ cup sugar
⅔ cup light brown sugar, firmly packed
1 teaspoon vanilla extract
¾ teaspoon baking soda
1 teaspoon kosher salt
1 teaspoon cinnamon
1½ cups all-purpose flour
2 large eggs
5 tablespoons milk
2¼ cups rolled oats (not quick-cooking)
1½ cups currants
1 cup chopped walnuts

Preheat the oven to 375°. Line two cookie sheets with parchment. Cream the butter, sugars, and vanilla together until light. Add the baking soda, salt, cinnamon, and flour and mix until smooth. Beat in the eggs and milk. Add the oats, currants, and walnuts and mix until smooth. With a soup spoon, drop about 2 tablespoons of the dough onto the prepared cookie sheets for each cookie. Leave 2 inches between cookies. Bake until the cookies are light brown, about 12 minutes. Set the cookie sheets on wire racks to cool for 5 minutes before removing the cookies.

Bull's-Eyes

I like to serve these delicate sandwich cookies, also known as Empire Biscuits, with tea. They are called "bull's-eyes" because the raspberry preserve filling shows through a round hole in the top cookie, making it look like a target.

MAKES ABOUT 30

1 cup all-purpose flour
⅓ cup cake flour
¾ cup plus 1 tablespoon powdered sugar
12 tablespoons unsalted butter (cold)
½ cup seedless raspberry preserves (see note)

Combine the flours and ¾ cup of powdered sugar. Cut the butter into 1-inch cubes. Using the paddle attachment of an electric mixer, a food processor, or your hands, work the butter into the dry ingredients until the dough comes together and is smooth and silky. Shape the dough into a 1-inch-thick patty, wrap it in plastic wrap, and refrigerate for 20 minutes.

Preheat the oven to 325°. Line 2 cookie sheets with parchment. On a well-floured surface roll out the dough and shape it into a 13- × 15-inch rectangle. Using a cookie cutter or an inverted glass, cut the dough into 2-inch circles. Place half of the circles on the cookie sheets, about 1 inch apart. These will be the bottoms. Bake them in the middle of the oven until lightly browned, 8 to 10 minutes. Watch them carefully to keep them from burning. Slide the parchment onto a counter or tabletop and let the cookies cool.

Line the cookie sheets with new parchment. Cut a ¾-inch round hole in the center of each of the remaining circles; a melon baller does the job neatly. Place the circles on the cookie sheets. These are the tops. Gather up the dough from the holes, roll it out, and cut more cookies, being sure you have an equal number of tops and bottoms. Bake until lightly browned, 8 to 10 minutes. Slide the parchment onto a counter or tabletop and let the cookies cool.

If the raspberry preserves are lumpy, process them for a few seconds in a food processor. Spread a rounded ¼ teaspoon of preserves on each cookie bottom. Put on the top and press very gently. Place the assembled cookies close together on a cookie sheet and sift the remaining tablespoon of powdered sugar over them. The sugar will slowly melt into the jam, leaving a clear red bull's-eye in the center of each sugar-dusted cookie.

NOTE   If you cannot get seedless raspberry preserves, you can remove the seeds from regular raspberry preserves by heating them gently and passing them through a strainer while still warm. Cool the strained preserves before proceeding with the recipe.

Sugar Cookies

Sugar cookies are so simple and unassuming they are the perfect accompaniment to almost any kind of ice cream or fresh or cooked fruit. Lightly scented with vanilla and lemon, these are also delicious accompanied by nothing but a glass of milk or a cup of tea or coffee.

MAKES ABOUT 70

7 tablespoons unsalted butter (soft)
½ cup plus 4 teaspoons sugar
1 large egg
¼ cup milk

¼ teaspoon baking powder
2 cups all-purpose flour
½ teaspoon vanilla extract
¼ teaspoon lemon extract

Mix the butter and ½ cup of sugar with a hand-held or countertop electric mixer. Add the egg and milk and mix until smooth. Add the baking powder, flour, vanilla, and lemon extract and mix until well combined. Remove the dough from the bowl, dust it lightly with flour, wrap it in plastic wrap, and refrigerate for 15 minutes.

Preheat the oven to 325°. Line 2 cookie sheets with parchment. On a lightly floured surface, roll the dough into a 14- × 18-inch rectangle; it will be about ⅛ inch thick. Cut out cookies with a 2-inch round cookie cutter or inverted glass.

Place the cookies on the lined cookie sheets. They don't spread much during baking, so you can put them close together. Sprinkle the cookies on each tray with 2 teaspoons of sugar. Bake until golden brown, 15 to 20 minutes. Slide the parchment onto a counter or tabletop and let the cookies cool.

Butter Cookies

These easy-to-make, buttery cookies are just right with ice cream or sorbet. They are also easy to dress up. For gifts and holidays, cut them into appropriate shapes with decorative cookie cutters and sprinkle them with colored crystal sugar.

MAKES ABOUT 4 DOZEN 1½- × 3-INCH COOKIES

12 tablespoons unsalted butter (cold)
¾ cup all-purpose flour
½ cup cake flour
¾ cup powdered sugar
2 teaspoons granulated sugar

Cut the butter into 1-inch cubes. Put it in a food processor with the flours and powdered sugar and process until the dough comes together. Remove the dough, wrap it in plastic wrap, and refrigerate for 20 minutes.

Preheat the oven to 375°. Line 2 cookie sheets with parchment. On a floured surface, roll the dough into a 10- × 12-inch rectangle. Using a fluted pastry wheel, cut the dough crosswise into twelve 1-inch-wide strips. Cut each strip into four 2½-inch lengths. Use a spatula to transfer the cookies to the cookie sheets. Arrange them about ¾ inch apart; they will expand during baking. Sprinkle them lightly with the granulated sugar. Bake until the edges are golden brown, about 10 minutes. The centers should still be pale. Cool in the pans.

Store cookies in a tightly closed tin or jar, at room temperature.

Scottish Shortbread

Shortbread is one of many European cookies American cooks have enthusiastically adopted. Buttery, thick, crumbly, and not too sweet, it is a perfect partner for ice cream or an afternoon cup of coffee or tea.

MAKES 12 WEDGES

10 tablespoons unsalted butter (cold)
2 cups all-purpose flour
½ cup plus 1 teaspoon sugar
2 tablespoons water

Preheat the oven to 350°.

Cut the butter into 1-inch cubes. Mix it with the flour and sugar in a food processor, with the paddle attachment of an electric mixer, or by hand until the mixture resembles coarse meal. Add the water and mix until the dough comes together.

Press the dough into a 9-inch round tart pan and smooth the top. Prick all over the surface with a fork, pressing the tines about halfway through the dough. Cut the dough into 12 equal wedges in the pan and sprinkle the remaining teaspoon of sugar over it. Bake until lightly browned and firm to the touch, 40 to 45 minutes.

Remove the pan from the oven and slide the shortbread out of the pan. Cut immediately into 12 pieces along the lines you cut before baking. Once it cools it will be too brittle to cut evenly. Cool the wedges on a wire rack.

Sicilian Fig Cookies

This recipe comes from Paula Schlosser of Albany, California, who based it on a recipe from her great aunt in Buffalo. Paula served the cookies at a Christmas party, and as soon as I tasted them I knew I had to add them to my repertoire.

MAKES 3 TO 4 DOZEN

FILLING

1 pound dried calimyrna figs, stemmed and
    quartered
⅔ cup walnut pieces, toasted in the oven un-
    til fragrant
½ cup raisins
¼ cup citron, coarsely chopped
Zest of 1 orange
2 tablespoons unsweetened cocoa powder
1 teaspoon cinnamon

1 tablespoon Galliano
1 tablespoon rum (light or dark)
½ cup honey

PASTRY

2½ cups all-purpose flour
½ cup sugar
2½ teaspoons baking powder
½ teaspoon kosher salt
8 tablespoons (¼ pound) unsalted butter
       (soft)
2 large eggs
½ teaspoon vanilla extract
¼ cup milk

ICING

1 cup powdered sugar
Zest of 1 orange
Water or rum as needed

FILLING

Combine all the filling ingredients in a food processor. Pulse until the mixture is finely chopped but not puréed. If the mixture is too thick to process, add 1 to 2 teaspoons of warm water. (If you prefer, you can chop the figs, walnuts, raisins, and citron with a knife then combine them with the remaining filling ingredients in a bowl.) The filling should be sticky and able to hold a shape. Set it aside to allow the flavors to mingle; it will keep a day in the refrigerator.

PASTRY

Sift the flour, sugar, baking powder, and salt together. Cut in the butter with a pastry cutter or 2 knives until the mixture resembles coarse meal. Mix the eggs, vanilla, and milk, and stir them in until the dough comes together. Gather it into a smooth ball. Roll it out on a lightly floured surface to slightly under ¼ inch thick.

Cut the dough into long, 4-inch-wide strips. Form a roll of filling, about 1 inch thick, a little way in from the long edge of one strip. Roll the dough around the filling, pressing the open edge of the dough into the roll with your fingers to seal it. Cut the roll crosswise into 1-inch slices. Repeat until all the dough and filling are used.

Preheat the oven to 400°. Place the slices seam side down on greased cookie sheets. Bake until lightly browned, 15 to 20 minutes. Cool on wire racks.

ICING

When the cookies are cool, make the icing by mixing the powdered sugar with the orange zest. Add water or rum a teaspoon at a time until you get a smooth, spreadable icing. Ice the top of the cookies. Let the icing dry before storing the cookies. They will keep in an airtight container for several weeks.

Peanut Butter and Bran Cookies

Peanut butter cookies are always popular with the younger set. The addition of bran makes these especially crisp and nutty, and irresistible to adults as well.

MAKES 3 DOZEN

½ cup bran
8 tablespoons (¼ pound) unsalted butter (soft)
½ cup dark brown sugar, firmly packed
¼ cup sugar
½ teaspoon vanilla extract
¾ cup all-purpose flour
½ teaspoon baking soda
1 large egg, beaten
½ cup peanut butter

Preheat the oven to 375°. Toast the bran on a parchment-lined cookie sheet for 10 minutes; set it aside to cool. Don't worry about the somewhat unpleasant smell; it will taste great in the cookies.

Cream the butter, sugars, and vanilla together until light and smooth. Sift the flour and baking soda. Add them, the bran, the egg, and the peanut butter to the butter mixture and blend well.

Line 2 sheet pans with parchment. Spoon on 1 tablespoon of dough for each cookie, leaving 2 inches between cookies. Press each cookie lightly with a fork dipped in flour. Bake until golden brown, rotating the pans for even baking, about 12 minutes. Slide the parchment onto a counter or tabletop and let the cookies cool.

Almond-Butter Cookies

These crisp, delicate little cookies are extremely easy to make, and are delicious served with ice cream or for afternoon tea.

MAKES 8 DOZEN

1 cup sliced almonds
12 tablespoons unsalted butter (cold)
1 cup cake flour
¾ cup powdered sugar

Combine all the ingredients and mix with the paddle attachment on an electric mixer until the dough comes together. On a lightly floured surface roll the dough into 2 logs, each 12 inches long. Wrap in plastic wrap and chill until firm, about 20 minutes.

Preheat the oven to 350°. Cut the logs into ¼-inch-thick slices. Arrange the slices, 1 inch apart, on parchment-lined cookie sheets. Bake until the edges of the cookies are golden brown, about 10 minutes. Slide the parchment onto a counter or tabletop and let the cookies cool.

Almond Tiles

These crisp and delicate cookies originated in France where they are called *tuilles*. Their arched shape is reminiscent of French terra-cotta roof tiles. They are the perfect accompaniment for ice cream or a fruity sorbet.

MAKES ABOUT 16

½ cup sugar
1 cup sliced almonds
2 tablespoons all-purpose flour
3 large egg whites, lightly beaten
1½ tablespoons unsalted butter (melted)
Unsalted butter for greasing the pan

Preheat the oven to 350°.

Stir together the sugar, almonds, and flour. Add the egg whites and butter and blend. Instead of a traditional cookie dough, you will end up with coated almond slices.

Butter a cookie sheet very well. Spoon 1 tablespoon of dough onto the sheet for each cookie, leaving about 6 inches between cookies. Only 2 or 3 cookies will fit on the sheet at one time. Use the tip of the spoon to spread each cookie into a circle about 3 inches in diameter and only one almond slice deep. Bake until golden brown, about 10 minutes.

To shape the tiles, remove the cookies from the pan immediately with a spatula and drape them over a small rolling pin to cool.

After each batch, wipe the pan clean with a cloth or paper towel and regrease it.

Almond Fingers

These delicate and delicious sandwich cookies start as the simplest of butter cookies—a quick blending of butter, sugar, and flour. They are filled with chocolate and topped with toasted almonds.

MAKES 32

12 tablespoons unsalted butter (cold)
1¼ cups all-purpose flour
¾ cup powdered sugar
1 egg
Rounded ⅓ cup sliced almonds
3 ounces bittersweet or semisweet chocolate

Cut the butter into 1-inch cubes. Process it in a food processor with the flour and sugar until the dough comes together. Wrap the dough and refrigerate for 20 minutes.

Preheat the oven to 350°. Line 2 cookie sheets with parchment.

On a lightly floured surface, work the dough with your hands until it starts to feel flexible, then sprinkle it with flour and roll it into a 10- × 16-inch rectangle. Trim the edges to straighten them. Using a pastry wheel, cut the dough lengthwise into four 2½-inch-wide strips. Then cut the strips crosswise into 1-inch lengths. Lift the cookies gently with a spatula and place them on the cookie sheets, 1 inch apart. (Some will be left for a second batch.)

Beat the egg with a fork and brush the cookies on one sheet lightly with egg. Leave those on the second sheet plain. Spread the top of each brushed cookie with almonds (about 16 slices per cookie). Place a sheet of parchment over the almond-topped cookies and roll a rolling pin very lightly back and forth over it to press the almonds into the dough (don't press hard enough to flatten the cookies).

Bake both sheets of cookies until the edges brown, 7 to 9 minutes. Slide the parchment onto a counter or tabletop and let the cookies cool. Brush half of the remaining cookies with egg and top them with almonds. Bake and cool all the remaining cookies.

Melt the chocolate in the top of a double boiler over boiled (not boiling) water. Turn the plain cookies bottom side up. Spread each with melted chocolate and top it with an almond-topped cookie. Set the cookies aside until the chocolate sets.

Chocolate-Almond Wafers

These are meringues, made without butter or egg yolks; they are light and low in fat. After I developed them, I was reminded that the combination of flavors—chocolate, almond, and cinnamon—is the same as in Mexican hot chocolate.

MAKES 4 DOZEN

4 ounces bittersweet chocolate
2 cups sliced natural (skin on) almonds
3 large egg whites
1 cup plus 1 tablespoon sugar
1 tablespoon cinnamon

Preheat the oven to 300°. Line 2 cookie sheets with parchment. Melt the chocolate. Crush the almonds in a food processor or chop them very fine by hand.

Beat the egg whites until foamy. Add the sugar slowly while beating, and continue beating to soft peaks. Beat in the cinnamon. Stir in the crushed almonds and then the chocolate.

Spoon a teaspoon of dough onto a lined cookie sheet for each cookie, leaving about 2 inches between them. Bake until lightly firm to the touch, about 7 minutes. Slide the parchment onto a counter or tabletop and allow the cookies to cool. Line the cookie sheets with new parchment and continue making cookies with the remaining dough.

Anise and Walnut Biscotti

Biscotti are dry, hard, twice-baked Italian cookies that beg to be dunked in coffee, milk, or (for a special treat) the sweet Italian wine called vin santo. These are flavored with orange and lemon zest as well as anise and walnut.

MAKES 48

1⅔ cups bread flour
2 cups cake flour
2 cups walnut pieces
½ teaspoon baking powder
¼ teaspoon baking soda
1 tablespoon anise seeds
8 tablespoons (¼ pound) unsalted butter
3 large eggs
1⅓ cups sugar
2 teaspoons lemon zest
2 teaspoons orange zest
½ teaspoon pure anise extract

Preheat the oven to 375°. Line a cookie sheet with parchment. Blend the flours, walnuts, baking powder, baking soda, and anise seeds in a bowl. Melt the butter and set it aside to cool.

Whip two eggs, one additional egg yolk, and the sugar until smooth. Reserve the extra egg white. Stir in the zests and anise extract. Add the butter and mix until smooth. Add the dry ingredients and mix to a smooth dough. Roll the dough into two 14-inch-long logs and place them on the lined cookie sheet. Press the tops of the logs to flatten them slightly; brush them with the reserved egg white. Bake until the logs are light brown but still give slightly when the tops are pressed, about 30 minutes. Remove the pan from the oven and reduce the temperature to 325°.

While the logs are still warm, cut them into ½-inch slices; cut on a slight diagonal, not straight across. Lay the slices on their sides, spreading them apart, and return the sheet to the oven. Bake until the cookies are brown, about 15 minutes. Cool completely on wire racks, then store biscotti in an airtight container.

Chocolate and Hazelnut Biscotti

These biscotti are dipped in chocolate, making them rich tasting and elegant. It is important to melt the dipping chocolate properly to keep it from blooming (becoming mottled with white) later on. Use a candy thermometer to monitor the temperature as you work.

MAKES 48

2 cups whole hazelnuts
2 large eggs
3 large egg yolks
1½ cups sugar
Zest of 1 orange, finely grated
½ teaspoon vanilla extract
2¼ cups all-purpose flour
¼ cup unsweetened cocoa powder
½ teaspoon baking soda
½ teaspoon kosher salt
Milk, if needed
8 ounces bittersweet or semisweet chocolate

Preheat the oven to 300°. Line a cookie sheet with parchment.
Toast the hazelnuts on an unlined cookie sheet in the lower third of the oven until light brown, 7 to 10 minutes. Transfer the nuts to a kitchen towel and rub them in the towel to remove any loose skins. Set the nuts aside to cool. Increase the oven temperature to 375°.
In a large bowl, whip together the eggs, yolks, sugar, orange zest, and vanilla. When the mixture is smooth and thick, add the dry ingredients and mix to a smooth dough. A small amount of milk may be needed to help the dough come together.
Divide the dough in half. Dust each half with flour and roll it into a 12-inch-long log. Place the logs on the lined cookie sheet, about 3 inches apart. Gently press the tops of the logs to flatten them slightly. Bake until the logs are light brown but still give slightly when the tops are pressed, 25 to 30 minutes. Remove the pan from the oven and reduce the temperature to 325°.
While the logs are still warm, cut them into ½-inch slices; cut on a slight diagonal, not straight across. Lay the slices on their sides, spreading them apart, and return the sheet to the oven. Bake until the cookies are brown, 15 to 20 minutes. Cool completely on wire racks.

Cut the chocolate into ½-inch chunks. Place two-thirds of it in a stainless-steel bowl. Spread the chocolate in an even layer over the bottom and up the sides of the bowl; cover the bowl with plastic wrap. Fill a medium saucepan one-third full of water. Bring the water to a simmer over high heat. Remove the pan from the heat and set the bowl of chocolate on it. Let it stand until about 80 percent of the chocolate has melted. Remove the bowl from the pan and wipe the sides and bottom dry with a towel.

Take off the plastic wrap and stir the chocolate with a metal spoon until all of it is melted. Add the remaining chocolate and continue stirring until it too melts. Do not let the temperature of the chocolate drop below 88° on a candy thermometer. If it does, place the bowl over a saucepan of warm water and continue stirring. Stir until the chocolate is smooth and glossy.

Have a clean sheet of parchment nearby. Dip half of each cookie in the chocolate; as you take it out, scrape the top and bottom against the side of the bowl to remove the excess chocolate. Set the cookies on the parchment until the chocolate sets, about 3 hours. Store the biscotti in an airtight container. They will keep up to a week.

Florentines

Florentines are crisp, lacy cookies full of almonds and fruit. They are often baked as round cookies and dipped in chocolate. I make mine as a sheet, cover the whole top with chocolate, and cut them into squares. These cookies need time to cool before adding the chocolate, and time for the chocolate to set. So start at least four to five hours before you want to serve them.

MAKES ABOUT 35

1½ cups sliced almonds
10 tablespoons unsalted butter
⅔ cup sugar
3 tablespoons honey
2 tablespoons whipping cream
3 tablespoons all-purpose flour
½ cup candied orange peel (page 211)
½ cup Candied Cranberries (page 211)
8 ounces semisweet chocolate

Preheat the oven to 300°. Bake the almonds on a cookie sheet for 12 minutes to dry them; do not let them brown. Set them aside to cool. Butter a 10- × 15-inch cookie sheet and line it with an 11- × 15-inch sheet of parchment. Increase the oven temperature to 350°.

Place the butter, sugar, honey, and cream in a 6-quart saucepan.

Cook over medium-high heat, stirring occasionally to blend the ingredients as the butter melts. Cook until the mixture registers 248° on a candy thermometer. Add the flour, orange peel, and cranberries and continue to cook, stirring continuously, until the mixture pulls away from the sides of the pan, about 1 minute.

While the mixture is still hot, spoon it onto the prepared cookie sheet and spread it evenly over the entire pan. Bake for 6 minutes. Remove it from the oven and let it cool for 15 minutes, then bake again until the sides are brown and the center bubbles, about 6 more minutes. Set the pan aside to cool for about an hour.

Cut the chocolate into 1-inch chunks. Put it in the top of a double boiler and cover it with plastic wrap. Bring 2 inches of water to a simmer in the bottom of the double boiler; do not let it boil. Remove the bottom of the pan from the heat and set the top on it. Let it stand until about 75 percent of the chocolate has melted. Transfer the chocolate to a bowl and stir until it is completely melted.

Pour the melted chocolate over the florentines and spread it evenly. Drag a fork through the chocolate to make wavy lines all across the top. Set the pan aside until the chocolate hardens, 2 to 3 hours. Take the florentines from the pan, remove the parchment, and using a Chinese chef's knife or other thin-bladed knife, cut them into 2-inch squares.

Hazelnut and Cinnamon Cookies

These crisp little cookies go well with ice cream or with afternoon coffee or tea. The mingled flavors of hazelnut and cinnamon are muted but intriguing. Eight dozen may sound like a lot of cookies, but once people taste them, they disappear very quickly.

MAKES ABOUT 8 DOZEN

1¼ cups hazelnuts
12 tablespoons unsalted butter (cold)
1¼ cups powdered sugar
1 teaspoon cinnamon
1 large egg
2 cups all-purpose flour

Toast the hazelnuts on a cookie sheet in a 350° oven until fragrant, about 10 minutes. Let them cool, then chop them in a food processor until fine.

Cut the butter into 1-inch cubes. Put it in a bowl with the powdered sugar, cinnamon, and ground nuts. Mix with an electric mixer. Mix in the egg. Add the flour and mix it in with a rubber spatula. If the dough is sticky, sprinkle on a little more flour. Work the dough into a smooth patty with your hands. If it feels damp, sprinkle on a bit more flour and smooth it in.

Place the dough on a sheet of parchment and pat it into an 4-× 8-inch loaf, about 1¼ inches tall. Wrap the parchment around it to cover it completely. Fold the parchment carefully at the corners, as you would gift wrap a package, so that the corners of the dough stay square. Refrigerate at least 30 minutes; the wrapped dough will keep in the refrigerator for 2 days.

Preheat the oven to 350°. Line 2 cookie sheets with parchment. Unwrap the dough and cut it in half lengthwise with a sharp knife. Cut each half crosswise into rectangular cookies, between ⅛ and ¼ inch thick. Each half should yield about 48 cookies.

Place as many cookies as will fit on the cookie sheets about ½ inch apart. Bake until they begin to brown around the edges, 10 to 12 minutes. Slide the parchment onto a counter or tabletop and let the cookies cool. Line the cookie sheets with new parchment and bake any cookies that remain. Store cooled cookies in a tightly covered tin or jar at room temperature.

Madeleines

Madeleines, of course, are French in origin. But American dessert lovers, who know a great cookie when they taste one, welcomed them into the American repertoire a long time ago. To be absolutely accurate, madeleines are not cookies at all, but little shell-shaped cakes. They are a great favorite among children.

You will need a special madeleine pan for baking them. This tin-lined pan should be washed before the first time you use it, then never again. After washing the pan, rub it with clarified butter and place it in a preheated 375° oven for 30 minutes. Set it aside to cool before pouring batter into it. From them on, after each use, rub the pan with a towel to clean it.

MAKES 18

½ vanilla bean
12 tablespoons unsalted butter (melted)
½ teaspoon lemon zest, chopped
¾ cup sugar
2 large eggs
1 cup all-purpose flour
Clarified butter for greasing the pans (see
        page 13)

Preheat the oven to 425°.
Split the vanilla bean lengthwise and scrape out ¼ teaspoon of seeds. Combine the butter, lemon zest, and vanilla seeds in a bowl. Add

the sugar, then add the eggs one at a time and beat until light and creamy. Add the flour and beat to a thick, smooth batter.

Grease a madeleine pan well with clarified butter. Using 2 spoons to transport the batter, fill each mold three-quarters full (about 2 teaspoons of batter per mold). Bake in the top third of the oven until the edges of the madeleines are golden brown and the tops are domed, about 10 minutes.

Spread a clean kitchen towel on a counter or tabletop. As soon as you remove a pan from the oven, hold it by the edges, turn it over, and tap it on the towel until the madeleines fall out. Transfer them to a wire rack to cool. Store leftover cookies at room temperature in a sealed jar or cookie tin.

Amaretto Macaroons

These scrumptious cookies are amazingly easy to make. All you do is mix the ingredients together and bake. Almond paste is sold in most supermarkets in 8-ounce cans. Don't substitute marzipan; it has too much sugar in it.

MAKES 4 DOZEN 2-INCH COOKIES

¼ cup sugar
½ cup powdered sugar
8 ounces almond paste
2 large egg whites
2 tablespoons Amaretto liqueur

Preheat the oven to 425°. Line 2 cookie sheets with parchment. (You will need enough parchment for several batches.) If your cookie sheets are thin, it is best to double them to avoid burning the cookies on the bottom.

Using the paddle attachment on an electric mixer, mix the sugars and almond paste together. Add the egg whites and mix until smooth. Add the Amaretto. Switch to the whisk attachment and whip at high speed for 5 minutes.

Spoon the dough into a pastry bag with a #4 plain tip. Pipe quarter-size mounds onto the parchment-lined cookie sheets about 2 inches apart. Bake until the tops and bottoms of the cookies are golden brown, about 10 minutes. Slide the parchment onto a counter or tabletop and let the cookies cool.

Chocolate Puffs

These light, chewy cookies get their chocolate flavor from unsweetened cocoa powder. They are simple to make, but they do need to be chilled before baking, so allow yourself enough time.

MAKES 60

6 tablespoons unsalted butter (soft)
¾ cup sugar
1 cup light corn syrup
2 teaspoons baking soda
¼ cup water
½ teaspoon kosher salt
2 cups all-purpose flour
1 cup unsweetened cocoa powder

Cream the butter with ½ cup of sugar and the corn syrup. Dissolve the baking soda in the water; add it to the butter and mix until smooth. Add the salt, flour, and cocoa powder and mix to a smooth dough.

Shape the dough into 60 balls and chill them for 30 minutes.

Preheat the oven to 375°. Roll the balls in the remaining ¼ cup of sugar and bake them on a greased cookie sheet until firm, 10 to 15 minutes. Cool on a wire rack.

Ginger Snaps

I like these gingery little cookies made with butter, but they are not hard like traditional snaps. If you want them to snap, use shortening. Either way, they will come out domed unless you flatten them. If you like your cookies flat, press the balls of dough down with a fork before baking. The flat cookies can be used to make delicious ice cream sandwiches; try them with the Cinnamon-Quince Ice Cream on page 169.

MAKES 60

6 tablespoons unsalted butter (soft) or
        shortening
¾ cup sugar
1 cup molasses
¼ cup water
2 teaspoons baking soda
¼ teaspoon kosher salt
1 tablespoon powdered ginger
½ teaspoon allspice
2 tablespoons crystallized ginger, chopped
3 cups all-purpose flour

Cream the butter and ½ cup of sugar together until smooth and light. Add the molasses and beat until smooth. Add the water, then the baking soda. (The batter will have dark particles in it at this point that make it look like brown mustard; that's okay.) Combine the salt, powdered ginger, allspice, and crystallized ginger and add them. Add the flour and mix it in with a rubber scraper. Wrap the dough in plastic wrap and chill it for 20 minutes.

Preheat the oven to 400°. Butter 2 cookie sheets. Form the dough into 60 small balls. Put the remaining ¼ cup of sugar in a small bowl and roll each ball in it before placing them on the cookie sheets. Bake until the cookies are lightly browned, 8 to 10 minutes. Transfer them to wire racks to cool.

Chocolate-Dipped Ginger Cookies

These are one of my favorite cookies to serve with afternoon tea or coffee. They are small and delicately flavored with ginger. A light milk-chocolate coating contrasts with the ginger without overpowering it.

MAKES ABOUT 9 DOZEN

¾ cup all-purpose flour
¾ cup cake flour
1 tablespoon powdered ginger
¾ cup light brown sugar, firmly packed
12 tablespoons unsalted butter (cold)
6 ounces milk chocolate
2 teaspoons pure vegetable shortening
1 ounce bittersweet chocolate

Combine the flours, ginger, and brown sugar in a bowl. Rub them together with your hands until well mixed. Cut the butter into 1-inch cubes. Using the paddle attachment of an electric mixer, a food processor, or your hands, work the butter into the dry ingredients until the dough comes together and is smooth. Shape the dough into a 1-inch-thick patty, wrap it in plastic wrap, and refrigerate for 15 minutes.

Preheat the oven to 350°. Line a cookie sheet with parchment. On a floured surface, roll out the dough and shape it into a 10- × 16-inch rectangle. With a pizza cutter or pastry wheel, using a yardstick as a guide, cut the dough lengthwise into thirteen ¾-inch-wide strips. Cut the strips crosswise into 2-inch lengths. Lift the cookies gently with a spatula and place as many on the cookie sheet as will fit, leaving ½ inch between cookies. Bake until they are light brown, 8 to 10 minutes. Slide the parchment onto a counter or tabletop and let the cookies cool.

When the cookies are cool, melt the milk chocolate in the top of a double boiler over boiled (not boiling) water. Melt the shortening separately in a saucepan. Stir the two together in a small bowl until smooth. Dip each cookie halfway into the chocolate, then lightly scrape the bottom of the cookie on the edge of the bowl to remove any excess chocolate. Set the cookies on a parchment or waxed paper–lined cookie sheet. Grate the bittersweet chocolate over the dipped half of the cookies; it will cling to the soft milk chocolate. Allow the cookies to sit until the chocolate is set.

Chocolate-Blackberry Cookies

These elegant chocolate sandwich cookies are pretty enough for a party, but simple enough to become a regular in your cookie jar. The cookies themselves are light and have a mild chocolate flavor. They are sandwiched together with blackberry jam, then dipped in melted chocolate.

MAKES 2 DOZEN

1 ounce unsweetened chocolate
11 tablespoons unsalted butter (soft)
¼ teaspoon kosher salt
¾ cup powdered sugar
1 large egg
1⅓ cups all-purpose flour
2 tablespoons blackberry jam
6 ounces bittersweet or *semisweet chocolate*
2 teaspoons pure vegetable shortening

Preheat the oven to 400°. Line 2 cookie sheets with parchment.

Melt the unsweetened chocolate in the top of a double boiler over boiled (not boiling) water. Whip the butter, salt, and powdered sugar with an electric mixer until light and smooth. Beat in the egg, then the warm melted chocolate; beat until smooth. Scrape the sides and bottom of the bowl.

Add the flour and work it in with a wooden spoon or a stiff rubber spatula. When the flour is completely incorporated, spoon the dough into a pastry bag with a #4 star tip. Pipe cookies out onto the lined cookie sheets, holding the bag so that the tip is about an inch above the paper. Start each cookie at the center (see illustration on page 153). Squeezing the dough out gently, move the tip about an inch from the starting point, then in a circle around the center. The finished cookie should be about 2 inches across. Leave an inch between cookies.

Bake until the cookies feel firm, about 8 minutes. Slide the parchment onto a counter or tabletop and let the cookies cool.

If the blackberry jam has seeds, heat it in a small saucepan over

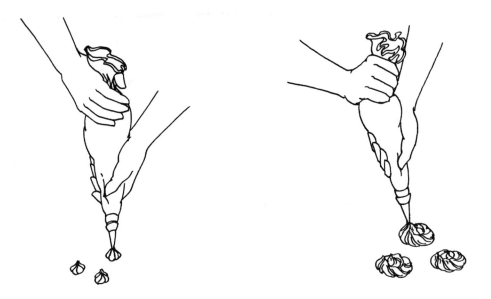

medium heat until it liquifies. Pass it through a sieve to remove the seeds, then let it cool. Turn half the cookies bottom side up. Spread each upturned cookie with ¼ teaspoon of jam, and top it with a right-side-up cookie.

Chop the bittersweet chocolate with a large knife or a Chinese cleaver. Melt it in the top of a double boiler over boiled (not boiling) water. Stir until smooth. Melt the shortening separately then stir it into the chocolate.

Line a cookie sheet with waxed paper or parchment. Dip each cookie sandwich into the chocolate to coat it halfway up both sides. Lay the cookies on the lined cookie sheet until the chocolate sets.

Pecan and Milk Chocolate Chip Cookies

These very chocolatey cookies are crisp on the outside and tender on the inside. Packaged milk chocolate chips do not taste as good or bake as well as high-quality milk chocolate. To make the best milk chocolate "chips," buy a thick bar of good milk chocolate and chop it into chunks with a cleaver or large French knife. Chop the pecans into pieces of about the same size.

MAKES 18

8 tablespoons (¼ pound) unsalted butter
   (soft)
¾ cup light brown sugar, firmly packed
1 teaspoon vanilla extract
1 large egg
1 teaspoon baking powder

½ teaspoon kosher salt
1 cup all-purpose flour
8 ounces milk chocolate in ½-inch chunks
    (about 1⅓ cups)
1 cup coarsely chopped pecans

Preheat the oven to 375°. Grease 2 cookie sheets.

Combine the butter, brown sugar, and vanilla in a bowl. Mix until creamy with a hand-held electric mixer or the paddle attachment of a countertop mixer. Add the egg, baking powder, and salt and mix well. Stir in the flour, chocolate chunks, and pecans with a wooden spoon.

Spoon rounded tablespoons of dough onto the cookie sheets. Since the batter is somewhat sticky, it is best to use 2 spoons, one in each hand. Use one to scoop up the batter and the other to push the batter off onto the cookie sheet. Flatten each cookie with the back of a spoon; you may need the second spoon to free the cookie if it sticks. Bake in the middle of the oven until the cookies are evenly browned, 10 to 12 minutes. Cool on wire racks. Store leftover cookies at room temperature in a sealed jar or cookie tin.

Vanilla Pretzels

These simple cookies always delight children because of their shape. For a special treat, slowly melt some white chocolate and let them dip the cookies to coat one side. Let the dipped cookies stand on parchment or waxed paper until the chocolate sets.

MAKES ABOUT 4 DOZEN

10 tablespoons unsalted butter (soft)
½ cup powdered sugar
½ teaspoon vanilla
⅛ teaspoon ground mace
1 large egg
2 tablespoons milk
1⅓ cups cake flour

Line 2 cookie sheets with parchment.

Whip the butter, sugar, vanilla, and mace with an electric mixer until smooth and light. Beat in the egg and then the milk. Add the flour and mix it in with a rubber spatula, pressing the dough against the sides of the bowl to work the flour in. Do not try to incorporate the flour with the electric mixer. When the dough is smooth, spoon it into a pastry bag with a #3 plain tip. Pipe the dough out onto the cookie sheets in pretzel shapes about 2 inches wide (see illustration on page 155).

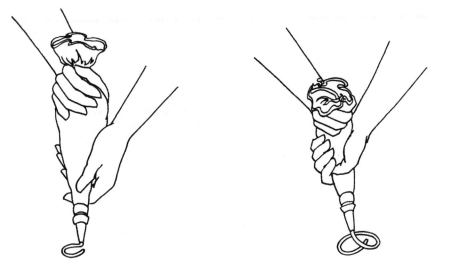

Refrigerate the sheets for 10 minutes while you preheat the oven to 400°. Bake the cookies in the middle of the oven until lightly browned, about 12 minutes. Slide the parchment onto a counter or tabletop and let the cookies cool.

Honey Wafers

These are cookies for people who love honey. They are thin, crisp, and slightly spicy, but mostly they taste like honey.

MAKES 4½ DOZEN

8 tablespoons (¼ pound) unsalted butter (cold)
½ cup honey
⅓ cup sugar
1 cup all-purpose flour
Pinch of ground cloves
Pinch of ground cinnamon

Preheat the oven to 300°. Line 2 cookie sheets with parchment.

Cut the butter into ½-inch cubes. Mix it with the honey and sugar until smooth. Add the flour, cloves, and cinnamon and mix until the dough comes together. Spoon teaspoons of dough onto the lined cookie sheets, about 1 inch apart. Fold a damp kitchen towel (not terry cloth) into quarters lengthwise. Grasp an end in each hand, with your thumbs flat on top and your fingers curled tightly underneath. Slap the tops of the cookies gently with the towel until they are shaped like fried egg yolks.

Bake the cookies until lightly browned, about 20 minutes. Cool them on a wire rack.

8

Ice Creams, Sorbets, Parfaits, and Sundaes

I THINK I ONCE MET a man who didn't like ice cream, but only once. Ice cream certainly must be the most popular dessert in the world. If you have an ice cream machine to do the churning, it is also one of the easiest to make. The machine doesn't have to be expensive, self-refrigerating, or even electric. Although the motorized machines are easiest to use, even the most basic models you fill with ice and salt then crank by hand turn out excellent ice cream with very little effort or mess. The canister-type machine that appeared on the market about five years ago works great, too. So there's no reason not to enjoy fresh, homemade ice cream any time you want it.

Be sure to use only the best fruits and flavorings in your ice cream; when a recipe is so simple, every ingredient shines through. Once you have mastered the basic techniques, you can easily adapt the recipes in this chapter to whatever luscious seasonal fruits you find in abundance at the market or on your tree. The Blackberry Ice Cream on page 159 could as easily be made with boysenberries; Orange Ice Cream (page 164) can be converted to tangerine or lime. Flavors that go well together in other desserts will almost always combine well in ice cream. Lemon and pistachio is a combination I often use in cakes; it is equally delicious in ice cream. I also especially like cinnamon with quince (see Cinnamon-Quince Ice Cream, page 169) and orange with chocolate (see Orange–Chocolate Chip Ice Cream, page 164).

When you want to emphasize the bright clear taste of a particular ripe fruit, try making it into sorbet. A simple fruit ice, usually containing only fruit and a sugar syrup, sorbet is an intensely flavorful and extremely light and refreshing dessert. Adding a contrasting liqueur gives new depth and dimension to the basic fruit flavor and can make a good sorbet extraordinary. Try the Cranberry-Campari Sorbet on page 171 or the Bing Cherry–Amaretto Sorbet on page 172 and you'll see.

Of course, the traditional way of adding a second flavor to ice cream is with a sauce. If the combination of flavors is unusual, and on the mark, an old-fashioned sundae can be an unexpected treat and the perfect ending for a special dinner. I like to top Maple-Butternut Ice Cream with strawberries (page 167) and Pistachio Ice Cream with a sauce made from white chocolate and crème de menthe (page 177). A new favorite, a sundae I first tasted in Hawaii, combines Coconut Ice Cream with chocolate, rum, macadamia nuts, and an assortment of tropical fruits (see Tropical Chocolate Sundae, page 175).

While sundaes are always popular, another of my favorite frozen desserts, the parfait, seems to have gone out of fashion. I hereby announce my intention to bring it back. Light, simple, and very pretty, the parfait deserves a permanent place on American dessert menus. Three very good ones are on pages 173 and 174.

Vanilla Ice Cream

There is just enough vanilla in this ice cream to mask the flavor of the eggs; it imparts vanilla tones without overpowering the wonderful natural flavor of fresh cream. It is very important to use a high-quality, pure vanilla extract. (I use Nielsen-Massey.)

MAKES 1 QUART

1 cup milk
2 large eggs
⅔ cup sugar
2 cups whipping cream (cold)
1 teaspoon vanilla extract

Freeze a clean 5-cup or larger container for storing the ice cream. Bring 2 quarts of water to a boil in a 4-quart pot; lower the heat to maintain a simmer.

Bring the milk to a simmer; turn off the heat and let it stand until needed. Select a 2-quart stainless-steel bowl that fits comfortably over the 4-quart pot. Whisk the eggs in the bowl until smooth. Stir in the sugar and place the bowl over the simmering water. Cook, stirring continuously with a wire whisk, until the eggs are as thick as mayonnaise, about 4 minutes (they should register 190° on a candy thermometer). Pour in the milk and continue whisking and cooking until thickened, about 4 minutes more. Remove the bowl from the pot and stir in the cream and vanilla.

Chill the mixture over a bowl of ice water until cool to the touch. Then freeze it in an ice cream machine according to the manufacturer's directions. Spoon the finished ice cream into the frozen container, cover with plastic wrap, and return it to the freezer for at least 1 hour before serving.

Strawberry Ice Cream

The tartness of strawberries makes it difficult to team them with just cream. I use vanilla to soften the sharpness of the berries; then I don't have to add a lot of extra sugar. If ripe fresh strawberries are not available, use frozen loose berries packaged in plastic bags. They are picked ripe and have more flavor than underripe (orange, green, and white-tipped) fresh berries. Sprinkling sugar over the berries helps to keep them from freezing to ice. This ice cream is best when made a day ahead; it gives the strawberry flavor time to travel through the cream.

MAKES 1½ QUARTS

1 pint ripe strawberries
⅔ cup plus 2 tablespoons sugar
1 cup milk
2 large eggs
2 cups whipping cream (cold)
1 teaspoon vanilla extract

FRESH BERRIES   If using fresh berries, wash them by floating them in a bowl of cold water. Gently remove them from the water onto a towel to drain and dry. Remove the stems, cut the berries into quarters, and place them in a bowl. Sprinkle on 2 tablespoons of sugar; cover and refrigerate. If it's a hot summer day, freeze the berries.

FROZEN BERRIES   If using frozen strawberries, defrost them for 1 hour in the refrigerator. Cut them into quarters and sprinkle them with 2 tablespoons of sugar. Cover and refrigerate until needed. Do not allow the berries to defrost completely. Put them back in the freezer if they become overly soft.

Freeze a 2-quart container for storing the ice cream. Bring 2 quarts of water to a boil in a 4-quart pot. Lower the heat to maintain a simmer.

Bring the milk to a simmer; turn off the heat and let it stand until needed. Select a 2-quart stainless-steel bowl that fits comfortably over the 4-quart pot. Whisk the eggs in the bowl until smooth. Stir in the remaining ⅔ cup of sugar and place the bowl over the simmering water. Cook, stirring continuously with a wire whisk, about 4 minutes or until the eggs are as thick as mayonnaise (190° on a candy thermometer). Pour in the milk and continue whisking and cooking until thickened, about 4 minutes more. Remove the bowl from the pot and stir in the cream and vanilla.

Chill the mixture over a bowl of ice water until cool to the touch. Then freeze it in an ice cream machine according to the manufacturer's directions. When the ice cream is frozen but still soft, add the chilled berries. Continue churning until the berries are blended in evenly. Spoon the ice cream into the frozen container, cover with plastic wrap, and return it to the freezer until ready to serve.

Blackberry Ice Cream

This ice cream has a color that is so electric it's hard to believe it's natural. You can make it with whatever type of blackberries are native to your area. On the West Coast I like using marion berries, which have a faint flower-like quality that gently lingers on the tongue.

MAKES 5 CUPS

2 pints blackberries
1 cup sugar
1½ cups milk
2 large eggs
1½ cups whipping cream (cold)

Freeze a 6-cup or larger container for storing the ice cream. Wash the berries in a bowl of cold water and drain them on a towel. Purée them in a food mill or food processor; stir in 2 tablespoons of sugar. Press the purée through a sieve to remove the seeds; use the back of a spoon to extract as much juice as possible. Set aside until needed.

Bring the milk to a simmer and set it aside.

Bring 1 quart of water to a boil in a 2- to 3-quart saucepan. Beat the eggs in a stainless-steel bowl until smooth. Stir in the remaining sugar until completely incorporated. Set the bowl over the simmering water and cook, stirring continuously with a wire whisk, until the eggs are as thick as mayonnaise (190° on a candy thermometer). Add the milk and continue cooking and stirring until thickened, about 4 minutes. Remove the bowl from the heat and stir in the purée. Add the cream and mix until smooth. Chill the mixture over ice water then pour it into an ice cream machine and freeze according to the manufacturer's directions. Spoon the finished ice cream into the frozen container, cover with plastic wrap, and freeze it until ready to serve.

Blueberry Ice Cream

Blueberries have a special spicy quality that I love. A little lemon juice added to the berry purée keeps their flavor bright and fresh and helps it to shine through the richness of the cream.

MAKES 5 CUPS

2 pints blueberries
1 cup sugar
½ cup water
1 tablespoon fresh lemon juice
1 cup milk
2 large eggs
2 cups whipping cream (cold)

Freeze a 6-cup or larger container for storing the ice cream. Wash the berries in cold water, drain, and remove any stems. Bring ½ cup of sugar and ½ cup of water to a boil in a medium saucepan. Add the blueberries and lemon juice. Reduce the heat to maintain a simmer and cook for 5 minutes; set aside to cool for 5 minutes. Pass the berries and their syrup through a sieve, pressing with the back of a spoon to extract all the juice.

Heat the milk to a simmer and set it aside until needed.

Bring 1 quart of water to a boil in a 2- to 3-quart saucepan. Reduce the heat to maintain a simmer. Beat the eggs and remaining ½ cup of sugar in a stainless-steel bowl until smooth. Set the bowl over the simmering water and cook, stirring continuously with a wire whisk, until the eggs are as thick as mayonnaise (190° on a candy thermometer). Stir in the milk and continue cooking until thickened, about 4 minutes.

Remove the bowl from the heat and stir in the blueberries and cream. Chill the mixture over ice water then pour it into an ice cream machine and freeze according to the manufacturer's directions. Spoon the finished ice cream into the frozen container, cover with plastic wrap, and freeze until ready to serve.

Chocolate Swirl Ice Cream

I use a simple syrup instead of the more traditional milk or cream to dilute the chocolate for this ice cream. I have found that this technique gives the chocolate a lighter texture that sets it nicely apart from the rich ice cream. A little corn syrup makes the chocolate slightly chewy.

MAKES 1 QUART

4 ounces semisweet chocolate
3 tablespoons water
1 tablespoon corn syrup
⅔ cup plus 3 tablespoons sugar
1 cup milk
2 large eggs
2 cups whipping cream (cold)
1 teaspoon vanilla extract

Chop the chocolate into small pieces and set it aside until needed.

Combine the water, corn syrup, and 3 tablespoons of sugar and bring them to a boil in a small saucepan. Reduce the heat and let the syrup simmer for 1 minute. Remove the pan from heat and stir in the chocolate until it has melted and is completely incorporated. Set the chocolate syrup aside to cool while you prepare the ice cream.

Freeze a 2-quart container for storing the finished ice cream. Bring a quart of water to a boil in a 2- or 3-quart saucepan. Reduce the heat to maintain a simmer.

Bring the milk to a simmer in a small pan. Turn off the heat and let the milk stand until needed.

In a 2-quart stainless-steel bowl, whisk the eggs until smooth. Stir in the remaining sugar and place the bowl over the simmering water. Stirring continuously with a wire whisk, cook the eggs until they are as thick as mayonnaise (190° on a candy thermometer). Pour in the scalded milk and continue whisking and cooking for about 4 minutes or until thickened. Remove the bowl from the pan and stir in the cream and vanilla. Chill the mixture over ice water. When cool, pour it into an ice cream machine and freeze according to the manufacturer's instructions.

When the ice cream is done, spoon it into the frozen container. Pour the chocolate syrup on top and swirl it into the ice cream by dragging a spatula or a spoon through ice cream and syrup. Cover with plastic wrap and freeze until ready to serve.

Raspberry Swirl Ice Cream

This is a festive ice cream. A ribbon of bright, fresh-tasting raspberry purée swirls through rich vanilla ice cream. I especially like to serve it with the Fig, Peach, and Raspberry Cobbler on page 75.

MAKES 5 CUPS

1 pint raspberries
½ cup plus ⅔ cup sugar
½ cup water
1 cup milk
2 large eggs
2 cups whipping cream (cold)
1 teaspoon vanilla extract

Freeze a 6-cup or larger container to store the ice cream. Wash the berries in a bowl of cold water. Drain. Then purée them in a food mill or food processor. Stir the purée, ½ cup of sugar, and the water together in a medium saucepan; bring the mixture to a boil. Reduce the heat to maintain a simmer and cook, stirring occasionally, until the syrup coats the back of a spoon. If you puréed the berries in a food processor, pass the syrup through a sieve to remove the seeds. Cool over ice water and set aside until needed.

Bring the milk to a simmer and set it aside until needed.

Bring 2 quarts of water to a boil in a 4-quart pot; reduce the heat to maintain a simmer. Whisk the eggs until smooth in a stainless-steel bowl. Stir in ⅔ cup of sugar. Set the bowl over the simmering water and cook, stirring continuously with a wire whisk, until the eggs are as thick as mayonnaise (190° on a candy thermometer). Pour in the milk and continue whisking and cooking for about 4 minutes or until thickened. Remove the bowl from the heat and stir in the cream and vanilla.

Chill the mixture over ice water, then pour it into an ice cream machine and freeze according to the manufacturer's directions.

Spoon the finished ice cream into the frozen container. Pour the berry syrup on top and swirl it through the ice cream with a spatula or spoon. Cover with plastic wrap and freeze until ready to serve.

Mocha Swirl Ice Cream

Mocha is the traditional and irresistible combination of chocolate and coffee. In this swirled ice cream, Frangelico liqueur adds an intriguing hint of hazelnut.

MAKES 5 CUPS

4 ounces bittersweet chocolate
3 tablespoons water
⅔ cup plus 3 tablespoons sugar
1 tablespoon corn syrup
2 tablespoons Frangelico liqueur
1 cup milk
1 tablespoon freshly ground coffee
2 large eggs
2 cups whipping cream (cold)

Chop the chocolate into small pieces and set it aside. Combine the water, 3 tablespoons of sugar, and the corn syrup in a small saucepan and bring them to a boil. Reduce the heat and let the syrup simmer 1 minute. Remove the pan from the heat and stir in the chocolate; stir until it has melted and is completely incorporated. Stir in the Frangelico and set the syrup aside until needed.

Freeze a 6-cup or larger container for storing the ice cream. Bring the milk to a simmer in a small saucepan. Add the coffee and remove the pan from the heat. Let it stand for 5 minutes, then strain the milk through a sieve to remove the coffee grounds. Set the milk aside.

Bring 1 quart of water to a boil in a 2- or 3-quart saucepan. Reduce the heat to maintain a simmer. Whisk the eggs until smooth in a 2-quart stainless-steel bowl. Stir in the remaining sugar and set the bowl over the simmering water. Cook, stirring continuously with a wire whisk, until the eggs are as thick as mayonnaise (190° on a candy thermometer). Pour in the milk and continue whisking and cooking for about 4 minutes or until thickened. Remove the pan from the heat and stir in the cream. Chill the mixture over ice water, then pour it into an ice cream machine and freeze according to the manufacturer's directions. Spoon the finished ice cream into the frozen container. Pour the chocolate syrup on top and swirl it in by dragging a spatula or spoon through the ice cream. Cover with plastic wrap and freeze until ready to serve.

Orange Ice Cream

For the best-tasting ice cream, use fresh juice oranges, such as Valencias. Navel oranges are too sweet.

MAKES 1 QUART

1 cup fresh orange juice
1 tablespoon orange zest
6 large egg yolks
¾ cup sugar
1 cup milk
1 cup whipping cream (cold)

Freeze a 5-cup container for storing the ice cream. Boil the orange juice and zest until the liquid is reduced to ½ cup. Strain out the zest.

Whip the egg yolks and sugar until light and smooth. Bring the milk to a boil in a large saucepan, add the yolk mixture, and cook, stirring continuously with a wire whisk, until thickened. Stir in the orange juice and the cream. Transfer the mixture to an ice cream machine and freeze according to the manufacturer's instructions. Spoon the ice cream into the frozen container, cover with plastic wrap, and freeze until ready to serve.

Orange– Chocolate Chip Ice Cream

High-quality semisweet chocolate tastes much better to me than any commercially packaged chocolate chips. So I make my own "chips" by chopping good chocolate into small chunks. For orange flavor equal to the chocolate, squeeze your own fresh orange juice from juice oranges, such as Valencias, not eating oranges. I like to serve this ice cream with Chocolate and Hazelnut Biscotti (page 145) or Almond Fingers (page 142).

MAKES 1 QUART

2 large eggs
⅔ cup sugar
½ cup orange juice
1 tablespoon grated orange zest
½ cup milk
2 cups whipping cream (cold)
4 ounces semisweet chocolate

Freeze a 5-cup container for storing the ice cream. Bring 2 quarts of water to a boil in a 3- or 4-quart pot. Reduce the heat to maintain a simmer.

Whisk the eggs until smooth in a 2-quart stainless-steel bowl. Stir in the sugar, orange juice, and zest. Place the bowl over the simmering water and cook, whisking occasionally, until thickened enough to heavily coat the back of a spoon, about 6 minutes. Stir in the milk and chill the mixture over ice water until cool to the touch. Stir in the cream. Pour the mixture into an ice cream machine and freeze according to the manufacturer's instructions.

While the ice cream freezes, chop the chocolate into ¼-inch chunks. When the ice cream is done, add the chocolate and continue churning just until blended. Spoon the ice cream into the frozen container, cover with plastic wrap, and freeze it until ready to serve.

Apricot and White Chocolate Chunk Ice Cream

Because of the richness of the apricots and the high fat content of the white chocolate, I use half milk and half cream in this recipe. It results in a better balanced ice cream. (Too much fat in ice cream will leave an unpleasant film in your mouth.) Choose only fully ripe apricots for the ice cream for this parfait, so that they will be tender and full of flavor.

MAKES 5 CUPS

1½ cups ripe apricots
1 tablespoon fresh lemon juice
1½ cups milk
2 large eggs
¾ cup sugar
1½ cups whipping cream (cold)
4 ounces white chocolate

Freeze an 8-cup or larger container to store the ice cream. Wash the apricots; cut them in half and remove the stones. Cut the halves into quarters. Toss them in a bowl with the lemon juice, cover them, and set them aside until needed.

Bring the milk to a simmer; set it aside until needed.

Bring 1 quart of water to a boil in a 2- to 3-quart saucepan. Reduce the heat to maintain a simmer. Beat the eggs in a stainless-steel bowl until smooth. Add the sugar. Set the bowl over the simmering water and cook, whisking continuously, until the eggs are as thick as mayonnaise (190° on a candy thermometer). Add the milk and continue stirring until thickened, about 4 minutes. Remove the bowl from the heat and stir in the cream. Cool the mixture over ice water, then pour it into an ice cream machine and freeze according to the manufacturer's directions.

Chop the chocolate into ¼-inch chunks. Spoon the ice cream into the frozen container and fold in the apricots and chocolate. Cover with plastic wrap and freeze until ready to serve.

Lemon Ice Cream

This ice cream has a wonderfully smooth texture. It is a great example of how contrasting flavors and textures can complement each other. The rich cream tames the tartness of the lemon while the lemon lightens the heaviness of the cream. I like to serve it with a caramel nut tart (see pages 68, 69, 70) or use it as the basis for the Lemon and Caramel Parfait on page 173.

MAKES 1 QUART

½ cup milk
2 large eggs
⅔ cup sugar
⅓ cup lemon juice
2 cups whipping cream (cold)

Freeze a 5-cup or larger container for storing the ice cream. Bring 2 quarts of water to a boil in a 4-quart pot; lower the heat to a simmer.

Bring the milk to a simmer; turn off the heat and let it stand until needed. Select a 2-quart stainless-steel bowl that fits comfortably over the 4-quart pot. Whisk the eggs in the bowl until smooth. Stir in the sugar and then the lemon juice. Place the bowl over the simmering water. Cook, stirring occasionally with a wire whisk, until thickened, about 6 minutes. Remove the bowl from the pot and stir in the milk; stir in the cream.

Chill the mixture over a bowl of ice water until cool to the touch. Freeze it in an ice cream machine according to the manufacturer's instructions. Spoon the finished ice cream into the frozen container, cover with plastic wrap, and return it to the freezer until ready to serve.

Lemon-Pistachio Ice Cream

In this tasty variation on Lemon Ice Cream, lemon and cream are background flavors for toasted pistachios. Toasting the nuts enhances their flavor and texture. Adding them at the end of the freezing cycle ensures that they'll remain crisp and not become soggy.

MAKES 5 CUPS

1 cup shelled pistachios
1 recipe Lemon Ice Cream (recipe above)

Freeze a 6-cup container for storing the ice cream. Preheat the oven to 325°.

Spread the pistachios on a cookie sheet and bake them until light brown and crisp, 7 to 8 minutes. Set them aside to cool.

Prepare the ice cream. Add the nuts when the ice cream is frozen but still soft. Continue churning only until the nuts are blended in. Spoon the ice cream into the frozen container, cover with plastic wrap, and return it to the freezer until ready to serve.

Maple-Butternut Ice Cream

Butternut trees are native to New England. Their nuts, which resemble walnuts, are rich in oil and have a delicate flavor that blends perfectly with New England maple syrup. Unfortunately, they aren't available commercially. If you can't befriend someone who owns a butternut tree, substitute walnuts.

MAKES 5 CUPS

1 cup butternut or walnut halves
1½ cups milk
2 large eggs
¾ cup grade A maple syrup
1½ cups whipping cream (cold)

Freeze a 6-cup container for storing the ice cream. Preheat the oven to 300°. Spread the nut halves on a cookie sheet and toast them in the oven until they are crisp but not browned, about 7 minutes. Set them aside to cool.

Bring the milk to a simmer; set it aside until needed.

Bring 1 quart of water to a boil in a 2- to 3-quart saucepan. Reduce the heat to maintain a simmer. Beat the eggs until smooth in a stainless-steel bowl; stir in the maple syrup. Set the bowl over the simmering water and cook, stirring continuously with a wire whisk, until the eggs are as thick as mayonnaise (190° on a candy thermometer). Stir in the milk and continue cooking and stirring for about 4 minutes or until thickened. Remove from the heat and stir in the cream. Chill the mixture over ice water then pour it into an ice cream machine and freeze according to the manufacturer's directions.

Chop the nuts into ¼-inch pieces. Spoon the ice cream into the frozen container and fold in the nuts. Cover with plastic wrap and freeze until ready to serve.

Anisette Ice Cream

Anisette is a liqueur flavored with anise seed. It makes an unusual, spicy ice cream that I like to serve with a Warm Pear Tart (page 51). Since alcohol doesn't freeze, it is necessary to burn it off before making ice cream.

MAKES 1 QUART

1 cup anisette
6 large egg yolks
½ cup sugar
1½ cups milk
1½ cups cream

Warm the anisette in a small saucepan. Light the top carefully with a long match and allow it to burn until the flame goes out. Keep the lid to the pan handy to smother the flame if necessary.

Whip the egg yolks with the sugar until light and smooth. Add the anisette and milk. Transfer the mixture to the top of a double boiler and cook it over simmering water until it thickens enough to coat the back of a spoon. Set the bowl in a larger bowl of ice water to cool. When it is cool, stir in the cream. Transfer the mixture to an ice cream machine and freeze according to the manufacturer's instructions.

Pineapple Ice Cream

Sweet, ripe pineapple makes a wonderfully delicate and fragrant ice cream. Choose your pineapple carefully; underripe ones are harsh tasting. The best pineapples are field ripened, and are often labeled as such. For a special treat, top each serving of ice cream with a drizzle of pure Vermont maple syrup.

MAKES 1 QUART

2 cups fresh pineapple, in ½-inch chunks
¾ cup sugar
3 large egg yolks
¾ cup nonfat milk
1 cup whipping cream (cold)

Toss the pineapple chunks with the sugar in a small bowl. Let them stand for 1 hour, stirring occasionally. Drain the pineapple and set it aside; save the syrup.

Whip the egg yolks with an electric mixer at high speed for 2 minutes. Boil the drained syrup until it registers 238° on a candy thermometer. Beat the hot syrup into the yolks at medium speed; continue mixing for 1 minute.

Bring the milk to a boil in a 2-quart saucepan over medium-high heat. Stir the egg yolks into the milk with a wire whisk. Reduce the heat to moderate and continue cooking, stirring continuously, for 8 minutes. Be sure to scrape the bottom and sides of the pan as you stir. (If you see any brown flecks, remove the pan from the heat.) Reduce the heat to low and continue cooking and stirring until the mixture is thick and silky-looking. Pour it into a bowl and set the bowl in a larger bowl of ice water to cool.

When the mixture is cool, stir in the cream. Transfer the mixture to an ice cream machine and freeze according to the manufacturer's instructions. Notice when the ice cream becomes firm. Freeze it for about 10 minutes longer, so that it can absorb air. Add the pineapple and continue freezing until it is blended in evenly. If adding the pineapple softens the ice cream, continue freezing until it is firm again.

Cinnamon-Quince Ice Cream

This is a smooth, subtly flavored ice cream. There is just enough cinnamon to bring out the lovely, soft flavor of the quince.

MAKES 1 QUART

2 cups water
⅔ cup sugar
½ teaspoon ground cinnamon
1 medium quince
2 large eggs
1½ cups milk
1 cup whipping cream (cold)

Bring the water, sugar, and cinnamon to a boil in a heavy-bottomed saucepan. Peel, quarter, and core the quince. Add it to the boiling syrup and continue boiling gently, uncovered, until the quince is tender, about 15 minutes. Remove the pieces of quince and finely chop them. Continue cooking the syrup over medium-high heat until it registers 235° on a candy thermometer.

Bring some water to a boil in the bottom of a double boiler; remove it from the heat. Beat the eggs and put them in the top of the double boiler, over the boiled water. Beat the eggs with a wire whisk until they are foamy and doubled in volume. Pour the hot syrup into the eggs in a thin stream while beating; be sure to scrape all the syrup from the pan. Continue beating until the eggs are light and bubbly.

Bring the milk to a simmer in the pan from the syrup. Bring the water in the bottom of the double boiler back to a simmer. Add the milk to the eggs and cook over the simmering water, stirring continuously with the whisk, be sure to scrape the bottom of the pan frequently. If the mixture rises up, just keep stirring. Cook until it is lightly thickened. Take the top of the double boiler off the bottom and continue whisking until smooth. Set the mixture over ice water to cool, stirring every few minutes.

When the mixture is cool, stir in the chopped quince and the cream. Transfer it to an ice cream machine and freeze according to the manufacturer's instructions.

Coconut Ice Cream

The rich, tropical taste of this ice cream goes especially well with a Brown Sugar Pineapple Crisp (page 79) or Cranberry Crisp (page 80). For instructions on how to deal with a fresh coconut, see the recipe for Coconut Cream Tart on page 63.

MAKES 5 CUPS

1½ cups milk
1 cup shredded fresh coconut
2 large eggs
¾ cup sugar
1 teaspoon vanilla extract
2 cups whipping cream (cold)

Freeze a 6-cup container for storing the ice cream. Bring the milk to a simmer in a medium saucepan. Stir in the coconut and remove the pan from the heat; let it stand until cooled. Strain the coconut from the milk, pressing it against the sieve to squeeze out all the liquid. Discard the coconut; its flavor is now in the milk.

Bring 1 quart of water to a boil in a 2- or 3-quart saucepan; reduce the heat to maintain a simmer. Whisk the eggs until smooth in a 2-quart stainless-steel bowl. Stir in the sugar and place the bowl over the simmering water. Stirring continuously with a wire whisk, cook the eggs until they are as thick as mayonnaise (190° on a candy thermometer). Stir in the milk and continue whisking and cooking until thickened, about 4 minutes. Stir in the vanilla and cream. Chill the mixture over ice water. When cool, pour it into an ice cream machine and freeze according to the manufacturer's instructions. When frozen, spoon into the frozen container and cover until ready to serve.

Peach Sorbet

This is a delicious, easy-to-make dessert and a great way to take advantage of summer's abundance of ripe peaches. To serve, put two small scoops of sorbet in a tulip cup or small stemmed glass and garnish with mint leaves.

MAKES 1½ QUARTS

10 medium peaches
2 teaspoons lemon juice
1¾ cups sugar
1¾ cups water

Wash the peaches, cut them into quarters, and discard the pits. Purée them with the lemon juice in a food processor. Strain the purée and set it aside.

Bring the sugar and water to a boil in a heavy saucepan. Boil just until the sugar dissolves; cool to room temperature.

Stir the purée and sugar syrup together. Transfer the mixture to an ice cream machine and freeze according to the manufacturer's instructions.

Raspberry Sorbet

This simple sorbet tastes like fresh, ripe raspberries. Serve it in glass bowls, if you have them, to show off its spectacular color.

MAKES 1 QUART

2 pints raspberries
1¼ cups sugar
1¼ cups water

Freeze a 5-cup or larger container to store the sorbet. Wash the berries by floating them in a bowl of cold water; soil and other foreign matters will fall to the bottom. Lift the berries from the water and drain them on a clean towel.

Purée the berries with a food mill or food processor. Press them through a sieve with the back of a spoon to remove the seeds.

Combine the sugar and water in a medium saucepan. Heat, stirring, until the sugar has dissolved. Bring the resulting syrup to a boil over moderately high heat. Remove it from the heat and stir it into the raspberry purée. Chill the mixture over ice water, then pour it into an ice cream machine and freeze according to the manufacturer's directions. Spoon the finished sorbet into the frozen container, cover with plastic wrap, and freeze until ready to serve.

Cranberry-Campari Sorbet

Campari, the bitter and slightly sweet Italian aperitif, adds a new dimension of flavor to tart cranberries in this refreshing sorbet. Serve Almond Tiles (page 142) alongside for a delightful dessert.

MAKES 1 QUART

1½ cups cranberries
1 cup sugar
2½ cups water
½ cup Campari

Freeze a 5-cup or larger container to store the sorbet. Wash the berries in cold water and remove any stems. Drain the berries on towels.

Bring the sugar and water to a boil in a medium saucepan. Add the cranberries and stir with a spoon to coat the berries with syrup. Continue boiling until the cranberries pop and soften. Remove the pan from the heat and stir in the Campari. Purée the mixture in a food mill or food processor. Press it through a sieve using the back of a spoon to extract all the juice. Pour the purée into a bowl and chill it over ice water. When cool to the touch, pour it into an ice cream machine and freeze according to the manufacturer's directions. Spoon the finished sorbet into the frozen container, cover with plastic wrap, and freeze until ready to serve.

Bing Cherry– Amaretto Sorbet

Sweet, dark bing cherries are one of the great joys of late spring and early summer. A touch of almondy Amaretto liqueur adds depth to their flavor in this marvelous deep-purple sorbet.

MAKES 1 QUART

3 cups bing cherries
1 tablespoon lemon juice
1½ cups sugar
2 cups water
2 tablespoons Amaretto liqueur

Freeze a 5-cup or larger container for storing the sorbet. Wash the cherries and remove the stems. Remove the pits with a cherry pitter or cut each cherry in half and remove the pit with the tip of a knife. Toss the cherries in the lemon juice. Purée them in a food mill or a food processor.

Bring the sugar and water to a boil in a medium saucepan. Add the purée and simmer for 3 minutes. Remove the pan from the heat and stir in the Amaretto. Strain the mixture through a sieve then cool it over ice water. When cool to the touch, pour it into an ice cream machine and freeze according to the manufacturer's directions. Spoon the finished sorbet into the frozen container, cover with plastic wrap, and freeze until ready to serve.

Lemon and Caramel Parfait

Somehow parfaits have been passed by and forgotten. I still consider them a perfect ending for an elegant summer dinner when a small amount of cool richness is just what's needed to top off the evening. In this one, rum-laced caramel is swirled around tangy lemon ice cream.

MAKES 6 PARFAITS

1 recipe Lemon Ice Cream (page 166)
1½ cups whipping cream
1 tablespoon light corn syrup
1½ cups sugar
2 tablespoons rum (Myers's Dark or Mount
    Gay Eclipse)
6 small White Chocolate Rum Truffles (page
    210) (optional)

Prepare the lemon ice cream.

Freeze 6 parfait glasses. Bring 1 cup of cream and the corn syrup to a simmer in a small saucepan.

Spread the sugar evenly in a heavy 6-cup sauté pan. Cook it over moderately high heat until it begins to melt into caramel or until you can see puffs of smoke through the sugar. Gently shake the pan to blend caramel and sugar. Once most of the sugar has melted, stir with a spoon to dissolve the rest. Cook to a medium, clear brown color. Remove the pan from the heat and slowly stir in the simmered cream mixture, pouring slowly so you add only as much at a time as you can easily control. Stir until blended. Add the rum and blend well. Pour the caramel into a bowl and cool it over ice water.

For each parfait, pour 1 tablespoon of caramel into the bottom of a frozen glass. Using a small scoop, scoop a ball of ice cream onto the caramel. Top with another tablespoon of caramel. Continue to alternate ice cream and caramel until you reach the top of the glass. Cover with plastic wrap and freeze.

Just before serving, whip the remaining cream to soft peaks. Top each parfait with a dollop of whipped cream and, if you wish, a small white chocolate rum truffle.

Orange–Chocolate Chip Parfait with Cointreau and Walnuts

This simple yet elegant dessert is always impressive. It is a boon to the cook because it can be made and frozen ahead of time. I like to serve it with Butter Cookies (page 138).

SERVES 6

1 quart Orange–Chocolate Chip Ice Cream
     (page 164)
½ cup whipping cream
½ cup walnuts
6 tablespoons Cointreau

Prepare the orange–chocolate chip ice cream.

Whip the cream to soft peaks and set it aside until needed. Chop the walnuts into ¼-inch chunks.

Pour 1 tablespoon of Cointreau into each parfait glass. With a small scoop, scoop 1 ball of ice cream into each glass, pressing it slowly to the bottom. This will bring some of the liqueur up over the ice cream. Sprinkle with walnuts. Continue alternating ice cream scoops and walnuts until you reach the rim of the glass. Top the parfait with a dollop of whipped cream and freeze it until 5 to 10 minutes before serving.

Apricot-Amaretto Parfait

This intriguing parfait combines an ice cream made from fresh, ripe apricots with Amaretto, a liqueur made from apricot pits. The richness of the ice cream both contrasts with and smooths the intense, slightly sharp flavor of its kindred liqueur. I like to serve Almond-Butter Cookies (page 141) alongside.

MAKES 6 PARFAITS

1 recipe Apricot and White Chocolate Chunk
     Ice Cream (page 165)
½ cup whipping cream
6 tablespoons Amaretto liqueur

Prepare the apricot and white chocolate chunk ice cream.

Whip the cream to soft peaks and set it aside until needed. Pour 1 tablespoon Amaretto into each parfait glass. With a small ice cream scoop, place 1 scoop of ice cream into each glass. Press it slowly to the bottom; this will bring the liqueur up around and over the scoop. Continue scooping and pressing all of the ice cream into the glasses; the liqueur should come up over each scoop.

Top each parfait with a dollop of whipped cream. Freeze the parfaits until 5 to 10 minutes before serving.

Tropical Chocolate Sundae

This sundae, made with coconut ice cream, chocolate-rum sauce, and tropical fruits, was inspired by my good friend Peter Deehan, executive pastry chef at the Mauna Lani Bay Hotel in Kawaihae, Hawaii. Peter is an expert at blending traditional and tropical flavors.

SERVES 6

1 recipe Coconut Ice Cream (page 170)
8 ounces semisweet chocolate
½ cup milk
2 tablespoons sugar
1 tablespoon corn syrup
2 tablespoons dark rum
¼ cup unsalted macadamia nuts
½ cup whipping cream
½ cup each banana, mango, and pineapple
    (cut into ½-inch chunks)

Prepare the coconut ice cream.

To make a chocolate-rum sauce, cut the chocolate into small pieces. Bring the milk, sugar, and corn syrup to a simmer in a small saucepan. Remove the pan from the heat and stir in the chocolate and rum until completely incorporated. Set aside until needed.

Preheat the oven to 300°. Toast the nuts on a cookie sheet in the oven until golden brown, 5 to 7 minutes. Set them aside to cool. When cool, chop them into ⅛-inch chunks.

Whip the cream to soft peaks.

To serve, place 2 scoops of ice cream in the center of each dessert bowl, pressing the second scoop on top of the first. Spread ¼ cup of fruit around the base of the ice cream. Pour chocolate-rum sauce over the top, add a dollop of cream, and sprinkle with chopped nuts.

Strawberry-Maple Sundae

This sundae, besides being delicious, is fun to eat because of its many different textures. The firm, smooth ice cream is covered with a satiny berry sauce then topped with juicy fresh berries, crisp sugared walnuts, and soft whipped cream.

SERVES 4

1 recipe Maple-Butternut Ice Cream, made
    with walnuts (page 167)
1 recipe Trefethen Maple-Sugared Walnuts
    (page 212)

½ cup whipping cream
2 pints fresh strawberries
2 tablespoons sugar

Prepare the maple-butternut ice cream and the Trefethen maple-sugared walnuts.

Freeze 4 glass bowls. Whip the cream to soft peaks; cover and chill it until needed.

Wash the berries in a bowl of cold water and drain them on a towel. Remove the stems and leaves and divide them in half, with the larger berries in one group and the smaller in the other. Cut the large berries in half. Purée them in a food mill or food processor with the sugar. Pass the purée through a sieve to remove the seeds. Cover and chill the sauce until needed.

If any of the small berries seem large, cut them in half. Place 2 scoops of ice cream in each bowl, pressing the second scoop on top of the first. Cover the ice cream with berry sauce, then sprinkle it with walnuts and strawberries. Top with whipped cream and serve at once.

Raspberry Sundae with Chocolate Swirl Ice Cream

Raspberry and chocolate is a beloved classic flavor combination. Here vanilla ice cream helps keep the two intense flavors separate and distinct, while at the same time bringing them together in delicious harmony. For a memorable dessert, serve the sundaes with Almond-Butter Cookies (page 141).

SERVES 6

1 quart Chocolate Swirl Ice Cream (page 161)
3 pints raspberries
1 tablespoon granulated sugar
1 cup whipped cream
1 teaspoon powdered sugar

Prepare the chocolate swirl ice cream.

Wash 2 pints of raspberries by dropping them into a bowl of cold water. Remove them from the water and let them drain and dry on a towel. Purée them with the granulated sugar in a food processor, blender, or food mill. Strain the purée through a sieve to remove the seeds. Chill the sauce until ready to use.

Wash the remaining pint of berries in cold water and drain and dry them on a towel. Whip the cream with the powdered sugar to soft peaks. Chill the cream until needed.

To serve, place 2 scoops of ice cream in each dessert bowl, pressing the second scoop on top of the first. Pour ¼ cup of raspberry sauce over the ice cream. Drop raspberries around the ice cream and top with a dollop of whipped cream.

Pistachio-Mint Sundae

The pale color of this pistachio ice cream may surprise you; commercial pistachio ice cream is usually tinted green with artificial food color. Use only natural pistachios, not the garish red ones, and not any that are salted.

SERVES 6

PISTACHIO ICE CREAM

1 cup pistachios
7 large egg yolks
1 cup sugar
1½ cups skim milk
1 vanilla bean, split lengthwise
1½ cups whipping cream (cold)

WHITE CHOCOLATE AND
   CRÈME DE MENTHE SAUCE

8 ounces white chocolate
1 cup whipping cream
¼ cup white crème de menthe

ICE CREAM

Preheat the oven to 350°. Toast the pistachios on a cookie sheet in the oven until fragrant, about 7 minutes. Set aside.

Freeze a bowl for storing the ice cream. Beat the egg yolks and sugar until pale yellow. Bring the milk and vanilla bean to a simmer in a 2-quart stainless-steel saucepan. Remove the pan from the heat and stir in the egg mixture. Cook over medium-high heat, stirring continuously with a wire whisk, until the center bubbles and the mixture has thickened. Pour the mixture into a cold bowl and cool to room temperature, stirring occasionally.

Remove the vanilla bean and stir in the cream. Pour the mixture into an ice cream machine and freeze according to manufacturer's instructions. When the ice cream is just about frozen, add the pistachios and continue churning until done. Spoon the ice cream into the frozen bowl, cover with plastic wrap, and return it to the freezer until ready to serve.

SAUCE

Place the chocolate and cream in the top of a double boiler over boiled (not boiling) water. When half of the chocolate is melted, stir with a spoon to help melt the rest. Remove the bowl and stir in the crème de menthe. Set aside to cool.

It is best to make the sauce a few hours ahead. When it has cooled, cover the bowl and refrigerate it. The sauce will keep for up to a week. When you are ready to make the sundaes, take out the bowl and stir the sauce.

To assemble the sundaes, put 2 scoops of ice cream in each bowl. Top with ⅓ cup of sauce. If you want, crown the sundae with a dollop of whipped cream.

9

Breads,
Breakfast Treats, and
Turnovers

IN MORE THAN TEN YEARS as a hotel pastry chef, I have developed a broad and varied breakfast repertoire. Breakfast is the meal guests are most likely to eat in the hotel, and the one they're most likely to remember, so it demands special attention. I've always felt that breakfast at home is special too, but it has become a meal on the run in many families. Most of us pause for a leisurely breakfast only on weekends and vacations. Whenever I can, I invite friends for breakfast for no particular reason; they always accept the invitation enthusiastically. A home-baked breakfast, it seems, is an occasion in itself.

The same principles apply to great breakfasts as to great desserts: use fresh, seasonal ingredients; match flavors carefully; and keep things simple. Breakfast should never be complicated. In its simplest form, all that's required is some fresh fruit, a pot of coffee, and something delicious from the oven. Muffins are usually my choice. I like to put fresh berries, especially blueberries, in muffins when they are in season. When they're not, I turn to what's best—rhubarb, cranberries, figs, oranges.

In a simple breakfast I like to offer some variety, so I often mix several kinds of muffins in a basket. Hearty bran muffins are a nice contrast to lighter fruit muffins. I discovered early on that toasting the bran before putting it into the batter makes better-tasting muffins (although the bran smells kind of bad during toasting). Sometimes I make bran muffins with pecans, for a more interesting texture and added flavor.

Muffins, coffee cake, scones, crumpets, sticky buns, and biscuits are all delightful ways to start the day. Any one, or a variety, can be the focus of a simple breakfast. When I feel like slightly more substantial fare, waffles or pancakes take center stage. Add a fruit topping or sauce, and they become a satisfying meal. I like to make blueberry pancakes in summer and apple in winter, but you can use any seasonal fruits that don't need much cooking.

Like most people, I have days when I have to rush off in the morning, so last year I set out to create a quick, nutritious breakfast I could eat on the way out the door. I came up with my own version of a breakfast bar (see page 198). Unlike supermarket bars, mine is soft, moist, and delicious. If you must eat a pit-stop breakfast, these are worth stopping for.

At breakfast or any meal, a loaf of good, fresh bread is always a treat. I love baking bread and have included a few of my favorite recipes here. The Walnut Raisin Bread and Orange-Walnut Bread (pages 204 and 205) are terrific for breakfast, served warm or toasted with butter and preserves. I developed the Braided Egg and Saffron Bread (page 201) and Easter Bread (page 202) for holiday meals, but they are wonderful any time. And then there is Focaccia with Sun-Dried Tomatoes and Garlic (page 205). This moist, fragrant Italian bread is practically a meal in itself. Cut it into squares and bring it along on a picnic, or serve it with a bowl of soup for a first-class lunch.

Country Blueberry Muffins

Blueberry muffins are at their best in summer, when plump, spicy blueberries are available fresh. But these cakey, all-American muffins are also wonderful made with frozen blueberries. Just be sure the berries are loose in the bag, like marbles, when you buy them. If they are stuck together they have defrosted and have been refrozen. Do not defrost blueberries before using them.

MAKES 18

10 tablespoons unsalted butter (soft)
½ teaspoon vanilla extract
4 large eggs
2 cups sugar
1 tablespoon baking powder
1 tablespoon kosher salt
¼ cup milk
2½ cups all-purpose flour
2 cups blueberries

Preheat the oven to 400°. Line the muffin tins with paper baking cups.

Using the paddle attachment on an electric mixer, cream the butter and vanilla until light. Add the eggs one at a time, adding ½ cup of sugar with each egg. Blend well after each addition.

Stir the baking powder and salt into the milk. Add the milk mixture, the flour, and the blueberries to the egg mixture, folding the ingredients together just until the flour is incorporated. The mixture will be a bit clumpy. Spoon the batter into 18 muffin cups, filling them about three-quarters full. Bake until the tops of the muffins are golden brown and the centers spring back when lightly touched, 30 to 35 minutes.

Cool the muffins in the pan for 5 minutes. Then spread out a clean kitchen towel, turn the pans on their sides, and tap the muffins out onto the towel. Let the muffins finish cooling on a wire rack.

Crunchy Blueberry Muffins

A sprinkling of cinnamon and sugar makes the top of these muffins bake up crisp and crunchy. Use only fresh blueberries in this recipe; the juice that leaks from frozen berries makes the batter too wet.

MAKES 12

5 tablespoons unsalted butter
1 large egg
7 tablespoons sugar
½ teaspoon kosher salt
1 tablespoon baking powder
½ cup milk
1¾ cups all-purpose flour
2 cups fresh blueberries
½ teaspoon cinnamon

Preheat the oven to 400°. Line a muffin tin with paper baking cups.

Melt the butter. Whisk it in a large bowl with the egg and 6 tablespoons of sugar. Add the salt, baking powder, milk, flour, and blueberries and fold gently until all the ingredients are mixed. Spoon the batter into 12 baking cups.

Combine the remaining tablespoon of sugar with the cinnamon and sprinkle about ¼ teaspoon onto each muffin (you will have a little left over).

Bake in the middle of the oven until the muffins are brown and lightly firm, about ½ hour.

Cool the muffins in the pans for 5 minutes. Then spread out a clean kitchen towel, turn the pans on their sides, and tap the muffins out onto the towel. Let the muffins finish cooling on a wire rack.

Rhubarb Muffins

When rhubarb is in season, I use it every way I can. Tart and slightly chewy, it adds interest to pies, cakes, and these moist, flavorful muffins. Field-grown rhubarb tastes better to me than hothouse-grown. I always use it if I have a choice.

MAKES 18

1 pound rhubarb
8 tablespoons (¼ pound) unsalted butter
    (soft)
1 cup sugar
¼ teaspoon vanilla extract
1 large egg

2 cups all-purpose flour
4 teaspoons baking powder
¼ teaspoon kosher salt
1 cup milk

Preheat the oven to 400°. Line the muffin tins with paper baking cups.

Trim the rhubarb, being sure to remove all the leaves and the green tips of the stems (they are poisonous). Wash the trimmed stalks and, using a sharp knife, cut them into 1-inch chunks. You should have about 2 cups.

Cream the butter, sugar, and vanilla until light in color and free of lumps. Mix in the egg. Sift the flour, baking powder, and salt together and stir half into the butter mixture. Add half the milk, then the rest of the flour mixture, and the rest of the milk, mixing after each addition. Continue folding and mixing with a rubber spatula until the dough comes together and has small lumps. Fold in the rhubarb.

Fill 18 muffin cups to just below the rim and bake in the middle of the oven until the tops spring back when lightly touched or a toothpick inserted in the center comes out clean, about 30 minutes.

Cool the muffins in the pans for 5 minutes. Then spread out a clean kitchen towel, turn the pans on their sides, and tap the muffins out onto the towel. Let the muffins finish cooling on a wire rack.

Cranberry-Fig Muffins

Unlike many healthful breakfast foods, these low-cholesterol muffins taste great. The cranberries and figs contribute a bright, rich flavor while supplying important vitamins and minerals.

MAKES 12

1½ cups water
½ cup oat bran
6 tablespoons canola oil
½ cup lowfat milk
4 large egg whites
⅓ cup sugar
1⅓ cups all-purpose flour
4 teaspoons baking powder
½ teaspoon salt
1 cup dried mission figs
1 cup cranberries

Preheat the oven to 425°. Line a muffin tin with paper baking cups.

Bring the water to a rapid boil in a small saucepan. Stir in the oat bran and remove the pan from the heat. Continue stirring until the mixture is free of lumps. Set aside to cool for 5 minutes.

Stir the oil and milk into the bran mixture. Beat the egg whites and sugar to soft peaks and fold them in. Sift together the flour, baking powder, and salt. Chop the figs so that each piece is about the size of a cranberry. Toss the cranberries and figs in the flour mixture to coat them, then fold fruit and flour into the batter.

Using a soup spoon, fill 12 muffin cups equally with batter. Put the tin on the middle oven shelf and reduce the heat to 375°. Bake until the tops are light brown and spring back when gently touched, about 20 minutes. If they feel like they are floating on a liquid center, continue baking for another 3 to 5 minutes.

Carefully turn the muffins out onto a wire rack; let them cool for 10 minutes before serving.

Almond and Orange Muffins

These are moist, light, tender muffins, topped with a sprinkling of crisp toasted almonds.

MAKES 18

1⅛ cups natural (skin on) sliced almonds
8 tablespoons (¼ pound) unsalted butter
        (soft)
1 cup sugar
1 tablespoon orange zest
¼ teaspoon pure almond extract
1 large egg
1⅓ cups all-purpose flour
4 teaspoons baking powder
¼ teaspoon kosher salt
1 cup milk

Preheat the oven to 400°. Line the muffin tins with paper baking cups. Spread ¾ cup of almonds on a cookie sheet and toast them lightly in the oven. Set them aside to cool completely.

Cream the butter, sugar, orange zest, and almond extract together until smooth and light in color. Add the egg and mix until blended. Scrape down the sides of the bowl with a rubber spatula.

Place the toasted almonds and the flour in a food processor; grind to a very fine powder. Add the baking powder and salt and pulse a few times to blend. Stir half the flour mixture into the butter mixture. Add half the milk, then the remaining flour mixture, then the rest of the milk. Mix with a rubber spatula until the batter comes together.

Spoon the batter into 18 muffin cups, filling them to just below the top. Sprinkle the remaining sliced almonds on top of each muffin. Bake until the centers spring back when lightly touched, 30 to 35 minutes.

Cool the muffins in the pans for 5 minutes. Spread a clean kitchen towel on a table, turn the muffin pans on their sides, and tap the muffins out onto the towel. Transfer the muffins to wire racks to finish cooling.

Bran Muffins

Many muffin recipes tell you to stir together the wet and dry ingredients with as few strokes as possible to avoid lumps, air pockets, and other disappointing results. I have always mixed my bran muffins with an electric mixer for a good five minutes. They come out smooth, dense, and richly rewarding

MAKES 12

1¾ cups wheat bran
1 cup currants
1½ cups buttermilk
3 tablespoons unsalted butter (soft)
½ cup sugar
½ cup molasses
2 large eggs
1 teaspoon kosher salt
1 tablespoon baking soda
1⅓ cups all-purpose flour

Toss the wheat bran and currants together in a bowl. Stir in the buttermilk and let the mixture stand about 20 minutes.

Preheat the oven to 375°. Line a muffin tin with paper baking cups.

With an electric mixer, cream the butter, sugar, and molasses together until smooth and light brown. Beat in the eggs one at a time, then add the bran mixture and mix until well blended. Add the salt, baking soda, and flour and mix at medium speed for about 5 minutes. Spoon the batter into 12 baking cups and bake until the centers spring back when lightly touched, about 20 minutes.

Cool the muffins in the pans for 5 minutes. Then spread out a clean kitchen towel, turn the pans on their sides, and tap the muffins out onto the towel. Let the muffins finish cooling on a wire rack.

VARIATION

You may substitute 1 cup chopped prunes and ¾ cup chopped walnuts for the 1 cup currants. Continue with the same directions.

Bran and Pecan Muffins

Toasting bran gives it a deeper, nuttier flavor that I especially like in muffins. Many people don't like the smell of toasting bran and wonder at that point if they are going to like the taste. Don't worry; once it's in the muffins it's delicious.

MAKES 12

1¾ cups wheat bran
¾ cup pecans
3 tablespoons unsalted butter
2 large eggs
½ cup sugar
½ cup dark brown sugar, firmly packed
½ teaspoon vanilla extract
1½ cups buttermilk
1 cup currants
2 teaspoons kosher salt
2 teaspoons baking soda
1¼ cups all-purpose flour

Preheat the oven to 350°. Line a muffin tin with paper baking cups.

Spread the bran out on a cookie sheet and toast it in the oven for 5 minutes. Take the pan out and stir the bran around a bit with your hand. Return it to the oven for another 5 minutes, then set it aside to cool.

Raise the oven temperature to 425°. Chop the pecans coarsely. Melt the butter.

Whisk the eggs and sugars together. Stir in the vanilla and melted butter. Stir in the buttermilk, then the bran and the currants.

Sift the salt and baking soda together and add them to the batter. Add the flour and pecans, and stir until well blended. Fill 12 muffin cups to the top with batter (an ice cream scoop does the job neatly). Put the muffins in the oven and immediately turn the temperature down to 350°. Bake until the tops spring back when lightly touched, about 20 minutes.

Cool the muffins in the pans for 5 minutes. Then spread out a clean kitchen towel, turn the pans on their sides, and tap the muffins out onto the towel. Let the muffins finish cooling on a wire rack.

Date and Oat Bran Muffins

These are substantial muffins, full of dates and nuts and the healthful bulk of oat bran. Serve them warm or at room temperature with butter or preserves.

MAKES 20

*8 tablespoons (¼ pound) unsalted butter
    (soft)
1½ cups pitted dates (about 24 medium
    dates)
½ teaspoon vanilla extract
1 large egg
1 cup oat bran
¾ cup cake flour
4 teaspoons baking powder
¼ teaspoon kosher salt
1 cup milk
1 cup chopped pecans
⅓ cup rolled oats (not quick-cooking)*

Preheat the oven to 400°. Line the muffin tins with paper baking cups.

Cream the butter, dates, and vanilla until the dates have broken up into pea-size pieces. Mix in the egg. Scrape the sides and bottom of the bowl.

Stir the bran, flour, baking powder, and salt together. Stir half into the butter. Add half the milk, then the remaining flour mixture. Add the rest of the milk and the pecans and mix with a rubber spatula until the batter just comes together (there will be a few small lumps).

Spoon the batter into 20 muffin cups, filling each to just below the rim. Sprinkle about 1 teaspoon of rolled oats on top of each muffin. Bake in the middle of the oven until the centers spring back when lightly touched, 25 to 30 minutes.

Cool the muffins in the pans for 5 minutes, then spread a clean kitchen towel on a counter, turn the pans over, and tap the muffins out onto the towel. Finish cooling the muffins on a wire rack.

Walnut Coffee Cake

I don't like very sweet coffee cakes, so I keep the sugar to a minimum in mine. This one is light and pleasantly spicy in the middle.

SERVES 8

*4 tablespoons unsalted butter
½ cup sugar
½ teaspoon vanilla extract
1 large egg
⅔ cup sour cream
1 cup all-purpose flour
1 teaspoon baking powder
1 cup finely chopped walnuts
¼ cup dark brown sugar (loose)
1 teaspoon cinnamon*

Preheat the oven to 375°. Grease a 9-inch round cake pan and line the bottom with a parchment circle.

Melt the butter. Add the sugar and vanilla and mix with an electric mixer until smooth. Add the egg; beat until smooth and light. Stir in the sour cream, then the flour and baking powder. Mix at medium speed until the batter is smooth. Do not overmix; if you do the vegetable gum in the sour cream will make the batter gummy. Set the batter aside.

To make the filling, rub the walnuts, brown sugar, and cinnamon together; be sure you break up any lumps and mix the ingredients well.

Spread half the batter in the prepared pan. Spread the walnut filling evenly over the batter, leaving a ½-inch border around the edge. Gently pat the filling down. Cover the filling with the remaining batter by dropping spoonfuls first around the edges, then spooning the rest into the middle. Spread the batter gently with the back of a spoon until the filling is evenly covered. This step takes care and patience.

Bake the coffee cake in the middle of the oven until the sides begin to pull away from the pan and a knife inserted in the center comes out clean, about 35 minutes. Cool in the pan on a wire rack, then turn out onto a plate.

Almond and Fig Coffee Cake

Almond paste in the batter brings out and complements the flavor of the figs in this unusual coffee cake. I like to serve it for brunch or in a breakfast bread basket with toasted homemade bread and crumpets. Do not substitute marzipan for the almond paste; it is too sweet.

SERVES 8

1½ cups dried mission figs
1 cup milk
8 tablespoons (¼ pound) unsalted butter
     (soft)
¼ cup almond paste
1 tablespoon sugar
2 large eggs
2 cups all-purpose flour
1 tablespoon baking powder
1 teaspoon kosher salt
½ cup sliced almonds

Preheat the oven to 375°. Butter and flour a 9-inch round cake pan or springform pan.

Chop the figs into ½-inch chunks. Combine them with the milk in a medium saucepan and bring it just to a simmer over moderate heat. Set aside to cool.

Mix the butter in a large bowl with the almond paste and sugar until smooth and light. Add the eggs and beat until blended. Sift together the flour, baking powder, and salt. Fold the dry ingredients and milk mixture into the butter mixture.

Spoon the batter into the prepared pan. Spread it evenly, smooth the top, and sprinkle on the sliced almonds. Bake in the lower middle of the oven until a knife inserted in the center comes out clean, about 40 minutes. Cool on a wire rack for about 45 minutes, then turn out onto a serving plate. Cut in wedges to serve.

Apple Coffee Cake

Soft apples such as Yellow Delicious, Royal Gala, McIntosh, or Rome Beauty are best for this cake. It's wonderful made fresh in the morning and served warm from the oven, but it's also fine served at room temperature.

SERVES 12

½ cup light brown sugar, firmly packed
1⅔ cups plus 3 tablespoons all-purpose flour
½ teaspoon cinnamon
11 tablespoons unsalted butter (soft)
2 medium-size soft apples
½ cup sugar
⅓ cup quick-cooking oats (not instant or old-fashioned)
1 tablespoon baking powder
¾ teaspoon kosher salt
¾ cup milk
2 large eggs
1 teaspoon vanilla extract
½ cup sliced natural (skin on) almonds

Preheat the oven to 350°. Butter the sides and bottom of a 9- × 13-inch baking pan.

For the topping, combine the brown sugar, 3 tablespoons of flour, the cinnamon, and 3 tablespoons of butter in a bowl. Mix with a fork until crumbly. Set aside.

Peel, quarter, and core the apples. Cut each quarter vertically into 3 wedges. Cut the wedges crosswise into thirds.

Combine all of the remaining ingredients except the almonds in a large mixing bowl. Mix with an electric mixer at low speed until the dry ingredients are well moistened. Mix at medium speed for 2 minutes. Pour the batter into the prepared pan. Arrange the apple chunks over the batter, then sprinkle the almonds on top. Spoon the topping evenly over all.

Bake until the sides of the cake begin to pull away from the pan and the top springs back when lightly touched, about 55 minutes. Cool in the pan on a wire rack for 15 minutes.

Place a dinner plate upside down on top of the cake; invert pan and plate together. Remove the pan. Place a second plate over the bottom of the cake and turn it right side up; remove the top plate. Wrap the cake until ready to serve.

Walnut Sticky Buns

These nutty, cinnamony buns are wonderful with an afternoon cup of tea or coffee. And, of course, they make any breakfast special.

MAKES 12

¾ cup milk
½ cup sugar
2 teaspoons (1 envelope) active dry yeast
½ teaspoon kosher salt
1 large egg, beaten
8 tablespoons (¼ pound) unsalted butter
        (soft)
2½ cups bread flour
½ teaspoon cinnamon
1 cup dark brown sugar, firmly packed
2 tablespoons honey
1 tablespoon all-purpose flour
2 cups walnut pieces
12 walnut halves

Place an oven shelf in the lowest position. Butter a 12-muffin muffin tin.

Warm the milk until lukewarm (about 110°) and stir in the sugar. Add the yeast and let the mixture stand until a foamy yeast raft forms on top, 5 to 10 minutes. Blend in the salt and egg. Melt 2 tablespoons of the butter and stir it in. Stir in the bread flour. Mix until the dough comes together and is elastic. (If mixing by hand, knead the dough until it is smooth and elastic.) Shape the dough into a ball and put it in a greased bowl; cover the bowl and let the dough rise in a warm, draft-free place until double in volume, about 1 hour.

Meanwhile, prepare the filling. Blend the cinnamon, brown sugar, and remaining butter until smooth. Add the honey and all-purpose flour and mix until blended. Set aside.

Punch down the dough. On a lightly floured surface roll it into a 12- × 8-inch rectangle; spread half of the filling over it. Cover the filling with the walnut pieces, pressing them gently into the dough. Roll the rectangle into a 12-inch-long log. Cut the log crosswise into 12 equal slices.

Divide the remaining filling equally among the 12 cups of the muffin tin. Press a walnut half into each cup and top with a slice of the log. Cover the pan with a damp towel and let it stand until the dough doubles in volume, 35 to 45 minutes.

Preheat the oven to 375°. Bake the buns until the tops are golden brown, about 20 minutes. Turn them out onto a sheet of parchment to cool. Serve upside down.

Potato Biscuits

Warm biscuits with butter slowly melting into them make any breakfast special. These potato biscuits are moist inside and crusty on the bottom. They can be made the night before and reheated for breakfast in just 10 minutes.

MAKES 15

1 medium baking potato
2 cups all-purpose flour
2 teaspoons baking powder
½ teaspoon kosher salt
4 tablespoons unsalted butter (cold)
1 large egg
⅔ cup milk

Wash and peel the potato and cut it into 2-inch chunks. Cook them in salted water until tender. Drain them, mash them until they are free of lumps, and set them aside to cool. Preheat the oven to 425°.

Blend the flour, baking powder, and salt in a large bowl. Add the potatoes and gently rub them into the flour with your hands. Cut the butter into small pieces and rub it into the flour.

Beat the egg. Stir the milk into it and add it to the flour mixture; mix only until blended. Turn the dough out onto a heavily floured surface. Dust the top of the dough with more flour and press or roll it to a ¾-inch thickness. Cut out biscuits with a 2½-inch round pastry cutter. Place the biscuits ½ inch apart on greased cookie sheets. Press the scraps of dough together and continue cutting. Bake the biscuits in the upper third of the oven until they are light brown, 20 to 25 minutes. Serve warm, with butter.

You can make the biscuits up to 2 days ahead, but they should be served warm, so reheat them for 10 minutes in a 375° oven before serving.

Onion-Walnut Biscuits

These savory biscuits will fill your kitchen with tantalizing aromas, especially appreciated on cold winter mornings. I like them any time, for supper as well as for breakfast

MAKES 15

1 medium baking potato
½ medium red onion
6 tablespoons unsalted butter (cold)
2 cups all-purpose flour
2 teaspoons baking powder
½ teaspoon kosher salt
1 large egg
⅔ cup milk
½ cup chopped walnuts

Wash and peel the potato and cut it into 2-inch chunks. Cook them in salted water until tender. Drain, then mash them until they are free of lumps, and set them aside to cool.

Peel and dice the onion. Melt 2 tablespoons of butter in a saucepan and sauté the onion until glossy but not browned. Set it aside to cool. Preheat the oven to 425°.

Blend the flour, baking powder, and salt in a large bowl. Add the potatoes and gently rub them into the flour with your hands. Cut the remaining butter into small pieces and rub it into the flour.

Beat the egg. Stir the milk into it and add it to the flour mixture. Pour the onion and nuts over the top and fold with a wide rubber spatula just until all the ingredients are blended.

Turn the dough out onto a heavily floured surface. Dust the top of the dough with more flour and press or roll it to a ¾-inch thickness. Cut out biscuits with a 2½-inch round pastry cutter. Place the biscuits ½ inch apart on greased cookie sheets. Press the scraps of dough together and continue cutting. Bake the biscuits in the upper third of the oven until they are light brown, 20 to 25 minutes. Serve warm, with butter.

You can make the biscuits up to 2 days ahead, but they should be served warm, so reheat them for 10 minutes in a 375° oven before serving.

Charleston Scones

Long before there was a United States the British were enjoying scones with their afternoon tea. Today scones are popular throughout America. These particular scones remind me of some wonderful biscuits I ate in South Carolina—they're crisp on the top and bottom, light and flaky inside. I like them best with butter and homemade preserves. Since they are rather small, each person will probably want three or four.

MAKES ABOUT 14

1 tablespoon plus 2 teaspoons sugar
1 cup all-purpose flour
¾ cup cake flour
½ teaspoon kosher salt
2 teaspoons baking powder
½ teaspoon orange zest, finely grated or
      chopped
½ cup currants
8 tablespoons (¼ pound) unsalted butter
      (cold)
½ cup milk (cold)

Place 1 tablespoon of the sugar on a small plate and set it aside. Combine the remaining dry ingredients with the orange zest and currants in a bowl. Cut the butter into 8 pieces and add it. Mix with the paddle attachment of an electric mixer or by hand until the pieces of butter are about the size of raspberries. (If mixing by hand, toss the butter and dry ingredients, then press the butter between thumbs and fingers to break it up.) Add the milk and mix only until it is absorbed. Press the dough gently against the bowl with your hand until it comes together.

FOOD PROCESSOR METHOD

Place 1 tablespoon of the sugar on a small plate and set it aside. Pulse the remaining dry ingredients to combine them. Cut the butter into 8 pieces and add it to the work bowl. Pulse until the pieces of butter are the size of raspberries. Transfer the mixture to a bowl. Add the orange zest and currants. Stir in the milk just until it is absorbed, then press the dough against the bowl with your hands until it comes together.

On a lightly floured surface, roll the dough out to about a ¾-inch thickness. Cut out scones with a 2-inch round cutter (a small juice or wineglass lightly dipped in flour works very well). Gently press any leftover dough together and continue cutting out rounds until the dough is all used. Touch the top of each round to the reserved sugar to coat it lightly. (You will probably have some sugar left over.) Line a cookie sheet with parchment and arrange the scones on it, about 1 inch apart. Chill for 15 minutes.

Preheat the oven to 375°. Bake the scones until light brown, about 20 minutes. Serve warm or at room temperature with butter and Strawberry-Rhubarb Compote (see page 200), or other homemade preserves.

Oat Scones

Oats in one form or another have always had an honored place on the American breakfast table. Since the discovery that oat bran helps to lower cholesterol, they have zoomed to new levels of popularity. I recommend these scones for breakfast because they are light and delicious. The fact that the oats are also good for you is a bonus.

MAKES ABOUT 14

1 cup plus 2 teaspoons rolled oats
1 cup all-purpose flour
3 tablespoons sugar
½ teaspoon kosher salt
1 tablespoon baking powder
1 teaspoon lemon zest, finely chopped
½ cup golden raisins
8 tablespoons (¼ pound) unsalted butter
    (cold)
½ cup half-and-half (cold)

Set aside 2 tablespoons of oats. Combine the remaining dry ingredients in a bowl with the lemon zest and raisins. Cut the butter into 8 pieces and add it. Mix with the paddle attachment of an electric mixer or by hand until the pieces of butter are the size of raspberries. (If mixing by hand, toss the butter with the dry ingredients, then press it between thumbs and fingers to break it up.) Add the half-and-half and mix just until it is absorbed. Press the dough gently against the bottom of the bowl with your hand until it comes together.

FOOD PROCESSOR METHOD

Set aside 2 teaspoons of oats. Pulse the remaining dry ingredients to combine them. Cut the butter into 8 pieces and add it to the work bowl. Pulse until the pieces of butter are the size of raspberries. Transfer to a bowl. Add the lemon zest and raisins. Stir in the half-and-half just until it is absorbed, then press the dough gently against the bottom of the bowl until it comes together.

On a lightly floured surface, press the dough into a 7- × 7-inch square; it should be about ½ inch thick. Cut the dough into rounds with a 2-inch round cutter dipped in flour. Gently press any leftover dough together and continue cutting rounds until all the dough is used. Sprinkle the reserved oats on top of the scones and press them lightly into the dough.

Line a cookie sheet with parchment and arrange the scones on it about 1 inch apart. Chill for 15 minutes.

Preheat the oven to 375°. Bake until the scones are light brown, about 20 minutes. Serve warm or at room temperature, with butter and homemade preserves or Strawberry-Rhubarb Compote (see page 200).

Crumpets

This is an American version of the popular English crumpet, with baking powder replacing the yeast and baking soda in the English original. Cooking the little cakes twice, once on the griddle and once in the toaster, makes them moist and soft in the center and crusty on the outside.

MAKES 6 OR 7

2 tablespoons plus 1 teaspoon vegetable
    shortening
2 teaspoons sugar
½ teaspoon kosher salt
1 large egg
¾ cup lowfat milk
¾ cup all-purpose flour
½ cup whole wheat flour
2 teaspoons baking powder

Combine 2 tablespoons of the shortening with the sugar and salt in a large bowl. Mix at low speed with an electric mixer until crumbly. Beat in the egg and milk. Combine the flours and baking powder and add to the bowl. Mix until smooth.

Rub a griddle or large heavy skillet with the remaining shortening. Heat it over low heat for 3 minutes, or until a hand held 2 inches above the surface feels warm within 5 seconds. (If using an electric skillet, set it at 300°.) For each crumpet, spoon ¼ cup of the batter onto the griddle, flattening and spreading it to about 3 inches in diameter and ¾ inch thick. Allow about 1 inch between crumpets. (It may be necessary to cook them in batches.)

Cook the crumpets until the bottoms are light brown, about 4 minutes, then turn. Press gently to flatten them slightly. Cook until light brown on the second side, about 4 minutes. Let cool on a wire rack, then wrap and refrigerate. Split and toast before serving. Serve warm with a little butter and honey or homemade preserves.

Blueberry Pancakes

Pancakes are supremely adaptable. By adding spices, nuts, or fruit to the batter you can vary them endlessly. In autumn I like pancakes studded with nuggets of apple (see page 196). In summer, I fold in fresh, plump blueberries. Pancakes are easy to make, so long as you are careful not to overmix the batter or make the griddle too hot. They will be gummy inside if you cook them too fast.

MAKES 16

2 cups cake flour
¼ cup sugar
2 teaspoons baking powder
½ teaspoon kosher salt
½ teaspoon baking soda
1½ cups buttermilk
3 tablespoons unsalted butter (melted)
2 large eggs, beaten
1½ cups fresh blueberries
4 tablespoons clarified butter (see page 13)

Combine the dry ingredients. Add the buttermilk and mix with an electric mixer or by hand until the batter is free of lumps. Stir in the melted butter, then the eggs. Fold in the blueberries. You should have about 3 cups of batter.

Heat a skillet or griddle over medium heat; when it is hot, add 1 tablespoon of clarified butter. The pan is ready when a little batter dropped onto the surface sizzles. Spoon the batter on to form circles 4 to 5 inches in diameter. Flip each pancake when it begins to get dry around the edges and the bubbles that rise to its surface start to burst. As you remove each finished pancake, carefully wipe the pan with a paper towel to prevent crumbs from burning and staining; add more butter as needed.

Serve immediately, with pure New England maple syrup.

Buckwheat-Apple Pancakes

We tend to think of buckwheat as Russian, imparting its special flavor to delicate *blini* topped with sour cream and caviar. In fact, buckwheat pancakes have been popular in America for centuries, especially as a fortifying wintertime breakfast. I like to add sautéed apples to provide contrasting texture and flavor.

MAKES 16

2 medium, tart apples peeled, cored, and cut
*   into ½-inch chunks (about 2 cups)*
5 tablespoons unsalted butter
1½ cups cake flour
½ cup buckwheat flour
¼ cup sugar
2 teaspoons baking powder
½ teaspoon kosher salt
½ teaspoon baking soda
1½ cups buttermilk
2 large eggs
4 tablespoons clarified butter (see page 13)

To tenderize the apple chunks and keep them from turning brown, sauté them in 2 tablespoons of butter for 1 minute over medium-high heat. Set them aside. Melt the remaining butter.

Stir the dry ingredients together. Add the buttermilk and mix with an electric mixer or by hand until the batter is free of lumps. Stir in the melted butter, then the eggs. Fold in the apple chunks with their butter. You should have about 3 cups of batter.

Heat a skillet or griddle over medium heat; when it is hot, add 1 tablespoon of clarified butter. The pan is ready when a little batter dropped onto the surface sizzles. Spoon the batter on to form circles 4 to 5 inches in diameter. Flip each pancake when it begins to get dry around the edges and the bubbles that rise to its surface start to burst. As you remove each finished pancake, carefully wipe the pan with a paper towel to prevent crumbs from burning and staining; add more butter as needed.

Serve the pancakes immediately, with pure New England maple syrup.

Sour Cream Waffles

I like to serve these light, crisp waffles topped with pure maple syrup or cut-up fresh fruit.

MAKES 8 TO 10 WAFFLES

8 tablespoons (¼ pound) unsalted butter
4 large eggs
½ cup sugar
¾ cup half-and-half
¼ cup sour cream
1¾ cups cake flour
1 tablespoon baking powder
¼ teaspoon kosher salt

Melt the butter in a small saucepan and keep it warm until needed.

Separate the eggs. Whip the whites with ¼ cup of sugar to soft peaks; set aside.

Blend together the yolks, half-and-half, sour cream, and the remaining ¼ cup of sugar. Sift together the flour, baking powder, and salt and stir them into the cream mixture until smooth and free of lumps. Blend in the melted butter and fold in the egg whites. Keep the batter covered in the refrigerator until ready to use.

Preheat the waffle iron. Spoon enough batter in the center to spread halfway to the edges of the iron. Lower the top; the batter will spread to the edges. Cook until golden brown. Do not press on the iron during cooking; it will make the waffle collapse. Serve waffles hot.

Buckwheat Waffles

Buckwheat gives waffles a faint nutty flavor that goes especially well with apples or other winter fruits. I serve them topped with apples—sautéed in butter until tender—and a dollop of sour cream.

MAKES 8 TO 10 WAFFLES

8 tablespoons (¼ pound) unsalted butter
4 large eggs
½ cup sugar
¾ cup half-and-half
¼ cup sour cream
1 cup cake flour
¾ cup buckwheat flour
1 tablespoon baking powder
¼ teaspoon kosher salt

Melt the butter in a small saucepan and keep it warm until needed.

Separate the eggs. Whip the whites with ¼ cup of sugar to soft peaks; set aside.

Blend together the yolks, half-and-half, sour cream, and the remaining ¼ cup of sugar. Sift together the flours, baking powder, and salt and stir them into the cream mixture until smooth and free of lumps. Blend in the butter and fold in the egg whites. Keep the batter covered in the refrigerator until ready to use.

Preheat the waffle iron. Spoon enough batter in the center to spread halfway to the edges of the iron. Lower the top; the batter will spread to the edges. Cook until golden brown. Do not press on the iron during cooking; it will make the waffles collapse. Serve waffles hot.

Breakfast Bars

These are nothing like the packaged "breakfast bars" sold in supermarkets. They are soft, moist, and brimming with fruit and nuts. They are nutritious, extremely convenient, and keep well in the refrigerator. Kids will love them as an after-school snack. I like them toasted.

MAKES 16

3 tablespoons unsalted butter (soft)
⅔ cup dark brown sugar, firmly packed
2 large eggs
1¾ cups wheat bran
1 cup buttermilk
1 cup all-purpose flour
2 teaspoons baking soda

½ teaspoon kosher salt
1 cup chopped walnuts
¾ cup currants
¾ cup dried figs, in ½-inch chunks
         or prunes

Preheat the oven to 375°. Butter a 13- × 9- × 2-inch rectangular baking pan.

Combine the butter, sugar, eggs, bran, buttermilk, flour, baking soda, and salt in a large bowl. Beat with an electric mixer at medium speed just until mixed. Stir the walnuts, currants, and figs or prunes in with a spoon. Spread the batter evenly in the pan.

Bake until the edges are lightly browned, about 20 minutes. Cool completely in the pan on a wire rack. Cut into sixteen 4½- × 1½-inch bars. Wrap the bars individually in plastic wrap and store them in the refrigerator.

VARIATIONS   You may substitute oat bran, rice bran, or lightly toasted wheat germ for the wheat bran. You may substitute raisins and chopped dried apples, golden raisins and chopped dried apricots, or golden raisins and chopped dates for the currants and chopped figs.

Apricot and Cornmeal Breakfast Bars

These tasty morning bars are highly nutritious without the bran content of those in the previous recipe. The basic texture is like corn bread.

MAKES 16

1 cup dried apricot halves, cut in eighths
1¾ cups lowfat milk
¾ cup yellow cornmeal
4 tablespoons unsalted butter (soft)
½ cup sugar
1 teaspoon vanilla extract
2 large eggs
1¼ cups all-purpose flour
1 tablespoon baking powder
½ teaspoon kosher salt
1 cup sliced natural (skin on) almonds

Preheat the oven to 400°. Butter a 13- × 9- × 2-inch rectangular baking pan and dust it with flour.

Place the apricots and milk in a small saucepan. Bring the milk to a boil, then remove it from the heat. Stir the cornmeal in until smooth. Cool the mixture to room temperature, stirring occasionally.

Cream the butter, sugar, and vanilla with an electric mixer. Stir in the cornmeal mixture. Beat in the eggs. Combine the flour, baking powder, and salt. Add the flour mixture and the almonds to the batter and mix at low speed until the dry ingredients are just moistened. Spread the batter evenly in the prepared pan.

Bake until the top begins to brown and the sides begin to pull away from the pan, about 20 minutes. Cool completely in the pan on a wire rack. Cut into sixteen 4½- × 1½-inch bars. Wrap the bars individually in plastic wrap and store them in the refrigerator.

Strawberry-Rhubarb Compote

This thick, slightly tart compote can be spread on scones or muffins like preserves or eaten by itself, plain or with a splash of fresh cream. It also works well as a filling for layer cakes (see Rhubarb and White Chocolate Cake, page 99). If your rhubarb is particularly tart you may want to add more sugar to the recipe. Taste the compote before taking it off the heat and stir in sugar if needed.

MAKES 1 QUART

1¾ pounds rhubarb
1 pint strawberries
1¼ cups sugar

Wash the rhubarb and cut off the ends, including any green (the leaves of rhubarb are poisonous). Do not peel; all the beautiful red color is in the skin. Cut the stalks into 1-inch lengths. You should have 4 to 4½ cups. Set aside. Wash the strawberries. Cut small berries in half, large berries in quarters.

Toss the rhubarb with the sugar and put it in the top of a double boiler over simmering water. Cook uncovered, stirring occasionally, until the rhubarb is quite soft and light in color, about 20 minutes. Add the strawberries and cook 10 minutes more, stirring occasionally.

Transfer the compote to a bowl or jar and allow it to cool to room temperature. When cool, cover and refrigerate.

Braided Egg and Saffron Bread

Saffron gives this bread a warm golden color and a subtle but distinctive flavor. Although expensive, it's worth the price for a special occasion. Don't skimp; if you do, you will get saffron color, but not saffron flavor.

MAKES 1 LARGE LOAF

1½ cups milk
2 teaspoons (1 envelope) active dry yeast
1 tablespoon sugar
2 teaspoons saffron threads
4¼ cups all-purpose flour
1 tablespoon kosher salt
1 large egg plus 1 egg white
8 tablespoons (¼ pound) unsalted butter (soft)

Heat the milk to 110°. Add the yeast, sugar, and saffron. Let the mixture stand until a yeast raft forms on top, about 10 minutes. Add 3 cups of flour and the salt. Mix until the dough is smooth and elastic. Add the whole egg, butter, and remaining flour. Mix until the dough is again smooth and elastic. Shape it into a ball and let it rise in a lightly oiled bowl covered with plastic wrap until double in volume, 1 to 1½ hours.

Punch the dough down and divide it into thirds. Shape each third into a patty, then roll it into a log with your hands. Continue rolling each log until it is a strand 18 inches long. Line up the strands side by side. Fuse the tops and braid the strands (see illustration).

Place the braided dough on a parchment-lined cookie sheet and brush the top with egg white. Cover the loaf with plastic wrap and let it rise until double in volume, 45 to 60 minutes.

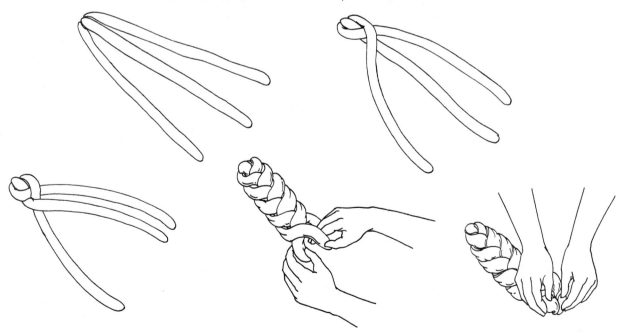

Preheat the oven to 375°. Bake the bread on the lower shelf until it is golden brown and sounds hollow when tapped on the bottom, 35 to 40 minutes. Cool on a wire rack before cutting.

Easter Bread

This rich holiday bread is filled with rum-soaked apricots and almond paste. Although it is traditional for Easter, it is delicious at any time of year.

MAKES 1 LARGE LOAF

½ cup rum
8 ounces dried apricots
¾ cup milk
4 teaspoons (2 envelopes) active dry yeast
3 tablespoons sugar
2 cups all-purpose flour
2 teaspoons kosher salt
1 large egg, beaten
10 tablespoons unsalted butter (cold)
4 ounces almond paste

Bring the rum and apricots to a simmer in a small saucepan. Remove the pan from the heat and let it stand until cool.

Heat the milk to lukewarm—not above 110°. Pour it into a medium bowl and stir in the yeast and sugar. Let the mixture stand until a yeast raft forms on top, 3 to 4 minutes. Stir in 1 cup of flour. Cover the bowl with plastic wrap and let it stand until the batter doubles in volume, about 1 hour.

Add the remaining flour, the salt, and the beaten egg. Mix until the dough is soft and elastic. Pound the butter with a rolling pin until it is soft. Roll the dough into an 8- × 12-inch rectangle. Cover half the surface with pieces of butter. Fold the other half over the butter and press the edges together; fold the sealed edge under the dough. Roll the dough into a 10- × 18-inch rectangle. Rotate the dough a quarter turn, fold it into thirds, wrap it in plastic wrap, and refrigerate 10 minutes. Roll it out to 10 × 18 inches again, turn, fold into thirds, and refrigerate again. Roll and fold the dough one more time, wrap it, and refrigerate it for 20 to 30 minutes. Each time you roll the dough, dust the top with flour as needed; brush the flour away before folding.

Drain the apricots and discard the rum. Chop the apricots and set them aside. Roll the dough to 8 × 12 inches and cover it with apricots. Crumble the almond paste evenly over the top. With your hands, roll the dough into a 12-inch-long log. Line a cookie sheet with parchment and place the log on it, seam side down. With a sharp knife, slash the loaf almost end to end, cutting about halfway through the loaf. Let it stand for 20 minutes.

Preheat the oven to 350°. Bake the bread until dark golden brown, about 30 minutes. Let it stand 15 minutes before serving. Serve warm or at room temperature.

Whole Wheat Farmer's Bread

This hearty and delicious bread is based on a starter, which takes two days to develop. So be sure to begin two days before you want to bake. Besides making the bread rise, the starter adds flavor, keeps the bread moist, and acts as a preservative. I like to form my loaves in reed baskets called *bannetons;* they are made in Hong Kong and are available in many cookware shops.

MAKES 2 LOAVES

1¾ cups warm water
Pinch of active dry yeast
1½ cups whole wheat flour
2½ cups bread flour
½ cup all-purpose flour
1½ tablespoons kosher salt
Cornmeal, for dusting

Prepare a starter 2 days in advance: Mix 1 cup of warm water, a pinch of yeast, and ½ cup each whole wheat and bread flour in a 6-cup bowl. Scrape down the sides of the bowl, cover it with plastic wrap, and let it stand in a warm place until the following day.

On the second day add ⅜ cup warm water, ½ cup whole wheat flour, 1 cup bread flour, and ¼ cup all-purpose flour to the starter. Stir, cover, and set aside in a warm place until the next day.

On the third day you are ready to bake. First, inspect the starter by smelling it; it should smell pungent and sweet. If it smells rancid or rotten, you have captured bad bacteria and the starter must be thrown away. Next, check to be sure the yeast is active. If it is, the starter will be foamy. If the night was warm, liquid may have formed on top of the starter. If so, tip the bowl until you can see the flour sponge beneath the liquid. Run a spoon slowly through the sponge, watching for bubbles as you go. The bubbles show that the yeast is active and your starter is ready to use. If the yeast is not active, you will have to throw the starter away and begin again.

Put 2 cups of starter in a mixing bowl. Add the remaining ⅜ cup of warm water, ½ cup whole wheat flour, and ¼ cup all-purpose flour. Mix until all the ingredients are blended, about 2 minutes on an electric mixer. Add the remaining 1 cup of bread flour and the salt. Mix until the dough is slighty elastic, about 5 minutes.

Take the dough out of the mixer and knead it on a lightly floured surface until it is smooth and elastic, about 10 minutes. Place it in a lightly greased bowl and cover it with a damp cloth. Let it stand in a warm place (80° to 90°) until it has doubled in volume, about 3 hours.

Turn the dough out onto a lightly floured surface and divide it in half. Form each half into a round loaf. Put each loaf in a floured circular basket or a lightly oiled bowl. Cover them with a damp towel and let them rise in a warm place until the volume has increased by 50 percent, about 2 hours.

Place an oven shelf in the lowest position and set a large bread stone or a heavy cookie sheet on it. Preheat the oven to 500°. When the stone or sheet is heated, dust it lightly and evenly with cornmeal and turn the loaves gently onto it. Score the tops of the loaves with a thin, sharp knife or a single-edged razor blade. Using a spray bottle, mist the loaves and oven with water until the loaves are slightly wet. Close the oven and wait 5 minutes, then mist again.

Bake for 5 minutes, then reduce the oven temperature to 400°. Bake until the loaves are well browned, 35 to 45 minutes. To test the bread for doneness, tap on the bottom; it should sound hollow. Cool the loaves on a wire rack.

Walnut-Raisin Bread

This is a nice variation on the Whole Wheat Farmer's Bread on page 203. The raisins make it slightly sweet and the walnuts give it crunch. It's great toasted and buttered or with jam.

MAKES 2 LOAVES

1¾ cups warm water
Pinch of active dry yeast
1½ cups whole wheat flour
2½ cups bread flour
½ cup all-purpose flour
1½ tablespoons kosher salt
1½ cups walnuts, coarsely chopped
1½ cups raisins
Cornmeal, for dusting

Follow the instructions for Whole Wheat Farmer's Bread (above), adding the walnuts and raisins with the last of the bread flour and the salt.

Orange-Walnut Bread

This is a rich, slightly sweet yeast bread, dotted with fragrant walnuts and orange peel. It is wonderful as is or toasted, especially with butter and jam. I suggest that you make a full recipe of candied orange peel, use a third of it in the bread, and keep the rest on hand.

MAKES 1 LOAF

⅔ cup water
1 cup milk
1 tablespoon sugar
2 teaspoons (1 envelope) active dry yeast
⅓ recipe candied orange peel (page 211)
1 cup chopped walnuts
1 cup chopped prunes (optional)
2 tablespoons unsalted butter (melted)
1 teaspoon kosher salt
4 cups bread flour

Combine the water and milk and heat them until warm to the touch. Add the sugar and yeast and let the mixture stand until the yeast rises and forms a raft on top, about 10 minutes.

Drain the orange peel and add it to the yeast mixture. Add the walnuts, and prunes if desired, and melted butter. Combine the salt and flour and add them. Continue mixing until the dough is smooth and elastic. Shape it into a ball and place it in a large oiled bowl. Cover the bowl with plastic wrap or a damp towel. Set it in a warm place until the dough doubles in volume. Punch it down and shape it into a loaf. Place it in a lightly oiled loaf pan and cover it with a damp towel. Set it in a warm place until the dough almost doubles again.

Preheat the oven to 350°. Bake the bread until it is golden brown and sounds hollow when tapped on the bottom. Remove the loaf from the pan and let it cool on a wire rack for 2 hours.

Focaccia with Sun-Dried Tomatos and Garlic

Focaccia is an Italian flat bread that is liberally anointed with olive oil before baking and is frequently flavored with herbs or vegetables. This version has sun-dried tomatoes and garlic scattered on top. Simply cut it into squares and enjoy it as is, or split it and fill it for spectacular sandwiches.

MAKES 15 SQUARES

4 teaspoons (2 envelopes) active dry yeast
1 teaspoon sugar
1 cup warm water (110°)

¾ cup olive oil
4 teaspoons kosher salt
2¼ cups all-purpose flour
1½ cups sun-dried tomatoes (not in oil)
4 medium garlic cloves

Dissolve the yeast and sugar in the warm water; let the mixture stand until a yeast raft forms on top, about 10 minutes. In a large bowl combine the yeast mixture with 6 tablespoons of olive oil, 2 teaspoons of salt, and the flour. Mix until the dough is smooth and elastic. Shape it into a ball and let it rise in a lightly oiled bowl covered with plastic wrap until double in volume, 1 to 1½ hours.

Blanch the tomatoes in 2 cups of boiling water for 2 to 3 minutes. Drain them and set them aside to cool. Peel and chop the garlic. Heat ¼ cup of olive oil in a small saucepan. Add the garlic and cook for 30 seconds. Remove from the heat and let cool. Cut the tomatoes into thin slices.

Grease a 10- × 15-inch cookie sheet with the remaining 2 tablespoons of olive oil. Punch down the dough and press it into the cookie sheet. Cover it with a damp kitchen towel and let it rise until double in volume, 45 to 60 minutes.

Preheat the oven to 450°. Press dents in the dough every inch or so over the entire surface with your fingertips. Spoon the garlic in oil over the top. Scatter the tomatoes evenly over the oil and sprinkle on the remaining 2 teaspoons of salt. Bake the bread until golden brown, 20 to 25 minutes. Cut it into 3-inch squares before serving. Serve warm.

Raspberry Turnovers

I add a small amount of tapioca to the raspberry filling. It prevents the juice of the berries from creating steam that can push the fruit from the shell, leaving an empty turnover.

MAKES 12

1 pint raspberries
⅔ cup sugar plus more for sprinkling
2 teaspoons quick-cooking tapioca
½ recipe Puff Pastry (page 50), cold
1 egg white

Wash the berries by submerging them in cold water. Drain carefully in a sieve or colander. Divide the berries in half. Dry half on towels and place them in a bowl. Cover and refrigerate until needed. Purée the remaining half, then pass them through a sieve into a bowl;

discard the seeds. Stir the sugar and tapioca into the purée. Let stand 10 minutes. Cook over slowly boiling water, stirring occasionally. When the tapioca has dissolved and thickened the purée, about 20 minutes, remove it from the heat and cool it over ice water.

Gently fold the berries, without crushing them, into the purée. Refrigerate until needed.

Dust a work surface lightly with flour. Remove the dough from the refrigerator, cut it in half, and place half in the center of the flour. Cover and refrigerate the other half. Dust the top of the dough with flour and roll it into a 10- × 15-inch rectangle, keeping the top and bottom lightly dusted with flour. With a soft brush, gently brush the top and bottom free of all flour. Cut the dough into six 5-inch squares. Using the edge of a rubber scraper or any stiff straight edge, gently mark each square with a shallow diagonal crease dividing it into 2 triangles.

Spoon 2 tablespoons of the raspberry filling onto each square, centering it on one of the triangles created by the crease. Spread the filling with a spoon, leaving about ½ inch on all 3 sides. Brush the egg white along the outside edge of the empty triangle, then fold it over the filled half and press the edges together with your fingers. Space the turnovers on parchment-lined cookie sheets, keeping them 1 inch apart. Brush the tops with egg white and lightly sprinkle with sugar. Chill until needed.

Roll out the other half of the dough and make 6 more turnovers. Chill 15 minutes. Preheat the oven to 400°.

Remove the turnovers from the refrigerator. Use a small sharp knife to cut a hole in the top center of each turnover. Place them in the oven and reduce the heat to 375°. Bake until golden brown, 30 to 40 minutes. Set aside to cool for 20 minutes before serving or cool completely, cover, and refrigerate until ready to serve. The turnovers may be reheated on a cookie sheet in a preheated 350° oven for 10 to 12 minutes.

Blueberry Turnovers

As children growing up in the rural lakes region of New Hampshire, my identical twin brother, Dan, and I would spend early summer mornings picking the wild blueberries that grew along the old stone walls lining the fields of our home. We'd return to our mother's kitchen with the promise of something blueberry for breakfast. Extra berries were delivered to our father's hotel pastry chef Lillian Drake, who would turn them into delicately light and tender turnovers. My turnover recipe was created from the memory of Lillian's perfection.

MAKES 12

1 pint blueberries
⅓ cup sugar

1 tablespoon quick-cooking tapioca
1 teaspoon lemon juice
½ recipe Puff Pastry (page 50)
1 egg white

Wash the berries by submerging them in cold water. Drain in a sieve or colander. Divide the berries in half. Dry half on towels and place them in a bowl. Cover and refrigerate until needed. Purée the remaining half. In a medium-size bowl, stir the sugar, tapioca, and lemon juice into the purée. Let stand 10 minutes. Cook over slowly boiling water, stirring occasionally. When the tapioca has dissolved and thickened the purée, about 20 minutes, remove it from the heat and cool it over ice water.

Gently fold the remaining berries into the chilled purée. Cover and refrigerate until needed.

Dust a work surface lightly with flour. Cut the dough in half and place half in the center of the flour. Dust the top of the dough with flour and roll it into a 10- × 15-inch rectangle, dusting the dough with flour when needed. Using a soft brush, gently brush the flour from the top and bottom of the dough. Cut it into six 5-inch squares. Press a diagonal crease in each one with a stiff rubber scraper or any stiff straight edge.

Spoon 2 tablespoons of blueberry filling onto the center of each square, centering it on one of the triangles created by the crease. Spread the filling with a spoon, leaving about ½ inch on all three sides. Brush egg white along the outside edges of the empty triangle, fold it over the filling, and press the edges together with your fingers. Space the turnovers on parchment-lined cookie sheets, keeping them 1 inch apart. Brush the tops with egg white and lightly sprinkle with sugar. Chill until ready to bake.

Roll out the other half of the dough and make 6 more turnovers. Chill 15 minutes. Preheat the oven to 400°.

Remove the turnovers from the refrigerator. Use a small sharp knife to cut a hole in the top center of each turnover. Place them in the oven and reduce the heat to 375°. Bake until golden brown, 30 to 40 minutes. Set aside to cool for 20 minutes before serving or cool completely, cover, and chill until ready to serve. The turnovers may be reheated on a cookie sheet in a preheated 350° oven for 10 to 12 minutes.

10

Confections for the Pantry

I'M ALWAYS emphasizing that dessert ingredients should be fresh. The items that follow, however, can all be made ahead and kept on the pantry shelf. It's nice to know that when you need them, they'll be there. Someday one may save the day for you by providing a last-minute cake decoration or a way to convert a quart of ice cream into an elegant dessert for unexpected guests.

White Chocolate–Rum Truffles

I like to use amber or golden rum to flavor these confections. Such dry rums have a pure flavor without a heavy syrup texture. Covering the bowl of white chocolate with plastic during melting and not using boiling water help to keep the chocolate away from direct contact with moisture which would cause it to seize.

MAKES 14 TO 18

5 ounces white chocolate
6 tablespoons unsalted butter
¼ cup powdered sugar
1 tablespoon amber or golden rum

Cut the chocolate into small pieces. Place it in a stainless-steel bowl in a single layer. Cover the top with plastic wrap.

Bring 2 cups of water to a simmer in a 6-cup saucepan and turn off the heat. Place the bowl of chocolate over the pan of water to melt.

Cut the butter into small pieces. When the chocolate begins to soften around the edges, remove the plastic and stir until melted. Remove from the heat and stir in the butter, 1 tablespoon of the powdered sugar, and the rum until smooth. If the cream separates or looks curdled, blend the mixture at low speed with a hand-held electric mixer or a wire whisk until smooth. Cover and chill until firm, about 1 hour.

Using a very small ice cream scoop (#100) or 2 coffee spoons, scoop 14 to 18 balls of cream onto a plate. Chill 1 hour or until firm. Sift the remaining powdered sugar twice into a bowl. Drop a truffle into the sugar. Cover the truffle with sugar and roll it with your hands into a perfect ball. Set it on a plate and continue rolling the remaining truffles. Cover and chill until ready to serve. They will keep 1 week.

Coconut Crunch

This crunchy toasted coconut can be pressed onto the sides of a frosted cake or mixed into pastry cream for a cake filling.

MAKES 3 CUPS

2 large egg whites
1 cup sugar
2 cups sweetened coconut flakes

Preheat the oven to 325°. Line a cookie sheet with parchment. Beat the egg whites and sugar until white and slightly thick, about

3 minutes. Fold in the coconut. Spread the mixture evenly on the cookie sheet. Bake in the lower middle of the oven until the edges and top are spotted with brown, about 6 minutes. Remove from the oven and turn the coconut with a spatula, blending brown and white. Bake for another 6 minutes. Remove from the oven and turn and blend again. Bake until evenly browned, about 5 minutes. Store in an airtight container for up to 1 week.

Candied Cranberries

Plump, homemade candied cranberries add sparkle to fruit cakes (see page 115) or a special batch of cookies (see Florentines, page 146). Stored in a cool, dark place, they will keep for up to three months.

MAKES 3 CUPS

3 cups sugar
1½ cups water
1 bag (12 ounces) fresh cranberries

Stir the sugar and water together in a 6-cup saucepan. Add the cranberries and bring to a simmer. Simmer gently, uncovered, for 30 minutes. Remove from the heat and let stand for 30 minutes.

Preheat the oven to 300°. Line a cookie sheet with parchment. Drain the berries, saving the syrup. Spoon the berries onto the cookie sheet and bake them for 30 minutes. Meanwhile, bring the syrup to a boil in a saucepan. Boil until it registers 230° on a candy thermometer. Set it aside to cool for 30 minutes. When the cranberries are baked, set them aside to cool.

If you are making the berries for Florentines, put them in a jar without syrup and keep them at room temperature. If they are for any other purpose, put the cooled berries into a jar and pour in the syrup. Cover the jar tightly and store it in a cool, dark place. If your storage place is too cold, the syrup may thicken so much it won't pour. If that happens, before using the cranberries, warm them in the syrup in the top of a double boiler until the syrup returns to pouring consistency.

Candied Citrus Peel

This recipe will work equally well for grapefruit, lemon, or orange peel. The candied peel will keep for 8 weeks in the refrigerator; make a batch when you have time and it will be ready the next time you want to use it in pastries or fruit cake.

MAKES 2 CUPS

8 large lemons or *6 medium oranges* or *2
      medium grapefruits*
3 cups water
4 cups sugar

Wash the fruit well with hot water and a dishwashing liquid. Rinse it thoroughly and pat dry. Peel off the skin with a vegetable peeler. Cut away as much white pith as possible, leaving only the colored outside skin. Cut the skin into ¼-inch squares. Squeeze ¼ cup of juice from the fruit and set it aside.

Bring 2 cups of sugar and 2 cups of water to a simmer in a 3-quart saucepan. Add the peel and cook just below a simmer for 15 minutes. Cool for 10 minutes, then drain the peel, discarding the syrup.

Preheat the oven to 275°. Line a cookie sheet with parchment. Spread the peel evenly on the cookie sheet. Bake for 15 minutes; cool for 15 minutes.

If you are making Florentines, cover the peel and keep it at room temperature. Otherwise, stir the remaining cup of water and 2 cups of sugar together in a saucepan. Boil until the syrup registers 230° on a candy thermometer. Stir in the reserved fruit juice. Put the peel into a jar and pour the hot syrup over it. Cover and refrigerate until needed.

Trefethen Maple-Sugared Walnuts

This recipe was inspired by the marvelous walnuts grown at the Trefethen Vineyards in Napa, California. I like to team them with ice cream, for the textural contrast (see Strawberry Maple Sundae, page 175).

MAKES 3 CUPS

3 cups walnut halves or pieces
1 cup pure maple syrup

Preheat the oven to 300°. Spread the nuts on a cookie sheet and toast them in the oven for 10 minutes. Set them aside to cool.

Heat the maple syrup in a heavy-bottomed saucepan until it registers 238° on a candy thermometer. Turn off the heat and add the walnuts. Stir until all the nuts are coated and the syrup begins to crystallize. Turn them out onto a sheet of parchment to cool. When cool, chop the nuts into ½-inch pieces. Store in an air-tight container for up to 2 weeks.

Maple-Butter Spread

This maple-infused butter is terrific with toast or special breakfast breads. It can also be used as a thin glaze for simple, unfrosted cakes or sweet breakfast breads.

MAKES 4 CUPS

32 tablespoons (1 pound) unsalted butter
     (cold)
2 cups pure grade A maple syrup
1 tablespoon corn syrup

Cut the butter into 1-inch cubes and set it aside until needed.

Bring the maple syrup and corn syrup to a boil in a 2-quart saucepan over moderately high heat. Cook until it registers 235° on a candy thermometer. Remove from the heat and stir with a metal spoon for 5 minutes to cool the syrup slightly. Add the butter piece by piece, stirring to melt and blend it with the syrup. Once the butter is fully incorporated, return the pan to the heat and bring the spread to a boil. Reduce the heat to maintain a simmer and continue cooking for 1 minute. Remove from the heat and stir for 2 minutes to cool.

Pour the spread into 1- or 2-cup jars. Cover tightly with lids and store refrigerated for up to 3 weeks.

To use as a glaze, slowly heat 1 cup of spread until liquid; brush it over the top of a cake or bread.

Index

215